District 9: Johannesburg as Nostalgic Dystopia

Contemporary Cinema

Series Editor

Martin P. Rossouw (*University of the Free State, South Africa*)

Editorial Board

Jaimie Baron (*University of Alberta, Canada*)
Maryann Erigha (*University of Georgia, GA, USA*)
Cynthia Felando (*University of California, Santa Barbara, CA, USA*)
Seung-hoon Jeong (*California State University Long Beach, CA, USA*)
Kathleen Loock (*Leibniz University Hannover, Germany*)
Tiago de Luca (*University of Warwick, UK*)
Ernest Mathijs (*University of British Columbia, Canada*)
Sheila J. Nayar (*University of Utah, UT, USA*)
Iain Robert Smith (*King's College London, UK*)
Christina Stojanova (*University of Regina, Canada*)
Aaron Taylor (*University of Lethbridge, Canada*)
Catherine Wheatley (*King's College London, UK*)
Dan Yacavone (*University of Edinburgh, UK*)

VOLUME 10

The titles published in this series are listed at *brill.com/coci*

District 9: Johannesburg as Nostalgic Dystopia

By

Landi Raubenheimer

BRILL

LEIDEN | BOSTON

Cover illustration: Photograph by the author, Landi Raubenheimer, 2008. Hillbrow, Johannesburg.

The University of Johannesburg, South Africa has generously funded the Gold Open Access of 5 chapters within this monograph: the Introduction and Chapters 3, 4, 5 and 7.

Library of Congress Cataloging-in-Publication Data

Names: Raubenheimer, Landi, 1981- author.
Title: *District 9*: Johannesburg as nostalgic dystopia / by Landi Raubenheimer.
Other titles: District nine
Description: Leiden ; Boston : Brill, 2025. | Series: Contemporary cinema, 1572-3070 ; volume 10 | Includes bibliographical references and index. | Summary: "Johannesburg, South Africa 2010: Wikus van de Merwe is an unimposing clerk working at the large company Multi National United (MNU). He has just been promoted and put in charge of relocating an alien refugee camp known as *District 9* further away from the city. The aliens and their mother ship arrived above the city of Johannesburg in 1982, and in 2010 it still languishes above the cityscape.
Identifiers: LCCN 2024045469 | ISBN 9789004525436 (hardback) | ISBN 9789004710955 (ebook)
Subjects: LCSH: *District 9* (Motion picture) | South Africa–Johannesburg–In motion pictures. | Nostalgia in motion pictures.
Classification: LCC PN1997.2.D584 R38 2025 | DDC 791.43/72–dc23/eng/20240930
LC record available at https://lccn.loc.gov/2024045469

Typeface for the Latin, Greek, and Cyrillic scripts: "Brill". See and download: brill.com/brill-typeface.

ISSN 1572-3070
ISBN 978-90-04-52543-6 (hardback)
ISBN 978-90-04-71095-5 (e-book)
DOI 10.1163/9789004710955

Copyright 2025 by Landi Raubenheimer. Published by Koninklijke Brill BV, Plantijnstraat 2, 2321 JC Leiden, The Netherlands.
Koninklijke Brill BV incorporates the imprints Brill, Brill Nijhoff, Brill Schöningh, Brill Fink, Brill mentis, Brill Wageningen Academic, Vandenhoeck & Ruprecht, Böhlau and V&R unipress.
Koninklijke Brill BV reserves the right to protect this publication against unauthorized use. Requests for re-use and/or translations must be addressed to Koninklijke Brill BV via brill.com or copyright.com.
For more information: info@brill.com.

This book is printed on acid-free paper and produced in a sustainable manner.

To Johannesburg with love

Contents

Acknowledgements   XI
List of Figures   XIII

Introduction: Unearthing the Johannesburg *'Genre'*   1
     Why *District 9*?   1
     Johannesburg in the Sands of Time   5
     A Rosetta Stone: Nostalgic Dystopia   7
     A Sublime Topography   10
     Excavating *District 9*   13
     A Map to the Site   17

PART 1
"District 9" in Context: Nostalgic Dystopia

1   **The City in Relief**   21
     1   *District 9* and Other Representations of Johannesburg   21
     2   Johannesburg   28
     3   Dystopia   32
     4   Nostalgia   35
     5   Speculating on the Sublime   38
         5.1   *The Post-industrial Sublime*   38
         5.2   *The Sublime in Post-apartheid and Post-colonial Contexts*   43
         5.3   *European Landscape Traditions in South Africa*   44
         5.4   *Sublime Potential*   48

2   **Digging Deeper**   53
     1   Analogue Aesthetics   53
         1.1   *Nostalgia for Analogue Media*   53
         1.2   *Authenticity*   56
         1.3   *Visual Effects in Film*   59
     2   Ruin Aesthetics   61
         2.1   *Post-industrial Ruins*   61
         2.2   *Formless*   64

PART 2
Analogue Aesthetics

3 Mockumentary: A Fly on the 'Stopnonsense' 71
  1   Skeletons in the Closet 71
      1.1   *Township Planning and Its Discontents: Chiawelo* 71
      1.2   *Land* 73
      1.3   *The States of Emergency* 74
  2   Analogue Landscape: A Parody of Documentary Conventions 77
      2.1   *Low-resolution Realism* 77
      2.2   *The Incidental Landscape* 89
      2.3   *Back to the 1980s* 98
            2.3.1   Landmarks 98
            2.3.2   Militarisation 103
      2.4   *What can Mockumentary Poetics Do?* 104

4 Township Nostalgia 109
  1   Analogue Nostalgia 109
      1.1   *Subversive Resistance* 109
      1.2   *'Native Nostalgia'* 112
      1.3   *Constructed History* 114

5 Sci-fi City 117
  1   Science Fiction Poetics 117
      1.1   *Retrofuturism and 'New Bad Future'* 117
      1.2   *Spaceship/Township* 121

PART 3
Ruin Aesthetics

6 Mining Landscapes 139
  1   A History of Mining 139
  2   Post-landscape 143
      2.1   *The Poison Belt* 143
      2.2   *Sublime and Formless Landscapes* 146

7 Urban Ruins 158
  1   A Sublime Johannesburg? 158
      1.1   *More than a Feeling* 163

    1.2   *Hillbrow: A New Jerusalem*   167
    1.3   *Ponte City*   171
    1.4   *Considering Entropy*   175

8 White Anxiety   179
    1   Hegemony in Ruins   179

Conclusion: The *District 9* Cache   194

Afterword   202
    Looking Back on *District 9* – An Interview with Neill Blomkamp   202

Bibliography   211
Index   237

Acknowledgements

It is thanks to my supervisors Annie van den Oever and Federico Freschi, that I could complete the research for this book, which originated in the work for my PhD. They both provided mentorship, guidance and countless cross-continental meetings over the last few years, and this book would not be here without their support. The feedback from the thesis examination panel has also been helpful: I am grateful to Susan Aasman, Amanda du Preez, Julian Hanich, Hilary Radner, Brenda Schmahmann and Theo Spek for their thorough and insightful engagements with my ideas.

I want to acknowledge funding received from the Accelerated Academic Mentorship Programme at the University of Johannesburg to complete this book. Previously, while I was working on the thesis, I also received funding from the University of Johannesburg and the South African Department of Higher Education and Training, as well as the Accelerated Academic Mentorship Programme, to undertake sabbatical travel to Groningen in 2016 and 2019, and teaching relief in 2019 and 2020. In addition, I obtained generous funding from the Foundation Study Fund for South African Students in Amsterdam, for which I am most grateful. Some of the research in this book has appeared in publications: aspects of Chapter 8 informed "Nostalgic Dystopia: Johannesburg as landscape after *White writing*" (2020), in the *Journal of Literary Studies* 36(4): 123–142, and to a lesser extent "Memorials, landscape and white masculinity: dialogic interventions in South African Art", co-authored with Karen von Veh (2022), in the journal *Image & Text* 36(1): 1–27. I also presented my research at various conferences, seminars and workshops during the writing of the thesis and the book.

I benefited from the support of colleagues when I was writing the thesis that would later lead to the research for this book: David Paton, who was a mentor to me during the time I was writing the book, Ruth Lipschitz and Karin Basel, who helped me manage my teaching while writing, and Brenda Schmahmann, who advised me when I was working on the thesis, along with several others. Christa van Zyl worked many hours on the layout and cover design for the thesis. Thanks also goes to Ahmed Wadee, who has been my coach and has had many conversations with me about academia and life. Colleagues at the University of Groningen were also of great help over the years, particularly Julian Hanich, who first suggested I write this book, along with Jakob Boer and Tom Slootweg. I am grateful to the series editor, Martin Rossouw, for the opportunity to publish this work, and for his unwavering support and kindness. Cynthia Felando's editing of the draft was an invaluable addition to Martin's feedback at a critical stage in the process. I also appreciate the faith that the publishers at Brill, Masja Horn and Iulia Ivana had in me, and for their willingness to engage with me on all the little details that writing a book requires. Elizabeth Rankin's insightful editing and enthusiasm for the project have been invaluable. I am grateful also for the opportunity to correspond with Neill Blomkamp in 2020, and for his generosity in sharing his thoughts and some of his process when making *District 9*. Many of the images that appear in this book were shared by practitioners themselves, and some, including Zander Blom and Jonathan Kovel, also engaged in substantial email exchanges with me.

I have been lucky to have the support of friends over the years as well, Julie, Jordan and Jules who have all heard far too much about this book, along with friends who know who they are. While many of those already mentioned have inspired my passion for Johannesburg, I learned most about the medium of film from my greatest supporter, Dillon. You are a true rock and have been my anchor in difficult times; thank you for being there through it all.

Figures

1 This image was captured during protests against apartheid in South Africa. Photograph by Paul Weinberg, 1980s   74
2 Composited newsreel footage from the 1985 state of emergency (Rui (channel), 2008). Still from the video. (South Africa State ... 2008)   79
3 An alien levitating a minibus. Still taken from *Alive in Joburg* (Neill Blomkamp, 2006)   80
4 Emulated newsreel footage. Still taken from *District 9* (Neill Blomkamp, 2009)   81
5 Composited archival footage depicting Johannesburg in 1974. Still taken fromThe kinolibrary (channel), 2017. (1974 Johannesburg Street Scenes ... 2017)   82
6 The inner city of Johannesburg. Still taken from *District 9* (Neill Blomkamp, 2009)   83
7 Introductory sequence. Still taken from *Gangster's Paradise: Jerusalema* (Ralph Ziman, 2008)   84
8 News footage depicting violence in Johannesburg. Still taken from *District 9* (Neill Blomkamp, 2009)   87
9 Ponte City visible from the rooftop of San Jose. Still taken from *The Battle for Johannesburg* (Rehad Desai, 2010)   89
10 Interview with Lael Bethlehem, director of Urban Renewal. Still taken from *The Battle for Johannesburg* (Rehad Desai, 2010)   91
11 Interview with Grey Bradnam. Still taken from *District 9* (Neill Blomkamp, 2009)   92
12 Wikus interviewed at MNU headquarters. Still taken from *District 9* (Neill Blomkamp, 2009)   93
13 Wikus addresses the camera while a prawn argues with an MNU officer. Still taken from *District 9* (Neill Blomkamp, 2009)   95
14 Lucky and Zakes near electricity pylons. Still taken from *Gangster's Paradise: Jerusalema* (Ralph Ziman, 2008)   96
15 *Johannesburg from the Southwest*. Photograph by David Goldblatt, 2003. Archival pigment inks, 98.5 × 123 cm   97
16 The mothership next to Ponte City as it leaves earth. Still taken from *District 9* (Neill Blomkamp, 2009)   99
17 *Cleaning the Core (360 Degree Panorama), Ponte City, Johannesburg.* Photograph by Mikhael Subotzky, 2008   100
18 The MNU headquarters with mine dumps in the background. Still taken from *District 9* (Neill Blomkamp, 2009)   102
19 MNU vehicles that resemble Casspirs. Still taken from *District 9* (Neill Blomkamp, 2009)   104

20	Still taken from *Rewind: A Cantata for Voice, Tape and Testimony* (Gerhard and Maja Marx, 2007)	105
21	Wikus addresses the camera while an informal structure burns behind him. Still taken from *District 9* (Neill Blomkamp, 2009)	105
22	*Power Park//Soweto*. Photograph by I See A Different You, 2016	110
23	*Johannesburg//Home*. Photograph by I See A Different You, 2016	111
24	*The Three Stages of Preparing Tea*. Photograph by Harness Hamese, 2014. Digital print	112
25	The mothership hovering over the township. Still taken from *District 9* (Neill Blomkamp, 2009)	122
26	The Lockheed F-117 Nighthawk Low-Observable / Stealth Strike Aircraft, first airborne in 1981. (Lockheed 2019)	124
27	Apartheid-era watch towers. Still taken from *District 9* (Neill Blomkamp, 2009)	125
28	*A Taste for Life, Baragwanath Terminus, Diepkloof*. Photograph by Santu Mofokeng, 1985. Silverprint, 30 × 45 cm, edition of 5	125
29	The mothership from below, with the command module beaming up. Still taken from *District 9* (Neill Blomkamp, 2009)	126
30	The mechanical robot from the series *Robotech* (produced by Carl Maceck, 1985). Still from video (Robotech-Intro... 2011, screenshot by author)	127
31	Wikus in the mechanical body armour suit. Still taken from *District 9* (Neill Blomkamp, 2009)	128
32	Humans break into the alien mothership to rescue the sick creatures. Still taken from *District 9* (Neill Blomkamp, 2009)	129
33	*Brazier, Joubert Park I – City in Transition Series*. Photograph by Andrew Tshabangu, 1994. Archival print. 120 × 84cm	130
34	Aliens huddle over braziers. Still taken from *Alive in Joburg* (Neill Blomkamp, 2006)	131
35	The command module drops from the mothership. Still taken from *District 9* (Neill Blomkamp, 2009)	132
36	The command module rises from the ground. Still taken from *District 9* (Neill Blomkamp, 2009)	132
37	The spaceship and mine dumps. Still taken from *District 9* (Neill Blomkamp, 2009)	140
38	*After the Mines*. Jason Larkin, 2013	140
39	Johannesburg's mining waste belt (Trangos & Bobbins, 2015)	141
40	A google maps rendition of the three Mooifontein mine dumps west of the city (on the left) (Mooifontein 225-IQ 2018)	143
41	Image 4/39 from *After the Mines*. Photograph by Jason Larkin, 2013	146
42	Image 28/39 from *After the Mines*. Photograph by Jason Larkin, 2013	150

43 Gold Tailings #1, Doornkop Gold Mine, Johannesburg, South Africa. Photograph by Edward Burtynsky, 2018. Pigment inkjet print on Kodak Professional Photo Paper, 121.9 × 162.6 cm. Toronto: Nicholas Metivier Gallery   151
44 *Legacy of the Mine. Riverlea Mine Dump, Main Reef Road, Johannesburg, Gauteng.* Photograph by Ilan Godfrey, 2011   153
45A Koobus approaches Wikus from behind. Still taken from *District 9* (Neill Blomkamp, 2009)   159
45B Wikus falls out of the alien mechanical suit. Still taken from *District 9* (Neill Blomkamp, 2009)   160
45C Wikus crawling from the wreckage of the alien mechanical suit. Still taken from *District 9* (Neill Blomkamp, 2009)   160
46 *The Destruction of District Six under the Group Areas Act, Cape Town 5 May 1982.* Photograph by David Goldblatt, 1982. Gelatin silver print, 27.9 × 34.8 cm. Manhattan: Museum of Modern Art   162
47 Lucky's taxi in front of Dunvista Mansions. Still taken from *Gangster's Paradise: Jerusalema* (Ralph Ziman, 2008)   168
48 Lucky staring out of the window. Still taken from *Gangster's Paradise: Jerusalema* (Ralph Ziman, 2008)   169
49 Trash and a police vehicle. Still taken from *Gangster's Paradise: Jerusalema* (Ralph Ziman, 2008)   170
50 Zukerman out of place in the street below his apartment. Still taken from *Berea* (Vincent Moloi, 2013)   180
51 *See Ya Later/Triple AVANT CAR GUARD on the Rocks.* Avant Car Guard, 2007. Photofiba print, 54.6cm × 39.8cm. Whatiftheworld Gallery, Cape Town   185
52 *AVANT CAR GUARD Dive into The South African Art Market.* Avant Car Guard, 2007. Photofiba print, 54.6cm × 39.8cm. Whatiftheworld Gallery, Cape Town   188
53 Stupid Fuckin' White Man. Avant Car Guard. 2007. Photofiba print, 54.6cm × 39.8cm. Whatiftheworld Gallery, Cape Town   189

Introduction: Unearthing the Johannesburg *'Genre'*

Why *District 9*?

Johannesburg, South Africa 2010: Wikus van de Merwe is an unimposing clerk working at the large company Multi National United (MNU). He has just been promoted and placed in charge of relocating an alien refugee camp known as District 9 further away from the city. The aliens and their mothership arrived above the city of Johannesburg in 1982, and in 2010 it still languishes above the cityscape. When the ship first arrived, the humans did not know what to do but, when nobody emerged from the ship and it became clear that its inhabitants were in trouble, they were rescued from the ship. The aliens were ill and starving. Put into a refugee camp, they were segregated from the citizens of Johannesburg for health and safety reasons.

In the years following the aliens' rescue from their dying ship, the camp quickly declined into a slum, where a paraplegic Nigerian warlord called Obesandjo now runs an illegal trade in food, weapons and sex workers. The aliens are abject, slimy, insect-like creatures, who love to eat cat food out of tins. They have been given the derogatory name 'prawns', because they resemble the insects *Libanasidus vittatus*, crickets known as Parktown prawns, endemic to Johannesburg's wealthy suburbs.

Wikus, overseeing the forced removal of the aliens from this slum, is almost a caricature of apartheid-era Afrikaner masculinity. He speaks with a heavy Afrikaans accent and his hair is conservatively parted. While he is diligent and well-intentioned, he is at heart racist and bigoted, and ultimately deeply afraid of the aliens.

As if fulfilling his fear of the aliens, Wikus encounters an alien substance while he is going from house to house in the camp, gathering signatures from the aliens who consent to being relocated. When he comes across the alien substance in one particularly chaotic dwelling, it sprays into his face by accident, and his transformation begins. He rapidly becomes ill and, when he returns home to a surprise party celebrating his promotion, he vomits a black substance all over the food. He also starts to notice that his body is changing. Soon it becomes clear that he is turning into an alien himself. His right arm and eye completely transform and he even starts to crave tinned cat food.

Wikus is admitted to hospital and becomes a test subject for the MNU personnel who want to harvest his DNA, now an amalgam of alien and human DNA. They also use him to experiment with alien weaponry, which humans cannot use. Wikus escapes and is forced to find refuge in the camp, where he meets the alien Christopher in the same chaotic dwelling where he originally encountered the alien substance. Together with his young son, Christopher is trying to repair a control module from the alien spaceship, which has been hidden under his shack for years.[1] Christopher promises to help Wikus reverse the DNA effects of the alien substance if Wikus helps him retrieve the substance from the MNU who had confiscated it. In this uneasy alliance, they join forces to break into the MNU headquarters to recover the alien substance that is necessary for completing the control module.

Targets of an aggressive pursuit, Wikus and Christopher flee back to District 9. Wikus finds he can use alien weapons and, in a climactic scene, he steals an alien mechanised suit of armour from Obesandjo to fight off the MNU's henchmen, to enable Christopher and his son to escape. The control module is finally beamed up to the mothership, while Wikus remains on earth, where Christopher has promised to come and find him, to help him return to human form. In the final scene of the film, we see Wikus as an alien, sitting on a waste dump, making a flower out of scrap metal, which he leaves at his wife's front door.

District 9, part mockumentary, part science-fiction film, is clearly an allegory of apartheid and the racism that was part of that regime, along with the forced removals that were ubiquitous in the government's enforced segregation between races. Wikus represents the regime's demise, but also, most significantly, the regime's hope of subsequent redemption. Much has been written about the film in relation to its allegorical merits. There has also been considerable focus on the character of Wikus and his own journey with abjection, and on the prawns as symbols of racial otherness. I am, however, interested in the other protagonist of the film: Johannesburg itself.

District 9 put South Africa – and Johannesburg – on the global map. As an audience member, watching it in the city where it was shot, I recall the uncanny and unusual feeling of seeing places I recognised. More importantly, the film captured Johannesburg in such a memorable manner. Inwardly I was exclaiming: "That is the Joburg I live in!" In my view, the film captured the gritty, ruinous and 'real' character of this dusty metropolis, with its post-industrial character that I had always found captivating and somehow inspiring. This is a city where life is a starkly quotidian affair, where survival and luxury overlap, and where things often seem to be 'going downhill', as Rehad Desai says in his documentary film, *The Battle for Johannesburg* (2010), released the year

---

[1] Shack is the colloquial term for informal structures in South African townships, often made of corrugated iron sheets. They are also sometimes referred to as a 'hok' in the Cape province (De Satgé & Watson 2018).

after *District 9*. What *District 9* captured for me as a viewer is the look of this city: browns, teals and oranges; vistas bleached by the year-round sunshine in the dry blue sky; buildings that date back to a monstrous modernity that is now haunting the city; and a landscape that reminds one that the open 'veld' is never that far away.[2] This film, no less because of how well-known it is, *is* Johannesburg, or at least *a* Johannesburg, one worth excavating from the remnants of recent history.

District 9 met with much anticipation, acclaim and academic interest after its release in 2009. It is one of the first Hollywood portrayals of contemporary Johannesburg, and local audiences were, like me, enthralled, fascinated and at times bemused. International audiences were likewise intrigued, regarding this as one of the first fictional depictions of apartheid South Africa on the big screen. While the film had a big impact relative to its small budget and the unknown director Neill Blomkamp, whom it propelled into the international arena, it has not yet been given its rightful place.

Aside from the merits of the film as an allegory of apartheid, and its portrayal of the protagonist Wikus van de Merwe, it should be considered as unique in that it is an important landmark depiction of Johannesburg in contemporary cinema. Its depiction of place is so convincing that this deserves special attention. This book is therefore invested in viewing *District 9* as a compelling portrayal of Johannesburg, rather than merely as a film set in Johannesburg, and is thus devoted to studying not only *District 9*, but Johannesburg in *District 9*. There are several reasons why this is merited, rather than an analysis of *District 9*'s plot and characters. First, *District 9* portrays contemporary Johannesburg in a style that borrows strongly from the documentary genre, and as such it reflects much of contemporary Johannesburg almost by default. As an imagining of the city that is axiomatic of its time, the film's portrayal of the city may therefore lead us to consider contemporary Johannesburg and its geopolitics and visual character anew. Second, it makes use of a distinctive visual vocabulary: this is strikingly familiar, because it also reflects much contemporaneous media, as it is not alone in doing so. The style, a 'visual idiom', is so well developed in *District 9* that I would go so far as to claim that to neglect its importance would be to forego a unique opportunity to study the Johannesburg 'idiom' that I call nostalgic dystopia, which emerges at the time. Situating the film within this larger visual idiom points to the importance of the film for understanding a particular post-apartheid moment in visual Johannesburg, and indicates that

---

2   The word 'veld' is a colloquial Afrikaans designation for grassy plains or undeveloped areas of landscape, typically used in other languages as well in South Africa.

Blomkamp is not alone in his vision of the city. Since this moment has not yet been the subject of substantial research, it is also an opportunity to explore the city's recent past from a visual point of view in a new way, drawing out the shared visions and strategies that filmmakers and photographers were using to imagine the city late in the first decade of the 2000s.

A further aspect that is unique to this film is how its use of particularly analogue media forms allows for a media archaeological interpretation of Johannesburg's visual identity after the transformation of South Africa's governance following the first democratic elections of 1994.[3] *District 9*'s analogue qualities cast the city's portrayal back to the apartheid era, and offer new insights into how the city was depicted historically, and how that continues to impact on its current image. Blomkamp's use of digital cameras to evoke an analogue aesthetic is a quintessential instance of so-called "analogue nostalgia" (Caoduro 2014, Niemeyer 2014), prevalent in film and photography during the years of the transition to digital media from analogue media, but used deliberately by Blomkamp in a self-reflexive manner. The film straddles this transition, and the strategies and effects of negotiating the media change are evident in how it gives form to Johannesburg as a city. Ultimately, this aspect of *District 9* also highlights the role media technologies[4] play in contributing to how cities are portrayed in popular culture, emphasising the importance of

---

3   The apartheid era is generally thought to have ended with the first official democratic elections which took place in 1994. Preceding that, F.W. de Klerk (then the president) delivered a speech to parliament on 2 February 1990, which marked the beginning of the legislative end of apartheid's laws and their undoing (Enwezor 2013: 20–22).

4   I take the term 'media technology' from the field of nostalgia studies, where, in discussions on analogue nostalgia, Dominic Schrey (2014) uses it to refer to analogue and digital cameras. Elena Caoduro (2014) refers to technologies in the same way, arguing that analogue cameras imparted particular features to photographs that are now nostalgically regarded by users of digital cameras. The term is also used by media scholar Lev Manovich (1995: 11) to discuss the advent of digital cinema as related to specific media technologies. He suggests that the "look" of older media technologies is often emulated in subsequent media technologies. Such changes in media technologies (like the shift from analogue to digital cameras) and their effects on culture, philosophy and film theory, is interrogated at length in the book *Technē/Technology*, edited by Annie van den Oever (2014). The book presents the complex debate in film and media studies around the terms technique and technology and explores whether they should in fact be regarded in ways that are more intertwined than what is implied in my use here, but engaging with this problem falls outside the scope of this book. It is important to note how the term technique is understood, however. It has its etymology in the Greek word *technikos*, which refers to the artful or skilful use of technologies (Van den Oever 2014: 16). See Benoit Turquety (2014, 2017), Rick Altman (1984) and Leo Marx (2010) for more on these terms, as well as the history of technology in relation to procedures of use (techniques).

studying media and media change even within the context of representations of urban space.

Films such as *District 9* often suffer from exhaustive interrogations into their allegorical qualities. Valid as these may be, *District 9* is more than its social narrative. The city in this movie is so complex that it prompted me to consider whether art historical landscape traditions are at play in how film and photography portray urban spaces. *District 9*'s Johannesburg is not just a difficult or contradictory place; it is also an urban landscape that ticks many of the boxes of sublime landscapes, because it is so fascinating at the same time. Seeing the city in this novel way unlocks a series of aesthetic repercussions that bring to light deeper and more nuanced aspects of how African cityscapes are imagined and portrayed. In my view, this can lead to further considerations of what difficult cities and 'hard' urban landscapes mean beyond first glance, unearthing their potential as possible sites of subversion and transformation.

Johannesburg in the Sands of Time

> Johannesburg is an ever-changing movie that no one has quite managed to produce. It is a screenplay in progress. Like movie directors, leaders are thrown up out of the soil of the surrounding area to try to bring a sense of order to what Johannesburg is. [...] Johannesburg is an unfinished movie.
>
> MATSHIKIZA 2004: 482

While some may say that Johannesburg is an unfinished movie, it may also be thought of as a ruin waiting to be excavated. Swallowed by the sands of history, the city has not yet taken concrete shape, or is perhaps waiting for urban 'archaeologists' to unearth its true foundations and brush away the dust of oppression and inequality. In a sense lacking shape, the city has been said to be unimaginable, to be a place that is unmanageable for planners and those who seek to represent it, and even "to have no *genre* of its own" (Gordimer 1958: 80). Nonetheless, since the end of the apartheid era, artists, filmmakers and photographers have sought to capture the city and its genus loci, as it grew towards the democratic future of the "New South Africa".[5] Perhaps it would reveal itself as a new Jerusalem?

---

5 See Okwui Enwezor (2013), Anthea Garman (2014: 222), Mellissa Thandiwe Myambo (2011), Mzwanele Mayekiso (1996) and Tom Penfold (2012), who are all critical of aspects of this notion and its effects in the country. A related concept is the notion of the Rainbow nation or

Looking back at *District 9* and a selection of film, photography and popular media produced since the end of the apartheid era, I am embarking here upon a project of excavating the recent past of Johannesburg's popular image – one that reveals itself to be quite unlike the utopian formulation of a "New South Africa", and which, perhaps surprisingly, is consistently dystopian. While many scholars have argued that the city is often portrayed as decaying,[6] I would venture, considering the yield of some light digging, that in recent years these depictions have become something of a trend, reaching a pinnacle in *District 9*. This 'trend' is evident in several other film depictions, such as *Gangster's Paradise: Jerusalema* (Ziman 2008). It also reverberates in popular culture developing around the city's image, as in the work of a photography studio in the regenerated inner-city district of Maboneng entitled "I was shot in Joburg", and in the music videos of local pop musicians Die Antwoord, and international musician and record producer Skrillex.[7] Time and again, Johannesburg is depicted as overwhelmingly dystopian: poverty-stricken, dirty, post-industrial and dangerously violent. Somehow, in spite of this, these depictions are visually compelling and even appear to have an aesthetic allure about them that is incongruous and questionable.

What these portrayals have in common when viewed together seems to be more than just a representation of characteristics of Johannesburg. They share a recognisable set of features that is unique to Johannesburg, depicting the city in a discomfiting nostalgic manner, and encouraging one to recall the city's fraught past. They foreground historic apartheid-era landmarks, architecture and motifs, and emulate the analogue media that captured the city at the height of apartheid. Furthermore, this visual language emphasises the dystopian elements of the city, its problems of poverty, inequality, urban decay and even ruin. It is in some ways representative of the current state of

---

Rainbowism, espousing the unity of different peoples in democratic South Africa, whatever their 'colour'. This is discussed critically by Zamansele Nsele (2019), who links it to restorative nostalgia and an ongoing violence perpetrated against Black bodies in contemporary South African media.

6   See the work of the following scholars, discussed in Chapter 1: Lindsay Bremner (2010), David Bunn (2008), Svea Josephy (2017: 67–85), Loren Kruger (2013, 2006), Martin Murray (2011), Sarah Nuttall & Achille Mbembe (2004), Alexandra Parker (2016, 2014, 2012), Jane Poyner (2011), Jennifer Robinson (2010) and Lucia Saks (2010).

7   Maboneng is a district in the inner city of Johannesburg that has been subject to some projects of regeneration that may be described as gentrification. Martin Murray (2011: 2) refers specifically to Saskia Sassen's terms "urban danger zones" and "urban glamour zones" that are the result of such practices in the city, often resulting in social segregation. See Tanja Winkler's (2009) article on gentrification in the inner city of Johannesburg for more on this phenomenon.

the country, caught between the ills of the apartheid past and the unrealised ideals of a democratic future. As such, it potentially creates cognitive dissonance for viewers of these depictions: they are both visually attractive, because they spark nostalgic responses to Johannesburg and the past, and repulsive, because they are so drenched in decay, poverty and violence. Viewers might further be left with a feeling of intense conflict, since nostalgia here implies nostalgia for the apartheid-era city and all it stood for. These depictions are indeed problematic on many different levels, and display elements of redundant stereotypes or binaries that may linger in depictions of the city and popular discourse around it. As such, they may reveal thinking that is questionable, contested, or reductive, implying racist, classist, sexist and even anthropocentric biases that should be brought to the surface and critiqued.

A Rosetta Stone: Nostalgic Dystopia

Considering *District 9* in the larger context of comparable portrayals of Johannesburg, I am concerned with the visual idiom of nostalgic dystopia, which I track across key representations from the late 2000s. Like a Rosetta stone, *District 9* serves as the key to Johannesburg as nostalgic dystopia, enabling me to unlock other instances of the idiom. One might also say *District 9* is the keystone which holds the idiom together, even if this was not the intention behind the making of the film.

'Idiom' is a term widely used by scholars from fields such as visual culture studies, art history and aesthetics, albeit in different ways.[8] The particular term "visual idiom", which I employ here, has been used in relation to film by Woei Lien Chong (1995: 81), discussing the visual vocabulary or "visual idiom" of the Taiwanese director Tsai Ming-liang. It is also sometimes used in relation to the visual arts. Writing about aesthetics and art, Paul Crowther (2009) employs the term in relation to the different artistic disciplines, seeing, for example, both sculpture and painting as idioms within visual art. Earlier writing by Joshua Kind (1964: 38–55), on the other hand, uses the term to identify a "Chicago visual idiom" in the artistic practices of artists in Chicago in the 1950s. In this context, it refers to the characteristics of works by a group of artists of a particular period and place, akin to how a school would be understood (such as the Hudson River School).

---

8   I have found only one South African scholar using the term "landscape idiom": Juliette Leeb-du Toit (2010: 189), writing about landscape painting in South African art history.

Visual culture scholar Moshe Barasch (1997: 28) provides one of the few more detailed explications of the term "visual idiom", discussing it as a concise visual representation, a "complex configuration" or a piece of "congealed syntax",[9] which is only retrospectively identifiable as an idiom. He points out that, as a combination of visual features that "congeal" into a recurrent form like a phrase, a visual idiom is not identifiable at the outset. Rather, it can be reconstructed when looking back on histories of particular representations, extracting their characteristics from the bedrock of representational history, so to speak. Visual idioms in Barasch's view are not as intentional as the use of iconographic symbols. More often, they rely on a seemingly inconsistent use of visual motifs or elements, which only cohere in retrospect (1997: 35). Further, a visual idiom is often used in a manner that makes it visually distinguishable in style from its context. In other words, it may be a historical quotation or reference, which may be anachronistic to some degree, standing out from contemporary styles of representation.

While scholars afford no consensus on the term, various aspects of these reflections are helpful. In general, I use the term idiom to investigate and analyse a particular visual vocabulary (in the sense Barasch uses it) in the depiction of Johannesburg in *District 9* and more broadly during the period in question.[10] The new idiom does not seem to have been intentionally shaped by Blomkamp or any of the other practitioners under discussion here; it must rather be seen as part of an emerging view of Johannesburg that began to evolve after the first democratic elections of 1994. It has become visible in depictions of the Johannesburg landscape over time, in the same way that a spoken idiom evolves spontaneously through the use of certain words and phrases. This idiom then stands on its own as an example of "congealed syntax" (Barasch 1997: 28) and I trace its appearance as a recurring visual vocabulary that characterises *District 9* and is used by various practitioners over the timeframe I am discussing – the post-apartheid era, with a focus on the later years of the first decade of the 2000s.

---

9   See also Yakov in Pinnavaia (2018: 1).
10 By way of clarification, I often refer to the idiom of nostalgic dystopia as a body of representations that depict Johannesburg in a particular manner, but I also use it in a second sense, which describes the depictions themselves as *evidencing* the idiom, by which I mean that images employ the vocabulary that is germane to the idiom as a body of representations. The idiom of course only exists in its identification, in this case by myself, and as such there is potentially a third sense in which I use it, as a unique occurrence I am identifying in the period under discussion.

What further interests me in the use of the term idiom is the cultural quality of idioms; that is, how they could refer to visual vocabularies that are particular to a moment and a place (Pinnavaia 2018: 6). In the context of linguistics, Laura Pinnavaia (2018: 7) explains that idioms reside within the minds of the speakers of a language, and that they survive in "lexicographical repositories". This aspect of an idiom as a shared vocabulary, or in this case as a visual phrase or expressive shorthand, is what draws me to this particular term. This visual cultural understanding of place – in this case, Johannesburg – exists in the minds of the viewers of these images, a notion that is well framed by yet another term that describes cultural understandings of place, namely Rob Shields' (1991: 1–27) "place-image".[11]

Place-images capture how places come to be known through the everyday practices of the people who frequent them, cementing them into shape through ritualistic use. They may not always relate logically to how space is designed and intended to function in urban contexts, or to how its appearance in representations conveys its character. Instead, place-images are often related to (fallacious) stereotypes – the socially maintained reputations of places – and as such are constructed through the collective meanings with which places are associated, regardless of their character in reality (Shields 1991). In his book on marginal places, Shields develops a threefold dialectic that explains how place-images come into being: spatial practices, discursive representations of space, and spaces of representation (or the social imaginary). Lived experiences of places, their social reputations and how they are represented in popular discourse interact with and inform each other to construct place-images.[12]

Furthermore, place-images may combine to form "place-myths" (Shields 1991: 61), which become apparent and coherent only when they appear in everyday discourse. Such myths abound in the case of Johannesburg, and predate *District 9*'s influential depiction. Apart from its colloquial nicknames, "Joburg" and "Jozi", it has variously been regarded in vernacular designations

---

11 Not to be confused with Gilles Deleuze's concepts of the movement-image or time-image in relation to cinema, as expounded in his books *Cinema 1: The Movement Image* (1983) and *Cinema 2: The Time Image* (1985).

12 Clearly Shields is inspired by different theorists in his study. He draws on Foucault's concept of the dispositive (see Foucault's 1980 'Two Lectures' in *Power/Knowledge*) to explain how the place-image reflects the structures that enhance the exercise of power within that context. In addition, Shields refers to Henri Lefebvre (see Lefebvre's 1974 'La production de l'espace' in *Homme et la société*) to enrich Foucault's concept of the dispositive, arguing that it could include the individual lived experience as well as individual, personal choices made around places, rather than merely institutional and edified social structures (Shields 1991: 46–51).

as *Egoli* or "place of gold" in Nguni languages (Wamba 2003: 11, Kruger 2006), Jozi *Maboneng* or "the city of lights" (Dlamini 2009: 129), "gangster's paradise" (Parker 2012), a "township metropolis" (Nuttall & Mbembe 2004: 197), and as a mining town (Chipkin 1993).[13] It has been described as "ugly" (Matshikiza 2004: 481), "uncultured" (Rogerson 2004: 16), "edgy" (Kruger 2006), and "anxious" (Falkof & Van Staden 2020). Nostalgic dystopia – as portrayed in *District 9* – is perhaps its latest guise.

A Sublime Topography

One may wonder why Blomkamp and so many practitioners chose to depict contemporary Johannesburg so negatively. Does it document the state of the city objectively, or merely glamorise decay and poverty in creating "ruin porn" or "poverty porn"? Or are there other reasons that this is an effective visual language to describe Johannesburg? The term ruin porn is widely thought to have been coined by Detroit-based photographer James D. Griffioen in the 2000s (Lyons 2018: 4–5).[14] The term could also evoke the related concepts of "war porn" or "disaster porn", as well as "slum tourism" and "dark tourism" (Whitehouse 2018: 11). All these terms have negative connotations, implying a gratuitous consumption of images of the suffering of others.

Representing nostalgic dystopia so axiomatically, *District 9* portrays and exaggerates the dystopian aspects of the city of Johannesburg. The film has also been analysed for its nostalgic portrayal of Johannesburg and the apartheid past, highlighting that depictions like this reveal the nostalgia prevalent in societies that are dealing with national trauma, such as formerly colonised countries and indeed post-apartheid South Africa (Walder 2014). When *District 9* was released, Dennis Walder (2014: 153) argues, it immediately evoked the apartheid past for both local and international audiences; thus, even at an allegorical level, it is fundamentally nostalgic (albeit in an ironic sense). The nostalgia evident in *District 9* is not unique: I would argue that, like a dystopian

---

13   I am of course not the first to draw up such a list, nor is it definitive; Addamms Songe Mututa (2020: 206) has a different list of Johannesburg's names, including "elusive metropolis" and a "city at war with itself".

14   Siobhan Lyons' book *Ruin Porn and the Obsession with Decay* (2018) is a very useful consideration of this relatively new term and topic, and I refer to it in subsequent chapters. I also refer to Svea Josephy (2017), who briefly discusses the term "ruin porn" in relation to the visually arresting photographs of the building Ponte City by Mikhael Subotzky and Patrick Waterhouse.

quality, nostalgia is also characteristic of an entire stratum of post-apartheid representation, established through particular formal features in these depictions. Nostalgia is also prominent in South African popular and academic discourse, especially in relation to the post-apartheid period.[15] In the international context, nostalgia studies has become an interdisciplinary field of great interest to contemporary film and media scholars, as well as art historians and those interested in cultural studies. It is worth noting that the nostalgia I identify in *District 9* resonates with this larger field. Particularly relevant here is the notion of analogue nostalgia.[16]

The ubiquitous evocation of the past evident in the idiom of *District 9* may be described in general as ironic, since neither Blomkamp, nor the other practitioners under discussion, could reasonably yearn for the overwhelmingly oppressive apartheid regime or colonial past of the country. Nostalgia is very particular in the idiom and has to be approached accordingly to grasp the nuances inherent in the contradictory qualities of this vocabulary.[17] Dystopia is likewise a term that needs qualification here: it is by no means only an imaginary place in *District 9*, but is rather based on the actual city *as* dystopia, which was already prevalent in both popular and academic discourse before *District 9* was made.

In order to further probe why portrayals such as *District 9* are so compelling, I am driven to consider the contradictory dynamic evident in the idiom – which has both dystopian and nostalgic elements. This fundamental tension within the idiom holds the promise that there may be more at work within these depictions than visual pleasure and titillation, moving its significance beyond notions of ruin porn or poverty porn. From the outset, therefore, I am interested in asking what its significance may be, and whether it may in fact harbour even the smallest glimmer of critical potential.

The contradictory dynamic or tension of nostalgia and dystopia is reminiscent of the tensions at work in the sublime as an aesthetic category, where viewers of sublime forces of nature are simultaneously attracted and repulsed, as described by Jennifer Peeples (2011), for example, writing on the

---

15 For more on this, see the work done in this field by Judith Lütge Coullie (2014), Pumla Gobodo-Madikizela (2012), Derek Hook (2014, 2012) and Eric Worby & Shireen Ally (2013).
16 Elena Caoduro (2014) and Katharina Niemeyer (2014) have considered analogue nostalgia in popular culture of the late 2010s, overlapping with the period during which nostalgic dystopia was at its most prominent in South African media.
17 This discomfiture is expounded in Jacob Dlamini's (2009) controversial book *Native Nostalgia*. Published in the year *District 9* was released, Dlamini's book reminisces in a reluctant and ironic manner about his apartheid-era childhood in Katlehong, a township near Johannesburg.

toxic sublime. Although not exclusively, the sublime is often associated with representations of landscape, and indeed Johannesburg as nostalgic dystopia seems to be such a landscape. It may seem unorthodox to regard a city as a landscape. Cities do have landscape elements and qualities embedded in their topography, however, and they may be regarded as artificial landscapes of a sort. After all, Johannesburg has the unofficial claim to being the largest artificial forest in South Africa.[18]

Urban legends aside, the separation between categories of rural (most often designated as landscape) and urban seems tenuous at best in contemporary cities. In addition, contemporary urbanisation is marked by peri-urban space – quasi-rural in character, while at the same time including post-industrial sites (Qviström 2012: 427–437). This is certainly the case in Johannesburg, as I expound later in considering the landscape of the city from the point of view of industry and urban planning. The sublime as an aesthetic category associated with landscape representation has more recently been applied to industrial sites, and provides a fitting lens through which to view these aspects of *District 9* and the idiom. In short then, I chisel away at *District 9*'s portrayal of Johannesburg by framing it within the landscape tradition and the aesthetic category of the sublime.[19]

The sublime as a category that is rooted in philosophical aesthetics has been formulated to interpret many different kinds of 'difficult' landscapes. These include landscapes that are not beautiful, but are overwhelming and awe-inspiring, as Edmund Burke and Immanuel Kant argue; those that are artificial or man-made; and even those shaped by industry that are now post-industrial ruins of some sort.[20] What these very different landscapes so clearly share is

---

18   See Louise Bethlehem's (2022: 345) reference to this popular notion, which appears in Lauren Beukes' (2010) dystopian novel, *Zoo City*, set in Johannesburg.
19   Since I am concerned with a visual idiom, I focus predominantly on landscape as a representational concept and particularly its articulation in the field of aesthetics, but it is important to note that the concept itself has historically been researched from geographical and historical perspectives also. The relatively new field of landscape studies combines cultural and geographical approaches to researching landscape as a concept, and geopolitics also informs this interdisciplinary field (see Antrop 2013). Along with aspects of landscape studies, such as those related to geographical interrogations of particular landscapes, I draw on urban studies in discussions of Johannesburg's planning, and on geopolitical and geographical research when discussing mining landscapes.
20   See Kant (2001: 5–42, 2007; 75–164) and Burke (1996: 131–132). For a discussion on Kant's and Burke's foundational writings on the sublime in relation to nature, see Gillian B. Pierce's book on the sublime (2012) and David Nye (1994) on the technological sublime. Dylan Trigg (2006) and Amanda Boetzkes (2010) offer useful considerations of how a 'post-industrial sublime' may be understood, which I draw on throughout this book to carve out Johannesburg's post-industrial qualities.

the embedded potential to challenge the viewer's interpretation of the landscape. In other words, I assume from the outset that *District 9*'s idiom of nostalgic dystopia has the potential, however unlikely, to challenge or transform how the city is regarded in the popular imagination. I investigate these dynamics embedded in the idiom through the particular aspects of transformation and subversion.[21] Both of these concepts may be understood in terms of a "freedom to" enact change within or upon a space, or in terms of how it is regarded, as Loretta Lees (2004: 23) frames it in her book *The Emancipatory City? Paradoxes and Possibilities*. From such a perspective one might also say the idiom has critical potential. The notion of critical potential is also grounded in the category of the sublime, and how contradictory effects evoked in beholding difficult landscapes may prompt the viewer to question entrenched notions of place.

Excavating *District 9*

In the coming chapters, I analyse *District 9* with a particular focus: its portrayal of Johannesburg. In looking back at the recent history of the city, I excavate the artefacts that have shaped its visual identity – its landmarks, its topography, but also the analogue media that have given it its nostalgic dystopian image. To better understand *District 9*'s Johannesburg I draw on the work of a range of filmmakers and practitioners, studying the features of nostalgic dystopia as it appears across these instances. In addition, I occasionally refer to historical material that predates the 1994 elections, such as artworks or popular visual texts, to provide contextualisation and to infer characteristics of the idiom at work. There may of course also be instances where practitioners

---

21 I refer to transformation as it is understood in discourse on the sublime (see Trigg 2006), and discourse on emancipation (see Lees 2004), but the word does have additional resonance in the South African context. The post-apartheid African National Congress (ANC) government has long held a mandate of socio-political transformation in the country to address social inequalities entrenched by apartheid's racist regime. Transformation is also of course at the top of the agenda at universities in the country and has been since at least 1994. Thiven Reddy (2004) presents an in-depth report on the role of universities in social transformation, and Joseph Seabi et al. (2014) discuss how students perceived transformation at universities post-1994. In more recent years (starting in 2015), the transformation of universities themselves has also become prominent in the #RhodesMustFall and #FeesMustFall protests led by students across the country, resisting rising university fees and questioning untransformed curricula among other things (Naidoo 2016). Transformation is further a widely used term in popular discourse in the country and is used in legal contexts pertaining to education, the financial sector and labour law, among other spheres.

use a comparable set of formal features and techniques[22] that fall outside the period I have circumscribed, as the idiom is not an absolute entity, but rather an organic reflection of the use of a repetitive visual vocabulary.

As will become evident, beyond *District 9* nostalgic dystopia appears mainly in photography and moving-image media, such as film, television, music videos and commercials (which I refer to collectively as popular media). It is rarely evident in paintings or in illustrations of Johannesburg, for example. I surmise that this is because nostalgic dystopia itself has a particular relationship to the act of documenting the city. In other words, part of the visual vocabulary relies on the use of a camera, often evoking analogue cameras.

The period between 2008 and 2010, when *District 9* was released, was particularly significant in the idiom's life, since a lot of material pertinent to it and its context was produced then. This may relate to political events in the country at the time. The year 2008 saw widespread xenophobic violence break out in townships and Johannesburg's inner city,[23] many political scandals and allegations of pervasive corruption, protests over service delivery, and growing fears around crime (Kapstein 2014: 157). In 2009 Jacob Zuma was elected president of the country, amid outrage over his indiscretions, which included charges of corruption and rape.[24] Concurrently, 2010 was the year that South

---

22 I use the term techniques in the sense of *technē* as explained in note 1; see also *Technē/Technology* (Van den Oever 2014). The term refers to the ways particular devices or media technologies are used by artists and practitioners. This use of the term is also embedded in discourse on analogue nostalgia where, for example, Niemeyer (2016: 27, 29) explores how distinctly recognisable features of analogue media are "fetishized" in analogue nostalgia, and how users of digital cameras employ particular techniques to emulate analogue photographs. Technique therefore refers to how filmmakers or photographers employ particular technologies to particular effect, in other words, how cameras or lighting are employed in particular ways, using particular knowledge or skills (Van den Oever 2014: 16).

23 See Matthew Wilhelm-Solomon (2022: 23) for more detail on xenophobic violence breaking out in Alexandra, and leaving 60 people dead.

24 Thembisa Waetjen & Gehard Maré (2009) interrogate the representation of gender and women's rights in Zuma's trial, which commenced in 2006, for the alleged rape of a younger, HIV-positive woman in 2005. They consider how Zuma was presented as a traditionalist, espousing supposed Zulu values, and how gender and sex were cast as private, customary matters in this context. Zuma was later acquitted of the crime. Before this, during Thabo Mbeki's presidency, Zuma was also accused of corruption, and as a result was fired from his position as deputy president in 2005, although later elected as president. Steven Friedman (2021: 1–24) provides a useful overview of sentiments in the country during the 'Zuma era'.

Africa hosted the Football World Cup to much acclaim.[25] Both the positive and negative events of the time garnered considerable popular media attention and fuelled academic discourse.

Along with *District 9*, I have selected films and photographs which assist me in analysing *District 9*'s portrayal of Johannesburg as nostalgic dystopia. At various stages of this book, I consider the films *Gangster's Paradise: Jerusalema* (Ziman 2008), *Berea* (Moloi 2013) and *The Battle for Johannesburg* (Desai 2010) alongside *District 9*. These films share much of the idiom's character with *District 9* and enable me to further probe and clarify particular aspects of the aesthetics of *District 9*. Like Blomkamp who was born in the city and lived there until he was eighteen, each of these directors has a relationship with Johannesburg, with Ralph Ziman growing up in the city, Rehad Desai returning to it after growing up in exile during apartheid, and Vincent Moloi growing up in adjacent Soweto.[26] Although representing diverse perspectives, these films all reflect on the city in ways that engage the documentary genre.

In addition, I concentrate on several photographers' work. I first consider those who are nationally and internationally renowned for their portrayal of Johannesburg, including David Goldblatt (1930–2018), who documented the city for many years throughout his life; Mikhael Subotzky (b. 1981) and Patrick Waterhouse (b. 1981), who are known particularly for their project documenting Ponte City (an infamous high-rise apartment building in Johannesburg); and Santu Mofokeng (1956–2020), a member of the anti-apartheid collective Afrapix, active in the 1980s and 1990s. Andrew Tshabangu (b. 1966) is another important photographer who has documented parts of the city. I also consider international photographers Jason Larkin (b. 1979) and Eva-Lotta Jansson, who both documented the mining landscapes, and I briefly refer to the work of emerging photographer Ilan Godfrey (b. 1980) in this regard. In addition, there

---

25   See Simone Brott (2013:31–32), Pier-Paolo Frassinelli (2015) and Human Rights Watch (2009) for more information on the political upheavals of the time in relation to *District 9*'s portrayal of the city.

26   Soweto is an acronym for South Western Townships and was first used in 1963 to describe the district to the southwest of Johannesburg, where there were several townships including Orlando (Dondolo 2018, Wagner 2015: 56–57). Townships are areas that were assigned to non-whites during apartheid, but they already existed in colonial cities. One of the first townships in Cape Town (an older colonial settlement than Johannesburg) was called Uitvlugt (founded in 1901). This township was populated mostly by descendants of enslaved people from West Africa, Angola and Mozambique (De Satgé & Watson 2018). It was typical for townships to be located far from city centres, and also for cities and townships to be separated by a green buffer zone (De Satgé & Watson 2018). This imposed a supposedly hygienic distance between the white residents of the cities and people of colour, the labour force, who were often stereotyped as carrying disease.

are groups of young amateur photographers publishing their work online, on Instagram and fashion blogs. These collectives (which I sometimes refer to as fashion bloggers, since many of them have blogs) include I See A Different You; Khumbula (which means "remember" in isiZulu); and the Sartists. Of note here too is the photographic documentation of performances by a visual art collective called AVANT CAR GUARD, whose members, although not photographers per se, use photography to capture Johannesburg in their artworks made in 2007 in a way that employs qualities of nostalgic dystopia. This selection is not meant to encapsulate Johannesburg photography of the period in question: one may think of other notable photographers, such as Mark Lewis, Guy Tillim and Gulshan Khan, who all engage with the idiom to some extent. While their work could also lead to productive research, the selection made here enables me to uncover the salient properties of *District 9* and the idiom most effectively for my purposes.

In order to get to the foundations of how *District 9* constructs Johannesburg, I am largely concerned with rigorous visual-stylistic analysis, focusing on the formal and generic features of the film and the work of the practitioners outlined above.[27] While such a concern with formal features and visual stylistics may be disparaged by those who consider it superficial and insensitive to the socio-politics of representation, pioneering scholars such as Lev Manovich (2017: sp) and David Bordwell (2008: 30) bemoan the fact that formal qualities, such as visual style, the visible implications of the use of particular visual technologies, and the shift to digital film and photography have been largely neglected in the field of media studies in the last few decades. Moreover, they reject the negative labelling of so-called formalist concerns in academic discourse, which implies that such a focus is superficial or frivolous. In addition, excellent arguments have been made for the value of studying formal elements in scholarship on visual media, arguing that this need not be as removed from social or political concerns as is often suggested.[28]

---

27   In this I am indebted to James Elkins (2015, 2013, 2012, 2005) who has done informative work on the intersecting methodologies and concerns of visual studies, art history and aesthetics, in particular pertaining to visual analysis.

28   This is maintained by, for instance, Patrick Colm Hogan (2016: 1–10) in his insightful discussion of the value of focusing on the analysis of formal features and aesthetics when conducting research on film and literature. Although Hogan works with a different system of aesthetics from mine, often drawing on cognitive neuroscience, he makes an excellent argument for the value of what might be seen as a formalist focus in research on visual media. Jacques Rancière (2013, 2009, 2004) is also known for his substantial arguments in favour of regarding aesthetics and politics as interdependent and inextricable in contemporary art practices and in film spectatorship.

It is the predominant existing focus on *District 9*'s allegorical and sociopolitical significance that led me to the conclusion that a visual focus would not only be advantageous, but is sorely needed in *District 9*'s case. My approach in this is also indebted to David Bordwell's historical poetics.[29] I am inspired by his method to examine representations of Johannesburg not only in terms of how they appear, but also to understand how they are made, what techniques were used, and the (generic) conventions and strategies that informed their making. In delving into the visual-stylistic characteristics of *District 9*, I also draw on approaches followed in the field of media archaeology, which is inspired by Foucault's use of the term archaeology. Such approaches see media history as non-linear, and importantly consider contemporary (digital) media by looking at media from the past (Elsaesser 2016: 17–45), apt for studying *District 9*, because the film is so engaged with media from the 1980s, which it emulates using digital techniques.[30]

I approach *District 9* in two ways: from the perspective of how it portrays Johannesburg, employing media in a particular manner, here with a focus on techniques and media technologies, and also from the perspective of which type of city it portrays in its focus on dystopian locations and landmarks. Here I consider the foregrounded characteristics of the urban landscape itself.

A Map to the Site

This book is divided into three parts, each made up of shorter chapters. Part 1 charts current views on depictions of post-apartheid Johannesburg, to probe the recurring concepts that arise, and to consider their usefulness for better understanding *District 9* and Johannesburg. I also draw attention to neglected aspects of *District 9* and representations of the city more generally. In Chapter 1, I identify the concepts of dystopia, nostalgia and the sublime in prevailing discourse on *District 9*, looking to inflect these terms in particular ways that make them unique to their appearance in the film and also in the nostalgic dystopian idiom. Chapter 2 considers the concepts that inform both how Johannesburg is depicted in the film, and which aspects of the landscape are foregrounded.

---

[29] Bordwell's *Historical Poetics* (2008) outlines his approach in great detail.
[30] See also Chrissy Thompson and Mark A. Wood's (2018) article on the 'creepshot', where they provide a useful summary of media archaeology as method. Seminal texts on the method and emerging field include *Media Archaeology: Approaches, Applications, and Implications* by Erkki Huhtamo and Jussi Parikka (2011), and *What is Media Archaeology* by Jussi Parikka (2012).

These concepts include analogue nostalgia and the post-industrial sublime, both of which are important in the analyses that follow in subsequent parts of the book.

Part 2 follows with the visual analysis of the film, and the formal features of depictions of the city. The chapters in Part 2 investigate the role of media technologies in shaping the image of the city in the film, broadly addressing the 'how' question: how is media used to construct Johannesburg in *District 9*? This focus on media is concerned with what I call analogue aesthetics, which is at work here. Taking into account the impact of historical media in contemporary contexts, Chapter 3 investigates the role that analogue media has played in how both *District 9* and its idiom represent Johannesburg, by looking at the mockumentary qualities of the film and the documentary qualities in other depictions. Chapter 4 considers analogue nostalgia in the work of amateur photographers who represent different perspectives on using this nostalgia to create an image of the city. Chapter 5 considers the aspects of the science fiction genre that dovetail with *District 9*'s analogue nostalgia, considering the traces of 1980s science-fiction films in its generic construction.

Part 3 addresses the role of sublime landscape conventions in shaping the city's appearance in depictions. Through visual analysis, I investigate how the features of the city itself, its geography and topography, have shaped its representation. In other words, this is the 'what' question: what is represented to give Johannesburg this particular appearance in *District 9*? Here I am concerned with sublime landscape conventions that appear latent in *District 9*, as well as many other contemporary depictions. These features appear mainly in the character of the city in decay or ruins, evidencing what I call ruin aesthetics. Chapter 6 is an exposition of the role of mining landscapes in nostalgic dystopian depictions of the city, considering them as difficult post-industrial sublime landscapes that articulate a new relationship between humankind and the environment. Chapter 7 considers urban ruins in the inner city and the townships as possible sites of sublime experiences as well. Here particular buildings and the inner-city suburb of Hillbrow are considered as sites where entropy might point towards a breaking down of oppressive planning regimes. Chapter 8 focuses on urban decay as a register for white anxiety. Here *District 9*'s protagonist Wikus van de Merwe and the township landscape he finds himself in for much of the film are seen as on the brink of painful and necessary transformation, which marks the collapse of apartheid's hegemonic whiteness. In conclusion, I revisit *District 9*'s nostalgic dystopia to consider what may be learned from its portrayal of Johannesburg.

PART 1

"District 9" in Context: Nostalgic Dystopia

∴

CHAPTER 1

The City in Relief

1 *District 9* and Other Representations of Johannesburg

Shot in 2008 and released in 2009, *District 9* is one of the first contemporary Hollywood depictions of Johannesburg. Though possibly not as impressive in its reputation as some other blockbusters, the film was released to rather surprising box office success.[1] Based on Blomkamp's earlier short film *Alive in Joburg* (2006), the film was produced by Peter Jackson after Blomkamp's opportunity to make the film *Halo* fell through (Robinson 2009). At the time of making *District 9*, Blomkamp was a relatively unknown director, fresh from studying filmmaking in Canada, where he had emigrated with his parents in his late teens.

The film elicited substantial reaction in South Africa, and also internationally, especially in forums interested in science fiction, such as the Comic-Con

---

1   The contrast between the film's relatively low budget of thirty million dollars, and its thirty-seven-million-dollar income during its first weekend of release in the US (Walder 2014: 150) probably contributed to it being described as a 'blockbuster' in the South African *Mail & Guardian* ("*District 9*" goes ... 2009). See articles in *The Guardian* (Hoad 2009) and by Reuters (Gorman 2009), as well as the Gauteng Film Commission's special feature on it (Special feature ... 2009), which likewise use this popular designation. In cinema studies, however, a blockbuster is often more specifically understood as a high budget genre film that grosses more than 100 million dollars at the US theatrical box-office (Eliashberg, Elberse & Leenders 2006, Schatz 2003, Neale 2003), and which features high-profile Hollywood actors (Schatz 2003). This definition pertains in particular to the two eras that are associated with Hollywood blockbusters, the 1920s to the 1950s and the 1970s to the 1980s (the so-called New Hollywood era). Steve Neale (2003: 55) argues that the notions of the Hollywood blockbuster and the New Hollywood blockbuster are in need of revision. While these eras of blockbuster films are characterised by studios producing high budget, high earning films, there are exceptions, especially in the contemporary film industry. Here some low to medium budget films (such as *District 9* perhaps) may become box office successes and may thus in a sense be thought of as blockbuster films, although they lack the production values, marketing and star performances usually characteristic of them (Schatz [2003]: 35] refers to such films as "star vehicles"). Grossing around 210 million dollars, *District 9*, with its small budget and unknown actors, was an unexpected box office success both in the US and in South Africa ("*District 9*" goes ... 2009). In 2010, it was ranked as the 29th highest domestic grossing film at the US box office of 2009 by *Variety* magazine (Domestic Top 250 2010). It must be noted, however, that it was not one of the top ten earning films of that year. In comparison, James Cameron's science fiction film *Avatar* was rated as the second highest earner in 2009, and by 2018 it was the highest grossing film of all time (Smith-Rowsey 2018:5).

conventions of 2008 and 2009 held in Las Vegas (Wagner 2015: 44). The fact that *District 9* was shot mostly in a South African setting in Chiawelo, in the township of Soweto, adjoining Johannesburg,[2] makes it unique in comparison to other science fiction films. Soweto is probably the most famous township in South Africa, with Vilakazi Street, including Nelson Mandela's and Desmond Tutu's former homes, a popular tourist destination.[3] Further, *District 9* may have contributed to the township's fame internationally.[4] The infamous District 9 as it is called in the film, which is depicted in an utterly dystopian way, became the *pars pro toto* for the whole of Johannesburg. The township itself has a long history of political upheaval and protests going back to the youth uprisings in the 1970s and the States of Emergency of the 1980s. More recently, in 2008, a section of the township was evacuated due to the xenophobic unrest in the city. It is therefore striking that this site was chosen to film the scenes in the alien refugee/detention camp. It has been suggested that Blomkamp used real interview footage, capturing xenophobic sentiments evident in townships at the time, and that part of this material ended up as so-called mockumentary footage in the film (Brott 2013: 31).[5] Even though it is a science fiction film with some genre-specific motifs and figures, as well as otherwise extraordinary characters in extraordinarily bleak surroundings, the depiction of the township in *District 9* also reflects aspects of the actual city.

Although the film's setting attracted some attention and set it apart in the science fiction genre, the setting is generally overlooked by scholars. Few have focused on the substantial role of Johannesburg in the film, although some combine remarks on its portrayal with discussions of the socio-political themes at work, and its allegorical significance in relation to South African history.

---

2   Soweto is one of the oldest and largest townships in greater Johannesburg. I return to a discussion of its history in Chapter 2.
3   See Luvuyo M. Dondolo (2018), Irma Booyens & Christian M. Rogerson (2019: 52–63) and Philip Harrison & Kirsten Harrison (2014: 293) for more on Vilakazi Street.
4   Bob Ma (in Booyens & Rogerson 2019: 52) suggests that films such as *District 9* have in fact contributed to 'slum tourism', where tourists visit impoverished areas. As such, one may wonder how beneficial the image portrayed in *District 9* has been to the township's reputation.
5   Simone Brott (2013: 31–32) takes this information from an interview Meredith Woerner (2009) conducted with Blomkamp. Notable in relation to xenophobia is that *District 9* includes some negative media attention about the depiction of Nigerians as criminals, involved in prostitution, illegal weapons trade and dubious business dealings. The film was banned in Nigeria on account of this portrayal. See BBC News (BBC News 2009), South African News24 (Nigeria bans … 2009), and an article by the Gauteng Film commission (Special feature … 2009). Several scholars, including Keith Wagner (2015), Helen Kapstein (2014), Pier Paolo Frassinelli (2015), Stefan Helgesson (2010) and Mocke Jansen van Veuren (2012), interrogate how the film portrays Nigerians in ways that evoke racist and xenophobic stereotypes.

Aghogho Akpome (2017) is one of few to focus overtly on how Johannesburg as a city is characterised in the film. Referring to Giorgio Agamben's (1998) "zone of indistinction", he argues that the city is represented in the qualities of the township, and that it portrays this space as fundamentally inhumane, untransformed and still reflecting apartheid inequality. Adele Nel (2012) refers to the setting of the film as well, describing Johannesburg as an "abject cityscape". She sees it as chaotic and repulsive, as do other scholars who briefly remark on its apocalyptic or dystopian qualities.[6] Pier Paolo Frassinelli (2015: 293–309) notes that *District 9* depicts Johannesburg as typical of the global North's view of African cities, but also resists such narratives, suggesting that African forms of urbanisation are the inevitable fate of other global urban centres. In addition, many refer to the allegorical significance of the name District 9 in relation to the forced removals that took place in the infamous area of District Six in Cape Town between the 1960s and the 1980s.[7]

There has been a decided focus on the compelling character of the film's protagonist, Wikus van de Merwe, who is allegorically representative of Afrikaner identity and, as I argue later, whiteness. Mocke Jansen van Veuren (2012) suggests, for example, that Wikus earns a form of allegorical redemption for apartheid's atrocities through his bodily suffering when his DNA mutates into alien DNA. Discussions of Wikus's body and the grisly (even abject) transformation he endures also appear in several studies. Helen Kapstein (2014) describes his bodily changes as comparable to those of a hysterical pregnant (female) body, rupturing, vomiting, bleeding and so forth. Nel (2012) and Jansen van Veuren (2012) highlight the abject depiction of the aliens in *District 9*, while Mireille Rosello (2016) focuses on the depiction of waste, along with the notion of

---

6   See Stefan Helgesson (2010: 174) and Mocke Jansen van Veuren (2012).
7   Lorenzo Veracini (2011), Dennis Walder (2014) and Adele Nel (2012) all discuss this aspect of the film's allegorical significance. Historically District Six was a part of Cape Town occupied primarily by so-called 'coloured' residents. This designation in apartheid South Africa referred in particular to people of mixed-race descent. The area was located near the city centre and in 1966 it was declared a white area under the Group Areas Act. This resulted in the forced relocation or eviction of residents, which took place over several years. The removals lasted until the 1980s, when there was little left on the land apart from a few places of worship (Jethro 2009). Around 50 000 people were forcibly removed from District Six and resettled in the Cape Flats and in the city in designated areas that were often rife with crime and poverty. District Six in contrast had been known for its cosmopolitan sense of community and for its cultural richness, and Duane Jethro's (2009) article on residents' recollections of the area considers these as mainly categorised under three forms of myth: Fairyland, Wasteland and a space of Exile. See *District Six Revisited* (Hallet & McKenzie 2007).

disgust for these creatures and how they live.[8] Keith Wagner (2015) makes the interesting further argument that there is a neoliberal agenda at work in the depiction of the aliens. They are not only allegorically representative of race, but also of immigrants and immigrant labour in South Africa, associated in recent xenophobic sentiments with an abuse of local resources and as a cause of unemployment. This is deeply resonant with South Africa's history as well, as immigrant labour was used in many of the industries that now underpin the economy: mining (in Gauteng) and agriculture (in Kwa-Zulu Natal).[9]

In addition to discussions of *District 9*'s dystopian depiction of Johannesburg, and a focus on its allegorical significance, hysteria and nostalgia are significant themes that recur in reflections on the film.[10] Like more recent depictions of Johannesburg, *District 9* is often regarded through the lens of the socio-political characteristics of post-apartheid South Africa. Generally, however, the focus is on the characters and their allegorical importance, rather than the city and the role it plays in this. I, on the other hand, argue that, far from being a mere dystopian setting in *District 9*, the city is iconically recognisable and it spearheads the nostalgic dystopian vocabulary peculiar to the period it represents in South Africa.

The films *Gangster's Paradise: Jerusalema* (Ziman 2008), *The Battle for Johannesburg* (Desai 2010) and *Berea* (Moloi 2013) are also important signposts on the larger map of nostalgic dystopia.[11] Made shortly before and after *District 9*, they have much in common with it, particularly in being characteristic portrayals of the city at the time. These films evince aspects of the nostalgic dystopian idiom in ways that I will untangle in relation to *District 9*. They may be regarded as important texts in the emergence of the nostalgic dystopian idiom, though they are diverse in generic orientation and intent. *Gangster's Paradise: Jerusalema* was a 2008 submission for a foreign language film Oscar, and was set to follow in the footsteps of Gavin Hood's *Tsotsi* (2005). The film was widely discussed and, unlike *District 9*, much academic consideration was given to its gritty portrayal of the city and the representation of the neighbourhood of Hillbrow, which Ziman described as being like Jerusalem, the promised

---

8   See also Michael Valdez Moses (2010) and Wanda Teays (2012: 67–73) for more discussions focused on Wikus.
9   See Goolam Vahed's chapter on indentured Indian labourers in South Africa in the book *Falling Monuments, Reluctant Ruins* (Judin 2021).
10 Dennis Walder's (2014) discussion of post-colonial nostalgia is pertinent in Part 2 of this book, when analogue nostalgia is discussed.
11 This is of course not an exhaustive list. For example, the film *Tsotsi* (Hood 2005) also engages this vocabulary, at least in part, along with films that are not set in Johannesburg, but are filmed there, such as *Judge Dredd* (Travis 2012).

city on a hill (Lehman 2011: 122). This portrayal of the "new Jerusalem" is ironic, however, since Hillbrow is depicted as having fallen from the grace of its promise; it is in a state of utter decay. Ralph Ziman, now living in Los Angeles, left South Africa in 1983 to avoid being called up to serve in the military (Ziman steals the screen 2008). He professes an interest in working with imagery that is "at once vivid and dark", and also in probing serious subject matter, such as the aftermath of apartheid in the city (Ziman 2021).[12]

Unlike *District 9*, *Gangster's Paradise: Jerusalema* is a low-budget independent film, and is perhaps less well-known to international audiences than Blomkamp's film. Like *District 9*, it is set in two temporalities, just after 1994 and 2007. The plot centres around a gangster, and is modelled on the Hollywood gangster genre perfected in such films as Michael Mann's *Heat* (Lehman 2011: 117). As it was released while *District 9* was being shot, it serves as an interesting comparison, particularly since the visual agenda is so strikingly engaged with comparable techniques, and it also presents many of the qualities of the nostalgic dystopian idiom.[13] Based on true events, *Gangster's Paradise: Jerusalema* relies on location shooting, and engages with notions of documentary authenticity in the ways it portrays Johannesburg in the early 2000s.

Rehad Desai's documentary film, *The Battle for Johannesburg*, came out in 2010, a year after *District 9*, and the same year the World Cup was hosted in South Africa. It investigates how the built environment was being prepared for the influx of tourists the event would bring. Far less academic attention has been devoted to this film than to Desai's best-known film, *Miners Shot Down* (2014).[14] However, his oeuvre presents several techniques and approaches to the documentary genre that allow for productive comparisons to *District 9*. One of these aspects relates to how he employs his own sense of nostalgia in different forms (Dlamini 2019: 41–53). The son of Barney Desai, an anti-apartheid activist, Rehad Desai grew up in exile in the UK and lived in Zimbabwe before returning to South Africa in 1990 (Moyer-Duncan, in Ian-Malcolm Rijsdijk and Andrew Lawrence 2019:58). He is an established documentary filmmaker and

---

12   His later work includes a project entitled *SPOEK I* that reclaimed a Caspir police vehicle and covered it in colourful crocheted yarn (Ziman 2021). These vehicles occur in many of the depictions of the city that are discussed here, and are recognisable symbols of the apartheid regime's militarisation of the city.
13   Daniel Lehman (2011: 114) describes the portrayal of Johannesburg in the film as "by turns gorgeous and horrifying".
14   *Miners Shot Down* has been written about by Pier Paolo Frassinelli (2022, 2016), Cara Moyer-Duncan (2015), Helene Strauss (2016), Claire Scott (2018) and Lieza Louw (2021).

has made more than a dozen documentaries (Moyer-Duncan: 2015: 58). In *The Battle for Johannesburg*, Desai focuses on several 'bad' buildings in the inner city and particularly Hillbrow; Ponte City and San Jose are two that are considered in some depth. He investigates how urban renewal is couched within the city council's rhetoric, amid forced removals and the construction of new stadiums, Soccer City and Ellis Park. He also interviews two developers who claim to be proponents of urban renewal in the city. The film provides an interesting mirror of the documentary techniques referenced in *District 9* and *Gangster's Paradise: Jerusalema* that preceded it. Although it is a documentary, it is nostalgic, with the director referring to Hillbrow's qualities before 1994 as a cosmopolitan and vibrant area where he spent many adventurous nights out in his youth. Overall, the film asks how Hillbrow could be restored to its former glory, implicitly conveying a sense of post-apartheid nostalgia.

Berea (Moloi 2013) is the last film I highlight here. This award-winning short film was made for the series *African Metropolis*, funded by the Goethe-Institut South, Guaranteed Trust Bank and the Hubert Bals Fund (Ryan 2016: 324). It has not received a lot of academic attention, despite it addressing such topical aspects of the post-apartheid inner city's transformation. The film engages with the notion of urban decay and white anxiety. Directed by Vincent Moloi, who grew up in Naledi, Soweto, and is a prolific director of television content, such as the award-winning *Tjovitjo* (2017), *Berea* follows the story of the fictional character Aaron Zukerman. He is an elderly Jewish man who, many years after the end of the apartheid era, finds himself living alone in the run-down suburb of Berea where few white residents remain. A recluse in his own home, his seemingly marred relationship with his urban surroundings is highlighted in the film. His troubled relationship with the transforming city plays out in his interaction with a Black prostitute, with whom he forms an awkward rapport, in turn leading to his own epiphany towards the end of the film. While *Gangster's Paradise: Jerusalema* and *The Battle for Johannesburg* provide points of reference for nostalgia in the idiom, the nostalgia portrayed here seems toxic, and presents an interesting portrait of white anxiety (also evident in *District 9*). Moloi wanted to capture a sense of the changes in the inner city from the perspective of a white male character, and he hints at the possibility that Zukerman could surprise the viewer in being more adaptable than he seems to be (SmartMonkeyTV 2014). All three films I have considered here engage with Johannesburg as setting and location. All are concerned with dystopian qualities in the city's post-apartheid character and they all convey associated nostalgic qualities – often related to the use of analogue media, which I discuss later.

Johannesburg has not only been captured on film. Documentary photography is an important part of Johannesburg's 'genre' too. In reflecting on local photography, Michael Godby (2014) argues that South African photographers are known in particular for the strength of their documentary work, and this may be because of the important role photography played in the resistance to apartheid. He suggests that, as a result, South African photography has an unusual commitment to social issues. Okwui Enwezor (2013: 34) refers to South African photography as "engaged photography" – especially since 1948 and the election of the National Party – engaged in responding to apartheid's new and developing strictures. Along the same lines, Bronwyn Law-Viljoen (2010) argues that there is a particular relationship between South African photography and violence. This is more than just the violence of the medium,[15] and is rooted in the violence meted out by the apartheid regime, documented by photographers such as Peter Magubane, Alf Khumalo, Bob Gosani and Omar Badsha, all photographers employed by the celebrated *Drum* magazine. The later social documentary collective Afrapix, which included Santu Mofokeng and the pure photojournalists of the 1990s Bang Bang club, Kevin Carter, João Silva, Greg Marinovich and Ken Oosterbroek, further contributed to documenting the regime's violence (Enwezor 2013: 30–31). Within the established tradition of documentary photography in South Africa, photographers such as Goldblatt and Mofokeng have captured the country's changing land- and cityscapes over long periods as a backdrop to apartheid-era history. Therefore, one can see a document of the city of Johannesburg over time in their work, as scholars like Enwezor are quick to point out. Such photographers are interested in the banalities of everyday life, as well as in the landscape itself, as it had been shaped by apartheid's laws and segregation. One could devote an entire book to the role of photography in shaping how cities are seen in South Africa but, alas, I cannot embark on that journey here. Instead, I can do little more than consider photography as a document of the city of Johannesburg, and one that has contributed greatly to the city's place-image during the period I discuss. The strong vocabulary of documentary photography is evident across diverse portrayals of the city, giving nostalgic dystopia the flavour of documentary grit and 'realism' that is so characteristic of the idiom.

---

15   Photography is often regarded as a violent medium. Scholars such as Susan Sontag (1977) and Laura Mulvey (1975) have made seminal contributions to the understanding of the act of photographing as potentially violent in relation to the object or person being photographed.

2 Johannesburg

Post-apartheid Johannesburg has been a subject of much interest to those who live there and those who aim to understand its problems academically. Prevailing discourse has centred around its recent depiction in literature, art and popular media, with a focus on its geopolitics.[16]

Contemporary depictions in film and photography, many have argued, reflect the city's dark past and often cast it along the same vein, as dystopian. Films such as *Tsotsi* and *Gangster's Paradise: Jerusalema* and the photography of Andrew Tshabangu, Santu Mofokeng, Mikhael Subotzky and Patrick Waterhouse, Guy Tillim, Mark Lewis and David Goldblatt (among a myriad of others) depict an extremely bleak view of the city. Notions of public and private space, and crime as a politicised problem, have become topical in writing on the city, as well as the township, as a space that exemplifies the uneasy union of many Enlightenment binary stereotypes, such as "primitive" and "civilised", "rural" and "urban".[17] There is also a focus on the ways in which Johannesburg

---

[16] The list of scholars scrutinising the city include Sarah Nuttall & Achille Mbembe (2004), David Bunn (2008), Jayne Poyner (2011), Alexandra Parker (2016, 2014), Fiona Siegenthaler (2013), Joseph Gaylard (2011) and Svea Josephy (2017). In particular, Mellissa Thandiwe Myambo (2018, 2011), Mzwanele Mayekiso (1996), Marie Huchzermeyer (2014), Martin Murray (2011), Leora Farber (2010), Lucia Saks (2010), Jennifer Robinson (2010), Jodi Bremner (2010), Loren Kruger (2013, 2006), Sally Gaule (2005) and Nikki Falkof & Cobus van Staden (2020) have interrogated the city as a post-apartheid and post-colonial site.

[17] Crime is a widely discussed topic in Johannesburg. After apartheid's demise many spatial changes took place, not least of which was white flight, when white middle classes left the previously affluent inner city, and poor Black residents moved into the buildings that were more or less abandoned as a result (Beavon 2004: 244–245). Scholars such as Martin Murray (2011), Jennifer Robinson (2010) and Loren Kruger (2013, 2006) have delved into the visible effects of high crime rates in the city; Murray (2011) discusses "siege architecture", for example, and Robinson (2004, 2010) writes about how the city has erroneously come to be seen as dystopian. Mzwanele Mayekiso (1996) recounts much of the unrest in townships throughout apartheid history, conveying the sense of danger that pervaded townships during this time. Author Ivan Vladislavić has written several celebrated novels set in the city: in *Portrait with Keys* (2006), whole sections are devoted to how important security is to the city's residents. Phaswane Mpe's novel, *Welcome to Our Hillbrow* (2001), is another fictional portrait of just how dangerous that area became in the 1990s. A useful study that examines the factors affecting crime in post-apartheid Johannesburg is the book chapter entitled "Violent Crime in Johannesburg" by Ingrid Palmary, Janine Rauch, & Graeme Simpson (2003). Gary Kynoch's article (2013) on the relationship between the perception of crime and race in South Africa sheds further light on how crime is perceived by diverse racial groups.

appears in film in particular, making for noteworthy overviews that relate to the themes mentioned above.[18]

As a city that is often given a descriptive designation (ugly, golden, a gangster's paradise, and so on), there is no lack of adjectives and phrases that have been used to capture the essence of Johannesburg. Loren Kruger (2006: 142, 2013), for example, uses the word "edgy" to characterise various aspects of the city. She argues that its "edges" or boundaries are difficult to distinguish and questions how public and private are differentiated in a city where such spaces often no longer fulfil their original intended functions (inherited from colonial and apartheid urban planning). The city has changed over the last few decades because the militant colonial and apartheid policing of boundaries between spaces, such as public and private, has lapsed. In addition, different kinds of spaces have evolved that no longer fit those categories, such as townships and informal settlements. The latter seem by their very nature disorderly and, although townships were historically planned, they have become far more complex than they were initially, developing hybrid and deregulated characteristics. The term "edgy" also relates to how important boundaries were to the mining industry, which still impacts the current functioning of the city. The ownership of property and land is related to historical inequalities in wealth distribution, that distinguish groups of people, such as the wealthy "Randlords" and mine owners from the labourers who worked in the mines in the late 1800s. It is important to bear in mind that these boundaries were always more complex than an impenetrable division between the rich and the poor, and white and Black people, so the ostensible edges are unstable.[19]

---

18 Loren Kruger (2006) and Alexandra Parker (2016, 2014) both examine Johannesburg in film. Another useful interrogation of film depictions is by Lucia Saks (2010), who writes about the film *Joburg Stories* (Schmitz & Tilley 1997), and how Johannesburg's fraught geopolitics are represented in this documentary.

19 Rather than use 'person of colour', which has been more widely adopted in US discourse on race, I opted for 'black' (see Catherine Manathunga [2018: 97] and Yuen [1997]). It has particular relevance in South Africa. During the 1970s the South African Student Organisation, the group from which Black Consciousness emerged purposely used the term 'black' in their constitution instead of the term 'non-white' adopted by government, and it may be seen against the political backdrop of apartheid South Africa to refer to those disenfranchised under that dispensation (see Thomas [2020: 192] and Enwezor [2013: 42]). In the post-apartheid context, according to the Broad-based Black Economic Empowerment Act of 2003, amended in 2013 (South Africa. The presidency 2014: 2), the term 'black' includes African people, those of Indian descent, people of mixed racial descent (described as Coloured in the Act) and, as amended later, of Chinese descent, and I use it in this way. Further, I choose to capitalise the word Black, as it is now commonly used by Black Feminist scholars and those concerned with Critical Race Theory, and also in Southern African contexts where emerging scholars studying gender and

The term "edgy" has a further, more emotive sense, which refers to the notion of contemporary feelings of anxiety related to crime and disorder in the city (Kruger 2013: 1–2). In much of the research on contemporary Johannesburg, the anxiety has been articulated around the white residents of the city who, in the wake of apartheid, no longer feel secure in suburban areas where crime has increased. As a result, many feel a lack of belonging in the contemporary city, as Murray (2011: 1–22) argues. I return to the notion of *white anxiety*, as the phenomenon has been designated, in Chapter 8.[20]

Examining the contemporary city's geographic and metaphoric edges, Kruger (2006: 142–143) argues that the city is incongruent and does not quite cohere; it is not quite suburban, nor completely urban. Martin Murray (2011: 1–22) makes a comparable argument that the city consists of isolated little citadels. Like Kruger, he refers to the collapse of public space in terms of the privatisation of spaces, such as shopping malls, residential complexes and office complexes. Shopping malls have become impenetrable to the general public by virtue of private security measures, which exclude most of the population of the city that cannot afford their luxuries. Furthermore "secure complexes" of dwellings exclude public access, since only residents and their designated visitors can access them. Large parts of the city thus reinforce the segregationist sensibility of apartheid spatial planning, although now informed by the new socio-politics of security and economic class structures, rather than the racial segregation that was previously enforced.[21]

---

race, have come to use it, though not as consistently (see, for example, Refiloe Makama, Rebecca Helman, Neziswa Titi & Sarah Day [2019]). Like Michael J. Dumas (2016: 12–13), I use blackness in lower case, and the same goes for whiteness. I want to point out that the use of capitalisation remains contentious and diverse arguments have been made for and against it. Kwame Anthony Appiah (2020) provides an insightful and measured perspective on the matter. Although he argues for the use of White, along with Black, to indicate the constructed quality of both concepts of racial identity, he notes that capitalisation is a matter of common use and consensus, as linguistic conventions are fluid. I therefore follow the convention at the time of writing, as required by my publishers.

20 Notions such as 'white anxiety' aim to describe certain socio-historical developments in Johannesburg society. But it does not mean that Black people living in Johannesburg do not feel anxiety in the face of its problems, as is explored in the recent book edited by Nikki Falkof & Cobus van Staden, *Anxious Joburg: The Inner Lives of a Global South City* (2020). The book postulates anxiety as a general affective state experienced by diverse residents of the city, which characterises the city itself. Phillipe Wamba's (2003) article about visiting Johannesburg from the US also explores the anxiety shared by Johannesburg's residents.

21 See Okwui Enwezor's (2013) eloquent analysis of how apartheid enacted segregation through strategies of normalizing its effects.

Poyner (2011) also focuses on public and private spaces in the city, arguing that there is a transgression of such boundaries in individual practices, as in informal street trading. This informality is considered in the writing of Sarah Nuttall and Achille Mbembe (2004: 197), which uses local architect Fanuel Motsepe's term "township metropolis". In their research, as well as in popular discourse, the township is a space that embodies many of the perceived problems with the city, such as its incongruent character and poor or failed planning. Townships are contradictory places where vibrant informal trade and poverty co-exist, where urban and rural collide, and where public and private are dubious functional categories. The township often represents the city as a whole in film, photography and art.[22] In the representation of Johannesburg, the township is a pivotal space, not only because it appears in so many of the depictions to which I refer, but also because most of the authors investigating Johannesburg's geopolitics devote a great deal of (critical) attention to it.

Alexandra Parker's (2014) work provides a valuable overview of the city's appearance in local films. Among other aspects, she focuses on the geography (which she refers to as the "materiality") of the city, and on crime, which is often portrayed in the township context. She also discusses the materiality of the city in a chapter of her book, *Urban Film and Everyday Practice* (2016), in which she concentrates on how films contribute to the way viewers construct a cultural notion of what a city looks like (Parker 2016: 65–97).[23] Referring to numerous films that have depicted Johannesburg, she argues that it has become recognisable through these images. Her research focuses on how viewers may or may not recognise the city in particular films. Parker also considers the portrayal of the townships as similar to how the "ghetto" has been constructed in American gangster films since the 1990s, by looking at the films *Gangster's Paradise: Jerusalema* (Ziman 2008) and *Four Corners* (Gabriel 2013).

How Johannesburg is recognisable in depictions is often predictably based on landmark buildings and how they appear in such portrayals. Svea Josephy (2017) reflects on the iconic building Ponte City, the decaying, and (at times in its history) slum-like high-rise building in Johannesburg.[24] She investigates

---

22 Loren Kruger (2006, 2013), Sarah Nuttall & Achille Mbembe (2007), Jordache A. Ellapen (2009), Alexandra Parker (2016: 83–97) and novelist Ivan Vladislavić (2006: 46–47) all suggest this in different ways.
23 This in some ways evokes the notion of place-image, as film depictions are an important part of the popular discourse on the city.
24 A slum, as defined by the UN, is a dwelling with more than three people per room, without access to clean water, sanitation, safety and shelter that is durable (UN-Habitat 2018: 2–5). I am fully aware of its derogatory connotations (see Huchzermeyer 2014) but employ it because it is widely used in urban studies discourse. It might seem prudent to indicate

the building in representations as a portrait of Johannesburg, through an analysis of the *Ponte City* book project by Subotzky and Waterhouse.[25] She argues that the building as it is represented there may reveal something about Johannesburg's character as a city, by exposing things that are not usually seen.

Johannesburg has come to be known as a city fraught with problems. It is frequently argued that it is incongruent and incoherent, and that it still perpetuates apartheid segregationist spatial politics in its geographies years after the regime ended. Often the township in particular is portrayed reductively as a site of poverty, decay and crime, problems that are evident in the inner-city slums that permeate the city's fabric as well. In short, many of the depictions of Johannesburg and much of the writing on the city paint it as dystopian.[26]

3   Dystopia

Since Johannesburg already has an established image as a dystopian city, whether in *District 9*, in other representations, or in discussions on the city's geopolitics, it appears that the film's nostalgic dystopia has its foundations in the prevalent gloomy view of the city.

The terms utopia (Thomas More's famous term for an idealised place, eutopia, which is a no-place) and dystopia (a term which only became widely used in the twentieth century) have a history of being associated with each other.[27] Both these notions of place are abstract, not referring to real places, but imaginary places that are seen either as idealised, or the opposite, as

---

its contested status by using scare quotes – 'slums' – but that becomes tedious. See also Wilhelm-Solomon (2022: 22) for the living conditions people inhabiting such buildings in Johannesburg's inner city in 2010 experienced, such as more than 200 people sharing one tap, and 84.5% of people living with severe overcrowding, far exceeding minimum standards.

25   The book project was the culmination of a six-year long interaction with Ponte City in which the photographers (South African Subotzky and British Waterhouse) documented the interior and exterior of the building. They also conducted interviews and used found and collected material along with architectural diagrams to investigate the building visually. The result was not only a book but also several exhibitions in Cape Town, Liverpool, Lubumbashi, Paris, Antwerp, Edinburgh and London (Josephy 2017: 69, 82).

26   Although that specific term is not always used, it is employed by Robinson (2010), Murray (2011) and in critical remarks on stereotypical views of the city by Nuttall & Mbembe (2004), as well as by Walder (2014), Nel (2012) and Frassinelli (2015) in relation to *District 9*'s depiction of the city.

27   Lyman Tower Sargent (2013: 10–13) provides a useful appraisal of these terms. Refer also to Gregory Claeys (2013: 14) and Gyan Prakash (2010: 2) for more on utopia and dystopia.

hellish. The concept of dystopia has often been associated with science fiction cinema. The genre typically depicts cities as sites of utopian or dystopian imaginings, as Andrew Milner (2004) writes. One may think of urban dystopias from the 1980s, as in *Blade Runner* (Scott 1982), *Robocop* (Verhoeven 1987), *The Terminator* (Cameron 1984), and so forth. These films are important contextual anchors for *District 9*, as Blomkamp grew up in the 1980s, and as *District 9* is, in part, set in the 1980s.

Unlike the films mentioned above, however, the dystopia depicted in *District 9* is an imagining of Johannesburg as a place that is not entirely fictional and is thus not solely a product of the science fiction genre at work in it. This imagining of place draws strongly on documentary modes of depiction that refer to documentary photography and newsreel footage of the city and, as will become clear, it relies on a 'newsreel realism' or a "low-resolution realism" (Lucas 2014:143–146). Dystopia here is thus related more to imagining or portraying the actual city of Johannesburg as dystopian than to science fiction, or an abstract imaginary version of the city. The township is the particular (albeit exaggerated) setting that achieves this notion of a "real" dystopia. Writing on *District 9*, Nel suggests that, despite its dramatization of the city, the film attempts to depict the "*real* world out there" (2012: 550). Other settings include inner city slums and abandoned buildings, or buildings that have degenerated and decayed, often due to the socio-economic ills associated with apartheid-era urban planning. These settings contribute to the impression of Johannesburg in *District 9* as "abject cityscape", a contemporary urban ghetto, unhygienic and claustrophobic (Nel 2012: 550–552).

Akpome's (2017) discussion of the depiction of the township in *District 9* is also fundamental to my interpretation of the setting as dystopian. He explores how *District 9* portrays the township as a "zone of indistinction" (Akpome 2017: 86), the phrase that Agamben (1998) uses to explain how camps, such as refugee camps, function as spaces of "bare life" conditions. Akpome goes on to discuss how Chiawelo, where *District 9* was shot, becomes representative of both Johannesburg and South Africa as an example of African urbanisation. As he argues, it is therefore highly problematic that District 9 is depicted as a slum, which may be understood to represent African urbanism (Akpome 2017:85–88). In the transition from an oppressive government to a democratic one, the townships have slipped through the cracks, so to speak, and both regimes (apartheid and democracy) have contributed to the poor conditions that persist and result in the "bestialisation of human subjects" (Akpome 2017: 94).

In line with Akpome's argument, it is interesting to note that the inhabitants of the camp in *District 9* are not in fact biological humans but are depicted as physiognomically alien, already lacking basic humanity. If anything, this reinforces their existence as one of bare life and not political life and therefore without human rights. Although I sketch the complexity of townships in subsequent discussions, it is notable that Murray (2008: 36) also describes them in a rather monocular manner as "sites of indistinction" where residents are excluded from the cosmopolitan city. In these instances, Agamben's "state of exception" (1998) becomes the norm, in which human rights and the law are no longer relevant. Residents of informal settlements are regarded as "guests, or unwanted trespassers" (Murray 2008: 36), rather than as citizens with a right to be in the city. The "state of exception" recalls the historical States of Emergency declared in South Africa in the 1980s, which enabled then-president P.W. Botha to impose military law and disregard the rights of township residents among others (Merrett 1990).

Johannesburg is not the only city that has become known through dystopian portrayals in art and the media. Dystopian depictions of cities elsewhere in the world have been explored extensively in urban studies, and in architectural and critical cultural discourse. Detroit is one of the most written about examples in relation to photography and ruin porn.[28] There are also substantial discussions of Delhi (Sundaram 2010: 241–257), Mumbai (Mukherjee 2017: 287–309), Lagos (Koolhaas 2002), and São Paulo (Opalach 1997: 35–50), and of the social and geopolitical problems these cities face as part of the global South.[29] In interrogating such cities, Anthony Vidler (1994: 167–176) refers to "dark space" as the opposite of the Enlightenment ideal of light modern urban spaces.[30] Most of these inquiries, like those on Johannesburg mentioned above, focus on how public and private spaces shape lived experiences of the city and how these contested categories came about.

A notable investigation of dystopian images of cities in film is Gyan Prakash's book, *Noir Urbanisms: Dystopic Images of the Modern City* (2010), in which he discusses the critical potential of the dystopian genre in film. For him there is often a utopian desire that underpins dystopian depictions (Prakash 2010: 2). Tom Moylan (2000) argues that dystopian depictions of place in the science

---

28   Refer to Mijs (2014), Lyons (2018), Rodney & Lauder (2018) and Steinmetz (2008).
29   The terms global North and global South are employed by Richard de Satgé & Vanessa Watson, who write on informal settlements in South Africa, not so much in geographic terms, but in terms of an orientation in relation to the world economy and socio-political factors. Former colonial powers are typically regarded as constituting the global North, whereas many of the countries that were their colonies are often seen as part of the global South, even if geographically in the Northern hemisphere. The global South is thus a critical perspective rather than an area (De Satgé & Watson 2018: 13).
30   See also Ravi Sundaram's (2010: 241–243) discussion on Anthony Vidler's concept. Vidler discusses nostalgia in relation to the uncanny as well.

fiction genre between the 1980s and 1990s are evidence of a prevalence of critical dystopias. Such dystopian depictions are fundamentally utopian in that they envisage transformation in society, or a wholesale questioning of the dystopian status quo. Most of Moylan's argument is centred on the narrative and plot structures of the literature and films he discusses, which differs from my focus on the formal features of *District 9*. Moylan and Prakash's work on the topic, however, reinforces my hunch that even dystopian depictions, although seemingly one-dimensional, could be probed for critical potential.

One of the most important concepts referred to in Prakash's book is the "slum", as Mike Davis conceptualises it in *Planet of Slums* (Davis 2006). Jennifer Robinson (2010: 218–240) looks critically at this concept and at what dystopian depictions of cities could reveal about cultural stereotypes, and which may in turn impact the ways cities are developed in the future. She also suggests that the dystopian genre should be reconsidered as one that offers hope, and not only doom (Robinson 2010: 220). She argues that Davis and others are in danger of perpetuating Enlightenment stereotypes about the "third world" and calls for a new critical discourse that offers space for imagining potential solutions to urban problems in perceived dystopian cities such as Johannesburg, instead of defining them as beyond hope. In light of this argument, I will consider the potential offered by the dystopian place-image of Johannesburg in *District 9* as more than an Enlightenment/colonial hangover, but rather as an image that harbours critical potential.

4   Nostalgia

Johannesburg is not only a dystopian city in prevailing discourse, but it has a particular character, also evident in visual representations that evoke poverty porn or ruin porn. Dystopian qualities seem to be tempered or even contradicted by the nostalgic tone evident in many of the depictions, which makes them in some ways both dystopian and repulsive, yet also nostalgic and alluring.

In the post-apartheid South African context, nostalgia itself has particular qualities, which influence how nostalgic dystopia functions. It is pervasive enough to define a particular moment of South African culture and critique (Worby & Ally 2013:457). Eric Worby and Shireen Ally refer to many different instances of nostalgia in popular culture, such as "struggle nostalgia" (2013: 457–458), in terms of which Soweto has become a site of touristic fetish, its role in the struggle against apartheid romanticised. One of the most important aspects of how Worby and Ally consider nostalgia in

South Africa, however, is the level of nuance and complexity they employ. They identify several kinds of nostalgic engagements with the past in South African popular culture, and in academic discourses. Some instances of nostalgia remember the past more hopefully in contrast to a rather disappointing present, as in historian Jacob Dlamini's book *Native Nostalgia* (2009). Others are more condemnatory and consider memories of the past in light of shameful complicity, as in research by Derek Hook (2014, 2012), Pumla Gobodo-Madikizela (2012) and Zamansele Nsele (2019). Yet others may think of the past effusively, or didactically, to enable the formulation of an ethics in relation to the past, the future and the present (Worby & Ally 2013: 458). There are also entanglements of nostalgia and memory particular to South Africa. In her book *The Frightened Land: Land, Landscape and Politics in South Africa*, Jennifer Beningfield (2006) argues that the notion of forgetting is particularly important to understanding the contemporary relationship of South Africans to the land and landscape. It may thus be that nostalgic views of the past are implicitly also views that forget particular histories or points of view.

There are several types of nostalgia identified in prevailing academic views on the topic, some more overtly than others, and they intersect in some ways with the range of sentiments outlined by Worby and Ally. First, and discussed in more detail in Chapter 2, is analogue nostalgia, which occurs in contemporary digital media. My interpretation of nostalgia focuses on the interaction between digital and analogue photography and film (evidenced in analogue nostalgia) in the post-apartheid era, and on how analogue nostalgia relates to notions of nostalgia found in depictions of Johannesburg. The second aspect of nostalgia relates to the cityscape of Johannesburg itself. Dominic Schrey (2014: 29) makes the argument that nostalgia can be evoked in either the content or the style of what is depicted. In the case of Johannesburg, the physical landscape of the city (the content of depictions) inherently lends itself to evoking feelings of nostalgia, since much historic architecture from the apartheid era remains in the city as dubious memorials to the past. This often contributes to photographers and filmmakers referencing the palimpsestic nature of the urban landscape itself, through signs of decay such as peeling paint, rusting metal and buildings in a general state of disrepair. The city is also nostalgic through references to iconic older representations, such as landscape depictions of the mining industry by well-known painter J. H. Pierneef, photographer David Goldblatt and, later, the artist William Kentridge.

There is however a tension at play here, as the past in South Africa is hardly neutral, let alone a time to romanticise. In this context, one may wonder with

Dennis Walder (2014: 144) why symbols of the apartheid past are evoked so nostalgically in *District 9*. How can *District 9* be nostalgic about such a fraught past? Probing this tension is central here. Worby and Ally (2013: 458) put it very eloquently when they argue that nostalgia should be considered as more than a sentimental longing for a past that was bad (forgetting the facts of how bad it was) or, conversely, by thinking that it can reveal that the past was not as bad as it seems, with the aim of restoring some kind of truthful version of memories of the past. For them, nostalgia is more usefully thought of as a practice that enfolds temporalities into each other – which sees forgetting as part of memory.

Nostalgia is not unique to the South African context and it has become influential in many fields, such as media studies, cultural studies and art history in recent decades. Svetlana Boym writes about the concept in her seminal book, *The Future of Nostalgia* (2001). She describes nostalgia as often having a utopian dimension. Arguing that it is not always directed to the past or future in a linear and logical sense, she suggests that it may extend laterally in an imprecise manner, so that one feels unsure of when or what it is directed towards. Boym further discusses nostalgia as a side-effect of modern life. One of the contemporary examples she cites is what she terms the "cyberpastoral" vocabulary of the internet, which includes glib references to the "global village" (2001: XVI–XVII). In tracing the concept's history, she discusses how the advent of high modernity in the nineteenth century coincided with the prevalence of nostalgia as an incurable affliction akin to melancholia. She traces its roots back to 1688 and the Swiss doctor Johannes Hofer (2001: 3), and emphasises the relationship between modernity's focus on progress and a romantic reaction against it, a longing for a return to a supposedly better world. She describes such nostalgia as unsystematic and unsynthesizable (2001: 13). In her view, nostalgia is a historical emotion that coincides with modernity and the birth of mass culture (2001: 16). Significantly, it was entangled with the advent of mass media from the outset.

Boym (2001: 41–48) proposes two types of nostalgia, one that is restorative and the other reflective. The former is often nationalist in emphasis and focuses on a shared longing for home and one's return there. The latter is more individual in emphasis and focuses on ambiguous collective and cultural frameworks of memory. The latter also defers the return to a real place, as the nostalgic feeling concerns the distance from home itself, not the place one longs for. She adds that such nostalgia is often ironic and self-reflexive.

The self-reflexivity and irony inherent in reflective nostalgia are precisely what is interesting to me. While one may think of nostalgia as indulgent, as psychoanalytic scholars have,[31] its prevalence in *District 9* and related depictions, points to an inherent critical potential that begs further investigation, as Worby and Ally (2013) and Lütge Coullie (2014: 207) suggest.

5 Speculating on the Sublime

The combination of nostalgia and dystopia in *District 9* is remarkable for its contradictory quality, which points to a unique dynamic at work. The dynamic of both repulsion and attraction has much in common with the dynamic of the sublime, as I explore here. At this point, readers might question my choice of a western aesthetic category to frame how Johannesburg is depicted in the film. It is a relevant question. Many scholars who investigate the dubious legacy of colonial town planning and apartheid laws in the city have interpreted the Johannesburg landscape in terms of its spatial politics, and an aesthetic category for describing landscape seems far removed from this. I have thought for some time, however, that the sublime may serve to deepen existing engagements with the geopolitics of the city, as it implies a greater focus on the formal features in depictions of the city, and the aesthetic effects to which they may contribute. Indeed, it is the contradictory effects – both nostalgic and dystopian – which depictions in the idiom seem to imply that first sparked my interest in the sublime as an aesthetic category, especially as the concept has been linked to challenging depictions of landscape in art history. Furthermore, contrary to what one might think, the sublime is not a static and dated concept. In what follows, I consider historical and contemporary versions of the concept in relation to Johannesburg as a post-apartheid and post-colonial city.

5.1 *The Post-industrial Sublime*
The aesthetic category of the sublime has played a central role in discussions of landscape depictions in many different temporal and representational contexts.[32] It is often contrasted with the category of the beautiful, a

---

31   Pumla Gobodo-Madikizela (2012) and Derek Hook (2014, 2012) have both engaged with this in great depth.
32   James Elkins' (2011) rather biting comments on the limitations of the concept of the sublime provides a good appraisal of its contemporary conceptual underpinnings. Elkins (2011: 15) discusses the complexity of the concept in particular, and how it relates to representations that are either evocative of the sublime or are sublime in themselves. His thoughts are useful for examining the discourse on the sublime rather than the concept itself, which he disparages.

complementary relationship formulated in the eighteenth century by Edmund Burke (1996) and Immanuel Kant (2001). Gillian B. Pierce (2012: VII) traces the concept of the sublime from Longinus' treatise on sublime writing, the *Peri Hypsous*, through the writings of Burke and Kant, to Hegel, de Man, Lyotard and Jameson, Nancy and Bourdieu.[33] Although for Kant the sublime was not associated with art or representation, it later came to be associated with landscape art, still later with avant-garde art (see Jean Francois Lyotard 1984a, 1990), and eventually even with industrialisation and digital technology (see David Nye 1994). I refer chiefly to a more recent formulation: the post-industrial sublime, which Dylan Trigg (2006) connects to post-industrial ruins, as do Jonathan Maskit (2007), Andreas Huyssen (2006), Amanda Boetzkes (2010), and Isis Brook (2012), whose research I return to in my analysis of *District 9*.

Four different historical interpretations of the sublime are pertinent, which I will outline as concisely as I can.[34] These moments in the concept's history do not begin to appraise the sublime's reach pertaining to landscape representation; that could of course be considered more fully than I do here, but would entail too lengthy a digression from my focus on *District 9*. In selecting these moments when the sublime is articulated in diverse ways, I do not consider them as progressions that build on each other, although they appear roughly chronological. Over time, scholars have built on seminal theories, despite often simultaneously regarding them as flawed and departing from them. Yet, while there seems to be no single contemporary version of what the sublime is, the category continues to offer tools (though no decisive answers) for understanding landscapes that confound viewers.

Both Kantian and Burkean notions of sublimity have been challenged, and my reference to them is limited to drawing out those aspects that remain to some degree relevant. The first interpretation concerns the notion of transcendence. For Kant (2001: 5–42), who is most often referenced in recent research on the sublime, the aesthetic experience of the sublime entails a triumph over the senses. When one beholds something impossible to comprehend, the faculty of reason enables one to achieve a sense of transcendence in the face of its incomprehensibility. This is the Kantian mathematical sublime.[35] The second interpretation relates to Burke's (1996: 131–132) equally

---

33   See also Jana M. Giles (2012: 15–16) and Herman Wittenberg (2004: 1–64) for discussions of the sublime's development.
34   See also Peter de Bolla (1989), Paul Crowther (1996) and Philip Shaw (2017) for representative accounts.
35   See Kant (2007: 78–87, §25–§26). For further reference, Bert Olivier (1998: 198–199) provides a useful summary of this concept.

well-known, slightly earlier formulation of the sublime. He describes a paradoxical experience of both terror and delight when, for example, one is confronted with a vast and destructive force of nature, but one is not physically endangered. The delight that one experiences is the sublime. In both cases, Bert Olivier (1998: 199) argues, the viewer may experience the same broad range of feelings: pain or displeasure, even terror, in the face of such threatening phenomena, which then transition into feelings of delight or pleasure of some kind. Amanda Boetzkes (2010) considers how these two important formulations of the sublime might be useful in a contemporary context, in her focus on sublime landscapes of industrial waste. One of the shortcomings to applying these historical formulations and, in particular, the Kantian version to contemporary sites of ruin, however, is that they rely on a resolution in the tensions they espouse. In other words, there is a resolution reached in how the faculty of reason transcends the incomprehensibility of the forces experienced. Such transcendence seems less tenable in the postmodern context, and perhaps even less so in the Anthropocene context.[36] Not all formulations, even if in the Kantian tradition, foreground such a transcendent experience, however.

Lyotard's postmodern sublime is the third interpretation of the concept relevant here. This sublime is fundamentally concerned with beholding something difficult to comprehend, and it is more open-ended than what Kant proposed. Lyotard (1984a) writes about the sublime in reference to avant-garde art, not nature, landscapes or their representations, later interpreted by Simon Malpas (2002: 199–200) as a denial of form, in that his sublime is not associated with figurative art. For Lyotard, sublime artworks deny the viewer the ease of interpretation that one associates with depictions of beauty, and yet they are compelling in a different manner. The sublime in Lyotard's interpretation concerns disruption, and the break with traditions and conventions that govern the spectatorship of art, and which produces new ways of seeing through a transformative process. Such a disruption carries with it a shock, a sudden rupture the viewer cannot control (Lyotard 1984a: 40, Shaw 2017: 167–189). In this interpretation of the sublime, there is no sense of resolution for the viewer,

---

36   See Sandra Shapshay's (2017: 164–174) appraisal of the sublime that responds to representations and physical experiences of landscapes, and discusses how the sublime remains a relevant concept through which to understand contradictory experiences of place. She engages in particular with the Kantian notion of transcendence, and questions of how it may be understood in the contemporary context. For her, outer space is one of the remaining sites where such a "thick sublime" may be experienced, as a frontier not yet domesticated by humanity (2017: 169–174).

as there is in the Kantian sublime, which, in a different way, artists prior to the avant-garde would have sought to achieve.[37]

This brings me to the last and most recent interpretation that is pertinent: the post-industrial sublime, as formulated by Dylan Trigg (2006). The post-industrial sublime does not stand alone, however, but alongside a historical precedent: the industrial sublime. David Nye (1994: 17–43, 126) considers the industrial sublime as a specific permutation of the sublime and industrialisation in the eighteenth- and nineteenth-century United States. He traces how industrialisation itself became a site of awe for the American public, and how it inverted many of the conventions associated with the Kantian and Burkean sublime, which he refers to as philosophical. For Nye the awe inspired by industrial feats, such as the construction of the Erie Canal in New York, and later industrial sites such as factory districts in their entirety, were characteristic of an American sublime. It was an experience available to everyone alike (and not associated more with masculine intellect than feminine emotion as the Kantian sublime is); it was experienced in crowds, and reinforced a nationalist sentiment. Instead of being associated with transcendence it became associated with religious revivalism. Here, one could argue, modernist spatial rationality was celebrated as sublime and as evidence of the prowess of human intellect and effort.

Michael J. Shapiro (2018: 101–132) also writes illuminatingly about the industrial sublime of the nineteenth century, which led to the contemporary post-industrial sublime. For him the emphasis in both is, perhaps surprisingly, political and post-colonial. He reads portrayals of the industrial sublime in the work of nineteenth-century American artists against the grain of that sublimity, as registers of the violence and dispossession inflicted upon native Americans, which was facilitated by processes of industrialisation that favoured white settlement of the country. He draws attention to how the sublime may be used to consider landscape critically, and this is what interests me in Trigg's formulation of the concept. For Trigg (2006), post-industrial sublime landscapes are fundamentally about decay, and for this reason stand in contrast to Kantian notions of transcendence. These sites do not represent a Kantian triumph of human reason but, unlike industrial sublime landscapes, a failure of human enterprise. According to Trigg, the contradictory effect of such contemporary sites is unsettling yet affirming because they represent another kind of

---

37 See Paul Crowther's (1996) critical appraisal of Lyotard's interpretation of the sublime, as well as Jerome Carroll (2008); they both see Lyotard as engaging with the Kantian sublime, though others, such as Philip Shaw (2017), argue that he departs from Kantian ideas.

disruption, namely the very *subversion* of modernist spatial rationality and, as such, they stand in contrast to historical formulations such as the industrial sublime (Trigg 2006: 150). Miles Orvell (2013) and Boetzkes (2010) also discuss the sublime with reference to contemporary industrial landscapes or places of urban decay, but with different emphases. Whereas Orvell focuses on what he terms the "destructive sublime", Boetzkes considers landscapes filled with industrial waste.

Thus, in summary, the sublime is historically associated with the notion of transcendence as well as an incongruous experience of both terror and delight. In line with this contradictory dynamic, it is further associated in postmodern thought with the disruption of visual conventions and traditions. Moving beyond Kantian formulations, it is finally regarded in contemporary post-industrial iterations as a disruption of, resistance to, or subversion of the spatial rationality of modernist urbanism. Although in essence a departure from the sublime (see Trigg 2006: 153 and Shaw 2017: 167–189), such disruption, as a post-sublime or a post-Kantian sublime (Shapiro 2018: 8), nonetheless offers "critical resistance against the enforcement of spatial rationality" (Trigg 2006: 150). In other words, a sense of the contradictory quality of its historical formulations remains even when the sublime tends to dissolve into something more unsettling. Importantly for my interpretation, Trigg (2006: 151) identifies the role that temporality plays in the perception of the post-industrial sublime. Post-industrial landscapes are characteristically unresolved and in a state of ongoing decay: they may exhibit some qualities that evoke contradictory responses but, as time passes, may end up the same as romantic historical ruins, as merely picturesque, having lost their sublime force (thus becoming more affirming than unsettling). On the other hand, a post-industrial landscape may also over time decay to the point at which it simply collapses into rubble and becomes merely unsettling to behold.[38] Since the post-industrial sublime is a slippery category because its objects are in a state of ongoing decay,[39] it makes sense to consider it along a sliding scale where the far end

---

[38] When writing about natural wonders in the US in the 1800s, Nye (1994: 14) discusses how sites that could be regarded as sublime may lose their impact on viewers over time, especially if they are widely reproduced in popular media; they may then disappoint instead of astonish. The point is important: sublime experiences of landscapes are never guaranteed, and they may change over time. While natural landscapes such as the Grand Canyon may evoke a sense of the eternal, post-industrial landscapes evoke the sure sense of their further decay.

[39] I discuss this later in more depth. Trigg (2006: 151) makes the argument that classical ruins do not function in the same way as contemporary post-industrial ruins. The former attain a semblance of stasis, which renders them more pleasurable than unsettling to behold.

is a complete collapse of sublimity into what Trigg (2006: 154) refers to as "the dissolute". At a later stage I consider this in more depth when another category of contradictory aesthetic experience becomes pertinent: the formless. The sublime is clearly not a fixed concept, and it has evolved throughout its different applications to nature, to art and to the human-made environment or Anthropocene. I will interrogate this further, but it is important at this stage to keep sight of its relevance for a better understanding of how *District 9* portrays Johannesburg as a post-industrial sublime landscape.

5.2 *The Sublime in Post-apartheid and Post-colonial Contexts*

Apart from questions around the sublime's contemporary qualities, one of the biggest concerns about the sublime is its origin in imperialist and colonialist theories. If the sublime holds any potential for critical resistance, or 'critical potential', then how does that potential reconcile with its ignoble foundations? In this regard, it is helpful to consider how post-colonial discourse has viewed the concept.

South African scholar Herman Wittenberg (2004) considers how theories of the sublime are entrenched in colonial discourse in South Africa. For him, the problem goes back to both Burke's and Kant's understanding of race. Both thinkers saw clear links between people's capacity for sublime experience and their supposed civilisation and education, and thus their status as Europeans (Wittenberg 2004: 57–60). Such ideas point to the uncritical racism that underpinned the thinking of eighteenth-century philosophers. Wittenberg argues that Kant believed that non-Europeans had no innate capacity to experience the sublime, and that African peoples in particular had no propensity for aesthetic experience. For Burke, on the other hand, the sublime is related to blackness as an environmental feature; however, in relation to Black bodies, it simply collapses into an experience of horror and aversion. One of the other concerns stressed in scholarly examinations of the topic is that Kantian aesthetic theory presupposed a universality of spectatorship that was obviously fallacious, because it essentially applied only to Europeans, and indeed only to European men (Spivak in Wittenberg 2004: 57, Gikandi 2001: 9, Nye 1994: 30–31).

Perhaps surprisingly in light of the above, John Su (2011: 65–86), as well as Gillian B. Pierce (2012: VII, 8), consider that there was a renewed interest in aesthetic theories in the humanities in the first decade of the 2000s, particularly in post-colonial studies. While Su (2011: 65) suggests that post-colonial studies first sought to devalue the aesthetic qualities of works, and to focus instead on socio-cultural and political elements, such as the representation of minority experience, there was a possible reversal, in which aesthetic concerns were once again considered important. There are clear risks with such an approach; for example, there is the danger of repeating the universalising tendency of colonial and Enlightenment discourse and, in so doing, denying the cultural differences, power relations and political concerns that are pertinent to specific settings (Su 2011: 66). Su argues, however, that post-colonial studies found a way to focus on both the aesthetic and the material aspects of cultural production. He considers how aesthetic categories can be redeployed and reclaimed in post-colonial settings, and argues that aesthetic concepts were often more valued by colonised individuals than the project of colonialism acknowledged. Scholars like Shapiro (2018) also pursue the political implications of aesthetic categories such as the sublime. In his book on the "political sublime", Shapiro engages with race, with histories of place, and with histories of the sublime from a critical perspective. He revives theories of the sublime to interrogate how industrialisation is historically implicated in racial inequality in the United States in literary and visual texts to demonstrate the concept's continued relevance for understanding landscape and geopolitics.

5.3 *European Landscape Traditions in South Africa*

The sublime is not just an aesthetic category, but also a landscape tradition. South African art history recognises varied traditions of landscape representation, many of them informed by colonial notions of landscape, as well as western aesthetic categories and conventions such as the sublime. It is important to note that these traditions were established by both Black and white artists, to emphasise that there is no singular landscape tradition in the country's art history, and that what I consider here is fragmentary at best. I tend to reflect more on settler interpretations of landscape, not only because they are dominant in the history of South African painting but also because they are relevant to the landscape *District 9* portrays and reveal the fraught relationship between whiteness and landscape.

It is vital, however, to be cognisant of developments in how Black artists depicted landscape in South Africa historically, because they too were influenced by western conventions. Juliette Leeb-du Toit (2010) discusses landscape traditions in the country between 1907 and 1948. She begins her discussion of African landscape representation by referring to Sol Plaatjie's 1915 *Native Life in South Africa* (1998), a book that marked the beginning of resistance to racially driven land loss in South Africa (Leeb-du Toit 2010: 188–189). The Natives Land Act of 1913, the Natives Act of 1923 and the Native Trust and Land Act of 1936 each contributed to the dispossession of land belonging to Black owners. The African National Congress (first known as the South African Native National Congress) was formed in response to the intentions promulgated in the 1913 Act, and opposition grew to these legislations, although it had little effect at the time. The fraught history of dispossession is implicit in landscape representation in South Africa, and it may be helpful to bear in mind that land and landscape are value-laden terms within the context of the country's history.

Poet Herbert Dhlomo's (1985) writing from the 1940s describes the landscape in Zululand (now KwaZulu Natal) nostalgically, as an idyllic pre-colonial place. His idealised view of landscape is echoed in the work of several Black artists at the time: John Koenakeefe Mohl, George Pemba, Simoni Mnguni, Jabulani Ntuli, Gerard Bhengu and Gerard Sekoto. Mohl is important here, especially as he produced some of the first 'township' landscapes (Leeb-du Toit 2010: 193). Over time, a particular tradition emerged in the work of some of these artists, who often seemed to value concepts of the landscape as rural, and to think of it in relation to urban environments (Leeb-du Toit 2010: 193). Generally in such works, urban spaces were seen as dystopian, while rural spaces were seen as utopian, thus constructing a binary that idealised rural life and implicitly preferred a pre-colonial view of the landscape.

Importantly, however, not all landscapes by Black artists were about the dispossession wrought by colonialism, and Bhengu's work seems to challenge such a view. His depictions represented African control over the realms of culture and agriculture, in the portrayal of real places where he had lived. His work became, in Leeb-du Toit's words, "a powerful metaphor for an aspirant political and social reality in a democratic society" (2010: 189).

While Leeb-du Toit makes a point of focusing on the unique voices developed by Black artists in South Africa in the twentieth century, many of the artists were trained in missionary schools, so they were in effect schooled in European art conventions. Elizabeth Rankin (2010: 93) suggests that many of the artists were to a large degree self-taught, and relied on their own observation and occasional mentoring, unless they furthered their studies abroad. Mohl, as well as Ernest Mancoba, Gerard Sekoto, Valerie Desmonds, Louis Maurice, Peter Clarke and Job Kekana, all worked and studied in Europe and Britain between the 1930s and the 1960s, and others, such as Selby Mvusi and Dan Rakgoathe, studied in the US. Under apartheid, Black artists could not gain access to South African institutions to further their studies, and there were very few who managed to do so abroad; even those who were able to study elsewhere rarely did so at the outset of their careers. The influence of European conventions in the work of many Black artists thus came about initially through contact with white mentors or teachers in South Africa who had in many cases been trained in Europe themselves. The same conventions also affected the work of artists of settler descent, such as Irma Stern, Maggie Laubser and J.H. Pierneef. In this sense, there is a lineage of grappling with

European conventions in the representation of the South African landscape in the work of both Black artists and white artists.

Author J.M. Coetzee's (1988) important text on landscape representation in South African literature and painting, *White Writing*, delves into the complex relationship in settler art between aesthetics and colonialism – or between European landscape conventions and the South African landscape. He explores how European aesthetics underpinned the work of white South African writers and painters, who tried to come to grips with the local landscape that they had either settled in or visited as part of the colonial project. He focuses on specific constructs through which landscapes were represented in European traditions, namely the pastoral, the picturesque and the sublime. Coetzee contends that the former two were fundamentally mismatched with the local landscape, and only the sublime offered an opportunity to adapt European conventions for South African purposes. He argues that the sublime could have evolved into an authentically South African set of landscape conventions. This was a missed opportunity, however, as the Dutch settlers in the Cape who sought to represent the terrain instead related to the landscape through pastoral notions of nature as "garden" (Coetzee 1988: 1–4). Coetzee discusses representations of rural and farm life in South African art and literature of the eighteenth and nineteenth centuries as idealised, and as a nostalgic reaction to the development of urbanisation. In a manner somewhat comparable to the work of later Black artists, farm life was often depicted as a pastoral idyll in contrast to the ills of urban life. In contrast to the work of Black artists and to settler notions of the landscape as garden (a tamed and productive landscape of sorts), the notion of South Africa as uncivilised wilderness emerged, a wilderness that had to be overcome to colonise the land. The wilderness was associated with the supposed idleness of the early indigenous inhabitants of the country, such as the Khoi and the San, who were not agriculturalists; the trope stood in opposition to pre-colonial notions of landscape, just as much as productive farm landscapes did. Wilderness, Coetzee argues, is an Enlightenment stereotype echoed in subsequent representations of landscape prevalent throughout English colonial rule that persisted during later expansion into the interior of the country. Colonial discourse held that territory belonged to those who made use of it and settled on it, and construed colonial expansion by white settlers as a justified moral imperative.[40]

---

40 See Coetzee (1988: 3–4), as well as Tom Scanlan (2005: 13–55) and Patrick Harries (1997: 171–191), for references to this colonial imperative.

For Coetzee (1988) then, there is a marked mismatch from the outset between the visual conventions applied to European landscape representation and the representation of the South African landscape, and it could be argued that it is also evident in different ways in the work of Black artists, such as those mentioned above. Coetzee (1988:36–62) discusses how the tradition of the picturesque and its conventions simply did not enable settlers to regard the South African landscape as beautiful or interesting. In the English picturesque, informed by the so-called Claudean tradition, there were specific visual schemas for both representing and interpreting the landscape in painting (Coetzee 1988: 39–40). The picturesque typically relied on a significant feature in the landscape's middle ground, such as a body of water or a ruin, for example. It also blended aspects of sublimity and pastoral landscapes to provide "variety, intricacy, wildness, and decay" (Brook 2012: 111). Paintings of the Lake District in the United Kingdom represented the pinnacle of the picturesque landscape in the British tradition. The South African landscape by contrast, and especially the interior from the arid Karoo region northwards, offered very little of visual interest to painters who were familiar with European conventions in the realm of the picturesque (Harries 1997).[41]

Coetzee's (1988:49–51) main concern in discussing these traditions is to consider why the sublime was not taken up more widely in historical representations of the South African landscape. He makes a comparison to the adoption of the picturesque and later the sublime in landscape painting and literature in the US, where he lived from 1965 to 1971 (J.M. Coetzee – Biographical 2003). He argues that the dramatic landscape of the US perhaps lent itself more readily to paintings in the tradition of the sublime than the other traditions under discussion here. It is a point also made by Nye (1994: 1–16) in his investigation of the American sublime tradition, which was orientated to appreciating the natural wonders of the United States such as the Grand Canyon. Focusing on the Hudson River School, Coetzee discusses notions of transcendence through these expansive and luminous representations of landscape.[42] Why did the sublime become so prevalent in the United States and not in South Africa?

---

41   I discuss these differences in more detail in Chapter 7, in the context of classical ruins.
42   A parallel stream of landscape photography developed alongside painting in this vein: early photographers such as William Henry, Timothy O'Sullivan and Carleton Watkins took up the language of the American landscape in the West of the country, and later Ansel Adams, working in the US in the 1950s and 60s, became known for it in his work in Yosemite National Park. See Jonathan Spaulding (1996: 615–639) on Adams' work in the Yosemite, and Kate Nearpass Ogden (1990: 134–153) for a discussion of painters and photographers working in the park in the nineteenth century.

His conclusion is that the lack of a sublime tradition in South African art and literature may be because the landscape baffled settler writers and artists who were drawing on predominantly European training, as well as the initial lack of artists and authors versed in the sublime tradition (1988: 55–56). By the turn of the nineteenth century in the US, some artists had been schooled locally and developed their own vocabulary for capturing the landscape, whereas, in South Africa, most artists were trained in Europe and therefore employed a mismatched set of schemas to the local landscape (Coetzee 1988: 56).[43]

Coetzee's work on the topic has had a considerable impact on research in this field. I revisit Coetzee's interest in the sublime to consider it anew in terms of what the aesthetic category and the landscape tradition of the sublime can offer to an understanding of depictions such as those in *District 9*. Although there is little exploration of this, I am not alone in revisiting Coetzee's ideas about the sublime. Jennifer Beningfield (2006) articulates aspects of contemporary landscape depiction in South Africa that have correspondences with my approach to *District 9*'s Johannesburg. She too refers to Coetzee, to explore the contemporary complexities of the South African landscape. Furthermore, she discusses land and landscape as fundamentally contradictory in the ways they are represented and imagined. This contradiction is part of what I propose might productively be understood through the lens of the sublime, which also arises from contradiction.

5.4 *Sublime Potential*

I now focus on one of the most important aspects of how the sublime has been conceived historically and in contemporary reflections. Considering how initially the sublime was associated with transcendence, with contradictory experiences of pain or terror as well as pleasure or delight, and more recently is seen as unsettling and affirming simultaneously, it is clear it represents a disruptive impulse, which subverts visual conventions and modernist urban rationality. Although associated with "the dissolute" (Trigg 2006: 153), and a true crisis in humankind's relationship to nature and landscape (Boetzkes 2010), as I explore in chapters to come, the experience of the sublime in the post-industrial context may be considered *potentially* productive, in that it fundamentally challenges the dominant order in society. This order might be urban planning, or visual conventions in artworks, or indeed the modernist rationality co-opted

---

43 This is not to say that there was no uptake of the sublime by later landscape painters. J.H. Pierneef's paintings are often understood as engaging with the tradition (Maré & Coetzee 2016), as I discuss later, and the argument has also been made that Moses Tladi's work could be seen as engaging the sublime landscape tradition (Coetsee 2013).

by colonial and then apartheid ideology, which can be critically revisited as a vestige of the past (Trigg 2006: 147–151). The sublime as a landscape category may also be used to interrogate spatial history and geopolitics, as Shapiro (2018) demonstrates. Looking at the concept diachronically, one may be tempted to ask whether the post-industrial sublime has such 'critical potential', since it is associated with a dissolution of reason rather than transcendence through reason. In my understanding of how contemporary scholars engage with the sublime, however, the question is not so much whether such potential remains, but rather how the sublime now works. Along the same lines, I find it less useful to embark on a comprehensive excavation of the sublime's most intricate machinations in this book, since that is a project of its own. Some scholars, such as Shapshay (2017) and Shapiro (2018), consider Kant as formative, but nonetheless formulate contemporary sublimity as post-Kantian, whereas others such as Boetzkes (2010) consider contemporary sublimes as wholly different because transcendence does not seem viable anymore. To me such considerations should be taken in context and for my purposes delving into such questions misses the point somewhat. What is pertinent here is that the concept prevails, and remains useful, especially in considering the aesthetic significance of post-industrial landscapes.

To flesh this out a little more, I return to the colonial couching of the concept of the sublime. Writing about aesthetics as a larger philosophical field of inquiry, Kenyan scholar Simon Gikandi (2001) discusses the inextricable and entangled relationship between the Enlightenment's aesthetic theories and the project of colonialism, as well as slavery and general racist notions of blackness that are evident in eighteenth-century Europe. He refers to this relationship as "troubled", but ultimately argues that the question is not straightforward enough to declare aesthetics incommensurate with post-colonial agendas (Gikandi 2001:1). By way of example, he refers to the poetry of twentieth-century African-American writer Robert Hayden, arguing that the writer's work functioned paradoxically within a western aesthetic canon. He goes on to acknowledge the emancipatory potential of Hayden's work, despite its being haunted by opposing notions such as enslavement. For Gikandi, race and the aesthetic are connected: he argues that ultimately it is the emancipation offered by art that may enable Black people to define their own subjectivity in colonial settings and, it may be inferred, in post-colonial ones.

It is not only within a post-colonial context that aesthetics can offer critical strategies and outcomes for the viewer or reader, however. The sublime has been associated with the notion of emancipation by scholars such as Hayden White, F. R. Ankersmit, Nicholas Brown and Amy J. Elias (Su 2011: 78). Moreover, it is theorised by Frankfurt School scholars (Adorno & Horkheimer 1993) and by Lyotard (1984a, 1990) in relation to avant-garde art, which has been regarded in critical theory as the true residence of emancipation.[44]

What exactly is the relationship between the post-industrial sublime and emancipation then? Since the post-industrial sublime is often regarded as post-Kantian, and there is no Kantian resolution-through-reason at work, I do not argue that there is an *emancipatory* effect per se at work in this contemporary sublime. Instead, it seems to me that the critical potential that Trigg (2006:150) refers to correlates with two particular dynamics that occur in how Johannesburg is represented in *District 9* and its visual idiom of nostalgic dystopia. The first is transformation and the second is "subversive resistance" (Farber 2015). Although I have not considered these concepts up to this point, they become important in the chapters that follow as articulations of the critical potential of the post-industrial sublime. Both transformation and subversive resistance may be seen as versions of what Lees (2004: 23) terms "freedom to". Lees (2004: 13–26) discusses urban freedom as an opportunity to be grasped, a "freedom to" impact and shape the city itself. It is a "freedom to" act, rather than a "freedom from" something, from apartheid and its aftermath, for example. Lees (2004: 23) bases the notion on Georg Simmel's description of freedom, which is understood not only in the negative sense that one is free from oppressive and restrictive forces in the city, but also in the positive sense that all individuals can express themselves and their being in the city in a unique and valid manner.

The emphasis that I draw from these diverse contexts and interpretations of the sublime is thus the *potential* for critical engagement that could be articulated in Johannesburg's difficult appearance. Jennifer Robinson (2004: 143), writing about the emancipatory potential of Johannesburg as city, cites transformative moments in South Africa's urban history and the present, as well as the notion that the city lends itself to "imaginative revisioning", especially in times of crisis. Robinson (2004: 151) refers to Henri Lefebvre when considering the representations of cities, and how they could contribute to transformation or be understood as transformative.[45] Along the same lines as Lefebvre, she argues that, through the way people live in cities, they can use spaces differently and so imagine them differently. She says that, despite the much problematised geography of Johannesburg, the diverse positions and histories of its citizens imply a vast potential for imagining the city in new ways. Later

---

44   See Theodor Adorno & Max Horkheimer (1993: 31–41) and also Stephen Eric Bronner (2011), who sketches a concise outline of the Frankfurt School's history and concerns, as well as Jerome Carroll (2008), who touches on Adorno's notion of emancipation.
45   See Lefebvre's *The Production of Space* (1991).

I consider how *District 9* imagines (a perhaps dubious) transformation in and of the city, and I also consider how other practitioners use nostalgic dystopia subversively. Engaging deeply with the post-industrial sublime's critical potential and measuring its outcomes would be a future step in this research, although beyond the scope of this book.

• • •

Johannesburg as it is represented in film, photography and popular media has been much written about. Why then my specific concern with *District 9*, given the varied and rich material already generated about the city over the last twenty years? Although the formal features of depictions of the city have been rather underemphasised up to this point, the city has become recognised by the use of specific formal features in visual depictions, which I see as a vocabulary peculiar to these media. *District 9* is one of the most emblematic examples of this and as such is a key node in a larger map of images of the city. Although the vocabulary itself has not been identified, consistent emphasis has been placed on the city's dystopian character, and on the city's past, exemplified in a recurring urge to look back at the city's sordid history, often in an incongruously nostalgic manner. This manifests in the geographic character of the city in representations, and in the attempts of scholars to make sense of the city's character in lived and portrayed capacities. These two elements – dystopia and nostalgia – are important qualities in *District 9*, which are reiterated in other representations to the point that their characterisation of the contradictory features of the nostalgic dystopian idiom has become an established visual shorthand. Another important quality that I probe here is how the sublime as an aesthetic category applied to landscape might present a frame that would prove helpful in approaching *District 9's* depiction of Johannesburg.

Regarding the depiction of Johannesburg, three important descriptive concepts that seem to inform *District 9's* Johannesburg – dystopia, nostalgia and the sublime – need to be articulated. Clearly, the dystopian qualities found in the film, and by extension in the larger visual context of the nostalgic dystopian idiom, are based on qualities of the actual city, rather than on mere notions of an imaginary place – a no-place, such as the terms utopia and dystopia would imply, or a fantastical place, as science fiction cinema would conceive it. Johannesburg is understood here as a "zone of indistinction", a real place where "bare life" conditions exist, and human rights are thwarted (Agamben in Akpome 2017: 89). There is more to such dystopian depictions, however, since there is ultimately a *critical* potential inherent in dystopian representations of cities, which is key in probing how nostalgic dystopia works. The nostalgia evident in *District 9* is also particular in that, within the post-apartheid context, it is a reluctant and self-reflexive nostalgia, which I propose may be understood as reflective nostalgia (Boym 2001: 41–48). This nostalgia is more than mere indulgence in longing; it implicitly contradicts the fundamentally dystopian qualities of the city.

From this paradoxical quality in the idiom, a contradictory dynamic arises, which, as my brief appraisal of the sublime revealed, is echoed in recent formulations of the sublime, such as the post-industrial sublime (Trigg 2006, Shapiro 2018). It is seen as both attractive and repulsive, but also as disruptive of established visual norms and rational urban order. To explore this effect, I consider how the disruption can give rise to certain forms of Lees'(2004: 13–26) "freedom to" enact change or transformation in how the city is regarded. The sublime is not perhaps the obvious choice for interpreting the post-apartheid and post-colonial cityscape of Johannesburg, as it is a decidedly western concept and thoroughly entrenched in the racist thinking of the Enlightenment. Recent scholarship in post-colonial studies, however, acknowledges and even welcomes a reconsideration of western aesthetics as a useful discipline within post-colonial contexts. The notion of a post-industrial sublime is not lacking in criticality either; it seeks to critique western urban planning and the rationalist biases that informed modern city planning. Finally, it is noteworthy that the sublime can be seen as an oversight of sorts, absent in the history of South African landscape representation, which I revisit to interrogate how Johannesburg is understood now. As such, a re-framed sublime presents a feasible and productive avenue to pursue to better understand *District 9*'s landscapes.

CHAPTER 2

Digging Deeper

1 Analogue Aesthetics

1.1 *Nostalgia for Analogue Media*

My approach to *District 9* focuses on both 'the how' and 'the what' of its representation of Johannesburg. Analogue aesthetics represents 'the how' – techniques that emulate analogue media and are fundamental to the film's portrayal of the city. The techniques largely rely on analogue nostalgia, and are part of a broader nostalgia trend in global popular culture. As scholars have noted,[1] this boom or wave manifests in photography, fashion and other design fields as well as film, and has been referred to as an "analogue renaissance" (Minniti 2020: 79).

What exactly is analogue media, however? Before I move on to discuss the analogue renaissance, I will briefly consider the distinction between the paradigms of analogue and digital media as I employ them in my discussion. In the first decade of the 2000s, Lev Manovich (2005) suggested that what he called "new media" might be understood as the move towards all media becoming increasingly computer-mediated. He describes the process as follows: "graphics, moving images, sounds, shapes, spaces and text [...] become computable, [as] computer data" (Manovich 2005: 44). Digital media has subsequently become a more widely used term and, in its popular and academic designations, refers to media that make use of binary code; in other words, computers are involved at some stage, whether in the creation of content or the technologies used (Cramer 2014: 17). Digital media is in this way also associated with electronic processes or technologies. In terms of the inception of digital media, Manovich (2005: 30–35) refers to the first computers used to work on 3D graphics in the 1970s, and the later arrival of the internet in the 1990s, as important turning points in the digital media paradigm. But he also draws out links between media from the 1800s (such as looms) and digital or "new media", so it is clear there is no precise moment when digital (new) media emerge as separate from analogue (old) media.

---

1 See Lowenthal (2015: 5), Schneider & Strauven (2013: 411–412), Niemeyer (2016, 2014: 1–26), Cook (2005), Bartholeyns (2014: 51–67), Schrey (2014: 27–38), Prince (2011), Sapio (2014: 39–50), DeLong et al. (2005: 23–42), Doss (2010: 58) and Caoduro (2014).

© LANDI RAUBENHEIMER, 2025 | DOI:10.1163/9789004710955_004

Many scholars have engaged with the concepts of new media or digital media. A decade after Manovich, Florian Cramer (2014) argued that society was already in fact "post-digital" because digital media were no longer seen as 'new' media. They had become ubiquitous by that time, and came to be regarded as merely 'media', while older media, such as analogue cameras, came to be referred to as 'analogue' (Cramer & Jandrić 2021: 985). Along with suggesting how artists and designers then began to make use of both digital and analogue media to meet their needs, and to enact a form of media nostalgia by embracing dated technologies, Cramer also takes issue with the terms analogue and digital. He argues that the very term digital media is misleading. In his view digital media are those that divide information into discrete numerical units, not necessarily binary code; they are digital in that they are countable. He suggests that even ancient floor mosaics and typewriters are digital, and that (analogue) film too is in practice digital since separate frames are used to create a moving image (Cramer 2014: 15–16). For Cramer, digital and analogue media are thus not as different as the use of the terms in the humanities and popular culture might indicate. He argues that digital devices are not digital at all, but actually converters of sorts, which convert media from analogue to digital and back to analogue forms (Cramer 2014: 20). In the context of the term post-digital, what one might take from such debates around digital media is how the paradigms of analogue and digital media are enmeshed, rather than two separate developments. The term post-digital, though thought-provoking, has been rather short-lived in academic discourse as Cramer himself later attests (Cramer & Jandrić 2021).[2] For this reason, I do not use it extensively here.

Since I am interested in popular media, and the popular use and understanding of media, I also do not interrogate the two terms in the way that Cramer does. Instead, I use the conventional designations, which refer to "computational electronic devices" and their media products as digital media (Cramer 2014: 20), while analogue media are those that predate such computation. Practitioners seem to regard analogue media as those that predate the advent of personal computers, and digital media are those that are part of the computational and electronic context which followed. In my use of the terms digital and analogue, I am less interested in further problematising how they historically developed as seemingly separate paradigms, than in probing the

---

2   The term is still in use, but with a different inflection and in a different context from Cramer's initial use of it. Kristin Klein (2021) discusses it in the context of art education, where it connotes a criticality towards digital media and its social, historical and economic effects. In this context the use of the term shifts and is no longer concerned with media nostalgia, but focuses more on the social context of post-digital and post-internet society.

first two decades of the 2000s, when the two paradigms productively overlap and interact in particular ways, to produce nostalgic effects that attest to the nostalgia boom mentioned above.

Digital television and cinema, or "moving image media",[3] have become sites for emulating styles and media from previous eras, with visual effects that evoke older media also mimicked in digital video and photography (Schrey 2014: 34–35). The title sequence for the American television series *Californication* (Kapinos 2007–2014) is a good example. Lens flares, bokeh, flash frames, scratches and visual splices, visible film grain and dissolving emulsion, perforation of the film strip, a limited round frame associated with 8mm home movies, and other visual devices are employed to simulate decaying analogue film stock (Schrey 2014: 33–34).

Such effects have become ubiquitous in contemporary film and television. The nostalgia boom is not limited to visual media, however, and an example many scholars cite concerns the way the shift from vinyl to cassette tapes in sound recording in the 1980s was interpreted subsequently: often the vinyl medium is described as sounding more vital, life-like, warmer and rounder than the succeeding medium of cassette tape.[4] The move to compact disc (CD) resulted in even greater loss of warmth. As many studies have argued, digital media of all kinds, including video, are likewise often regarded as colder and less life-like than analogue media.[5]

Katharina Niemeyer (2014: 1–26) writes that a nostalgia for the past is often embedded within contemporary media, and that nostalgia is evoked to heal or address a pining for the past in users or audiences. She argues that in contemporary representation nostalgia can represent a past that one did not experience, and that "nostalgi[s]ing" the past in this manner is an act *facilitated* by media (Niemeyer 2014: 10). In this way, past media may stand in for past experiences one may not have had access to, and may bring experiences closer through representation in a seemingly Benjaminian manner, something I explore below. Scholars have asserted that it is this yearning for a supposedly more authentic time and experience of life that underlies the nostalgia boom in popular culture (Caoduro 2014, Niemeyer 2014). Benjamin is a key theorist in nostalgia studies; Niemeyer and Caoduro both refer to notions of authenticity that resemble his famous concept of the aura of authenticity, and several other

---

3   See Gaudreault & Marion (2015: Chapter 3, p 15).
4   The fascination analogue media holds for users of digital media is discussed by Dominic Schrey (2014: 27–38) and Gil Bartholeyns (2014: 51–67).
5   Refer to Schrey (2014: 31), Prince (2011: 32) and Gaudreault & Marion (2015: Chapter 3, p 10), and also Florian Cramer (2014: 13–14).

scholars also make reference to his work. In engaging with Benjamin's writings on history, both Dominic Schrey (2014) and Giuseppina Sapio (2014) suggest that an example of this yearning for a more authentic time is the way in which temporality may be evoked in a completely artificial manner in digital texts, a way that does not make chronological or temporal sense. The past becomes a collection of visual styles to select from, as it were, that lend representations a sense of historicity rather than a true temporal setting.

1.2 *Authenticity*

In light of the above, it seems there is a fetishization of analogue aesthetics in digital media and the visual techniques they employ (Schrey 2014: 34–35). Schrey refers to this as remediation, a term established by David Jay Bolter and Richard Grusin (2000) in their book *Remediation: Understanding New Media*. The process takes place when digital media employ the style of older media to evoke nostalgia for a perceived lost past (Schrey 2014: 27–38). In this context, Bolter and Grusin (2000) use the concept hypermediacy to refer to the emphasis on mediatic qualities within the process of remediation. Here the material qualities of a medium are emphasised instead of concealed, to draw attention to the aspects of analogue media that are referenced. Remediation does not develop in one direction only, however. Sergio Minniti (2020), writing about Lomography and "polaroidism", refers to how the two analogue photography movements may be regarded as less of a nostalgic development than an innovation in how analogue and digital photography co-exist and are imbricated with each other in the digital age. He traces how it has become important for amateur enthusiasts of these practices to use photography as a form of resistance to the perceived lack of materiality and authenticity of digital media. He argues that, rather than a nostalgic urge, this could be seen as a form of "technological resistance" (Minniti 2020: 93–94), which pursues analogue materiality through the physicality of the medium. Nonetheless, the effect is often nostalgic, and evokes the previous lives of these media forms.

As discussed above, the preoccupation with evoking historicity that is prevalent in analogue nostalgia has been related to Benjamin's concept of authenticity by several scholars. What is at stake in current thinking is a varied use of the term authenticity rather than a direct reference to Benjamin's concept of the aura of authenticity, although it seems to be either implied or explicitly referenced in many discussions on analogue nostalgia. For nuance and clarification, I find it helpful to devote some time to the concept.

In the 1930s, at a time when paradigmatic media change was unfolding – as it currently is again with the advent of digital media – Benjamin (2004: 791–811) suggested that film as a new medium associated with mass reproduction had less aura of authenticity than the older medium of painting. In ways that evoke many aspects of Benjamin's thinking at the time, analogue film is heralded now as more authentic than digital video.[6] Benjamin's (2004: 793) reflections on the aura of authenticity of artworks explore the experience of an object's unique existence in time and space, and thus its rootedness in tradition and ritual. For him, the aura, informed by an artwork's uniqueness, was depreciated by how easily accessible filmic and photographic media would make representations available in the 1930s. As a consequence of media such as photography and film, he argued, the original artwork held much less fascination, or aura, for the audience. As a result, the aura would be something that audiences nostalgically longed for, in the future of cinema as he saw it (Benjamin 2004: 804).

It is noteworthy that Benjamin's use of the term aura varied throughout his work, and that it is not a concept to be transposed wholesale into current media contexts without careful nuancing. It is therefore useful to ask whether Benjamin's notion of the aura of authenticity is relevant at all to the discussion of authenticity in current writing on analogue nostalgia. Noah Isenberg (Isenberg & Benjamin 2001: 119–150) discusses the relationship between Benjamin's work on the aura and contemporary media. He considers why the impact of Benjamin's work is so prolific by arguing that it is at heart interdisciplinary, and thus able to influence many different fields. Along with the aura of authenticity, Benjamin's concepts of "monad", "constellation" and "dialectical image", and his thinking on photography, have been influential in cultural criticism and media studies (Isenberg & Benjamin 2001: 135). Isenberg refers to several scholars who were interested in Benjamin's relevance for the information age before the current literature on analogue nostalgia came into play. They include Rosalind Krauss, in her article on photography Reinventing the Medium (1999), Janet Wolff (1993), Susan Sontag (1980), Hannah Arendt (1973) and Miriam Hansen (2008, 1987). He suggests there is an emerging field entitled Benjamin studies, in what he refers to as the "Benjamin industry" (Isenberg & Benjamin 2001: 120). The use of authenticity by Caoduro (2014), Niemeyer (2014), Sapio (2014) and Schrey (2014) thus seems to be aligned with several earlier scholars who turned to Benjamin to consider contemporary discourse on media developments.

Benjamin first mentions the aura in his 1931 essay entitled *A Short History of Photography* (Benjamin 1972) and reflects on it in the *Arcades Project* (2002), which was published posthumously. German-born expert on Benjamin,

---

6 Refer to Gaudreault & Marion (2015) and John Belton (2008) for more on this perceived difference between analogue and digital media.

Miriam Hansen (2008, 1987), unpacks aura in relation to his use of the term the "optical unconscious", and to the notion of mimesis as articulated by the Frankfurt scholars. The former concept is pertinent here because it refers to the ability of photography and film to capture aspects of the visual world that are not visible to the naked eye, or not consciously perceived, such as the way a person walks, or movements that occur in split seconds. As such the camera can reveal a different world, or indeed a world of unconscious visual information (Benjamin 1972: 7, Benjamin 2004: 220, 236–237, Hansen 1987: 208–210).[7]

The notion of aura is unpacked in three distinctly different ways by Hansen: first, the "unique appearance of a distance, however near it may be" (Benjamin 1972: 20, 2004: 795); second, the ability of the object or phenomenon to return the gaze of the viewer. Third, referring to Benjamin's friend and contemporary Gershom Scholem, Hansen proposes another interpretation of aura, by suggesting that Benjamin was inspired by Jewish mysticism and that his understanding of aura borrowed from thinkers in that field, such as Alfred Schuler and Ludwig Klages of the Munich Kosmiker circle. Within this realm, authenticity has a wider, more esoteric inflection, and references the atmosphere or energy that infuses every object and being (Hansen 2008: 339–363).

The notion of the aura is thus multi-dimensional. But what is most important here is the fundamental historicity and retrospective quality implied by aura (since it connotes uniqueness in time and place), which, as contemporary media scholars argue, is emulated in the use of digital photography and film. Because digital media has lost a sense of authenticity, as Caoduro (2014: 73–76) suggests, users turn to analogue media as repository for authenticity, and regard analogue media nostalgically as the locus of a lost link to the past. Caoduro (2014: 74) argues that users may "simulate" a sense of authenticity in digital media. Benjamin himself distinguishes between what he refers to as genuine aura and simulated aura (1972: 19). Even though Benjamin's "Artwork essay" (as Hansen refers to the 1936 essay) proposes that photography and film are in opposition to an aura of authenticity, he discusses aura in relation to photography in his 1931 essay on photography (1972). There he suggests that early photography was more auratic than later photography. The latter, which he defines as from the post-1880 period, simulated some of the auratic (poorer) quality of earlier photography, which resulted in more murky images than later

---

7 I do not apply this notion of aura here, although it may be useful to pursue further in relation to digital film and photography at another stage, especially given the relationships between nostalgia and psychoanalysis (within which the unconscious is canonical) in a post-colonial setting. The unconscious has also been used to consider how cinema itself works mimetically, particularly in the seminal writings of Christian Metz (1977).

crisper-looking photography (1972: 19). He cites the use of retouching to add more atmosphere to newer photographs. It is thus in line with such reflections by Benjamin that contemporary scholars, such as Schrey (2014) and Caoduro (2014: 67–82), consider practices of artificially creating an aged analogue look in digital photography.

Schrey argues that the aura of authenticity supposedly found in analogue media, indeed their historicity, may thus be simulated in digital media, when digital media employ what is now discussed under the label of "analogue nostalgia" (2014: 28). Analogue media products decay through use, and hence move into the realm of what is called *pentimenti* in art history: traces of the history of their use are left in the media themselves.[8] For example, film stock degrades with each viewing, and scratches appear, just as vinyl records may become scratched over time, which may be heard in the fuzzy noise that results when they are played. Schrey (2014: 34) employs the metaphor of ruins and argues that digital media users often try to emulate signs of ruin, creating virtual ruins that emulate indexicality and the flaws of analogue media that leave traces of decay on the artifacts over time. Such ruins then signify aura, the presence of time in the medium. Digital media texts, however, do not decay over time in an analogue way, because they exist as data; they seem removed from the ravages of time, and lack an aura of authenticity.

In summary, nostalgia for analogue media may thus be understood as nostalgia for authenticity, sought by digital media practitioners or users in the creation of virtual ruins or simulated visual historicity in digital media. The notion of ruins is noteworthy, because it connects nostalgia to the aesthetic category of the sublime in landscape representation, to be considered in later chapters.

1.3   *Visual Effects in Film*

A question that must be addressed is whether analogue nostalgia is a phenomenon particular to amateur practices. Although scholars in nostalgia studies, such as those discussed above, often focus on amateur photography, they do consider more industry-driven and institutionalised media such as film (see Sapio 2014), which demonstrates that analogue nostalgia is not the outcome of amateur practices alone. I would take this further to suggest that the use of visual effects in cinema over the last two decades shares many of the driving

---

8 Benjamin describes how an 1850 photograph depicting Joseph von Schelling is infused with such a trace of time, even visible in the shape of Schelling's coat, which itself becomes infused with time's traces (1972: 17).

impulses at work in analogue nostalgia, and that analogue nostalgia can be seen as important to understanding contemporary films, such as *District 9*.

Stephen Prince (2011) writes extensively on the significance of visual effects in contemporary cinematography. He refers to "visual effects" created through various digital post-production processes that affect the final appearance of a film. He is concerned with the "digitalizing" of film (a term I borrow from André Gaudreault & Phillippe Marion [2015]), as a process that has unfolded since the late 1980s in Hollywood film.[9] Along with Christopher Lucas (2014: 132–157), who also writes on digital film and cinematography, Prince discusses visual effects as distinct from special effects. The latter is understood as effects that create spectacle in film, such as explosions, or unrealistic and fantastic representations of non-existent beings (Prince 2011). He argues that, by contrast, visual effects are often not meant to be conspicuous to the viewer at all (as a spectacle) and can be applied to create a greater impression of realism. In other words, the effects could enhance the verisimilitude of a film, without drawing the viewer's attention. At the extreme end of the scale, visual effects can be used to emulate analogue film effects too, such as motion blur, grain and other response curves of celluloid film stocks (Prince 2011: 4). Digital processes can emulate analogue film techniques and technologies so faithfully that they are visually virtually indistinguishable from an analogue film. Such processes may satisfy audiences' nostalgia for film, which is often perceived as "warmer", more alive, and more organic than digital video, as discussed previously (Gaudrealt & Marion 2015: Chapter 3, p 6–10).[10] The "film look" was sought after and remained a benchmark, even after the so-called digital turn in Hollywood cinema, with directors such as Steven Spielberg and Christopher Nolan and cinematographers such as Christopher Doyle professing its superiority to digital video (Lucas 2014: 139–146).

What interests me, however, is the impact visual effects can have on manipulating colour and lighting in films. Referred to here as grading, the technique originated in cinema as digital grading, or the digital intermediate (DI). The

---

9 Gaudreault & Marion (2015: Chapter 1, p 20) refer to digitalizing rather than digitizing, to encapsulate the transition in filmmaking from analogue to digital and all its permutations, which include 'the digital intermediate', where analogue film is scanned to digital format, manipulated, and then printed on film again to be screened. Because filming itself, cameras and projectors transitioned to digital formats at different times, digitalizing is a more accurate term than digitizing, which would only imply turning an analogue text into a digital one. The transition to digital film is also sometimes called the digital turn or revolution (2015: introduction, p 10–18).

10 Some scholars use the term 'digital video' to refer to filmmaking on digital cameras, which produces a completely digital text.

process first occurred when film stock could be scanned and then manipulated as a digital file to alter the overall appearance of the footage (Lucas 2014: 134). With digital footage (shot on digital cameras), this process is used too, except that scanning is not required. An emblematic example of grading often discussed in studies on cinematographic practices is the film *O Brother, Where Art Thou?* (Coen & Coen 2000). Director of photography Roger Deakins opted for a sepia grading to create a washed-out tone across the whole film to evoke the Depression era in the United States during which the story is set (Lucas 2014: 135). Digital grading is important here because, as I argue, colour and lighting are manipulated in *District 9* to evoke visual nostalgia (indeed, analogue nostalgia) in viewers. It occurs in comparable depictions of Johannesburg in general, but particularly in *District 9*, recalling the 1980s newsreel footage of apartheid Johannesburg to which Blomkamp refers.

2   Ruin Aesthetics

2.1   *Post-industrial Ruins*

Johannesburg is a city with a mining history, and the mining landscape and so-called mine waste areas (MWAS) play no small role in depictions of the city before and after 1994. In fact, these landscapes seem to have become synonymous with Johannesburg. The same goes for the slums of various kinds, such as illegally occupied buildings or buildings in severe disrepair in the Central Business District (CBD), as well as sections of townships and informal settlements that have slum-like characteristics. Such recognisable landscapes of urban and post-industrial ruins characterise the content of *District 9*'s portrayal of the city and fit easily under the aesthetic umbrella of ruin aesthetics. Daryl Martin (2014: 1037–1046) and Caitlin DeSilvey and Tim Edensor (2012: 465–485) discuss the critical potential of ruins in such contexts. Moreover, Trigg (2006) and Maskit (2007) both deal specifically with post-industrial landscapes, considering how they could be regarded as akin to classical ruins in some respects. An important distinction here is that post-industrial ruins – such as the ones under discussion – are not abandoned the way ruins are abandoned in so many accounts from the global North. As opposed to them, the ruins in urban settings in Johannesburg are part of daily life, and may be inhabited, mainly out of necessity, and they are often referred to as slums. The texture of ruin is not entirely limited to the inner city or townships, however. It is not uncommon to see large open ditches on street corners in even the wealthy suburbs, where the local municipality has repaired water pipes but has delayed filling the cavities and repairing the sidewalk for months on end. There is also the ongoing complaint about potholes in the city's roads. Such neglect is so prevalent in Johannesburg and South Africa in general that the right-wing political party, Freedom Front Plus, employed the slogan "Stop the decay" in their municipal election campaign in 2021 (Gerber 2021). The party represents a conservative and arguably racist white constituency, but their campaign is a testament to the viability of the viewpoint of the city as decaying, from a white perspective at least.

Johannesburg is haunted by the notion of ruination. How then are ruins to be understood in this context? Tanya Whitehouse (2018: 12), for example, defines contemporary ruins as abandoned structures that have decayed, and no longer perform the functions for which they were originally intended. Such urban ruins have been documented in South African photography by, for example, Goldblatt and Subotzky and Waterhouse. Slums like those in Johannesburg frequently display a great deal of the decay and the subversive practices of use that are associated with industrial and urban ruins: no longer inhabited or used by their intended residents, they are often occupied illegally by new residents.

One of the biggest concerns with the contemporary appreciation of ruins in the depiction of Johannesburg is the notion of ruin porn. The term is also enmeshed in discussions around depictions of Johannesburg as dystopian, as discussed earlier. The perverse aestheticisation of ruined urban landscapes in glossy coffee-table photography books may underplay the socio-economic contexts and histories underpinning the creation of those spaces in the first place. The often-expressed critique is that such aestheticisation may lead to a passive or gratuitous consumerist gaze on such spaces, thus serving a capitalist agenda rather than a critical purpose.[11]

Despite the implications of the superficiality of the term ruin porn, sites of industrial ruin are understood by many scholars to harbour critical or indeed aesthetic potential.[12] For many scholars, images of ruin are a register of anxiety in society. Although they associate such anxiety with postcapitalist crises, such as climate change, terrorist attacks, fears around the growing power of

---

11 The literature on ruin porn is more extensive than one might expect, as in the work of Caitlin DeSilvey and Tim Edensor (2012: 470), Lee Rodney & Adam Lauder (2018: 76), Siobhan Lyons (2018: 4–5) and Carl Lavery & Christopher M. Gough (2015: 1–8). Lyons' (2017) book entitled *Ruin Porn and the Obsession with Decay* is a useful source on the relatively new concept, along with Tanya Whitehouse's (2018: 53–55) *How Ruins Acquire Aesthetic Value*, which also includes a section on the concept.

12 See the work of Siobhan Lyons (2018), Caitlin DeSilvey & Tim Edensor (2012), Kate Wells (2018), Miles Orvell (2013: 647–671), Daryl Martin (2014), Andreas Huyssen (2006), Carl Lavery & Christopher M. Gough (2015: 1) and Whitehouse (2018: 11–18) in this regard.

digital media industries, and nuclear warfare, it resonates within the rubric of nostalgic dystopia as well. In the South African context, the fears seem to complement particular forms of anxiety, such as white anxiety about the future of the country.

For Trigg (2006) and Huyssen (2006), there is aesthetic potential in ruinous post-industrial landscapes because they are in a state of becoming and are unresolved, and as such they challenge the viewer more than classical ruins can. Classical ruins are typically Greek or Roman, dating back to antiquity, and were popular in neo-classical revivals in the eighteenth and nineteenth centuries. In art history, classical ruins have been understood by Alois Riegl (1996: 73) and others as sublime, in that they are beautiful and yet disconcerting to behold. Such ruins seem to indicate that empires are not eternal and that even great civilisations fall and crumble eventually (Murray 1971: 17). For scholars like Trigg (2006), however, such ruins are more agreeable to the viewer than they are discomfiting, because they may appear arrested in time, fixed in their ruinous state, and hence they may offer space for detached contemplation.

Post-industrial ruins, on the other hand, are understood by Trigg (2006), Huyssen (2006) and Maskit (2007) to offer the viewer a more complex engagement than classical ruins in the western tradition, perhaps because they create more possibilities for disruption. They open up subversive interaction through the notion of "freedom to" (Lees 2004). Tim Edensor (2005), for example, discusses how industrial ruins can become spaces of play, and even illicit activities, since they are often abandoned and not under surveillance. From a conceptual point of view, these spaces are also more open to interpretation and individual interference because they have no designated function, and even their material structure may be undefined. Since they may decay further, they are also difficult to apprehend aesthetically. In essence, therefore, these spaces are fundamentally spaces of potential, which leads me to consider even the seemingly dystopian landscapes of mine waste areas and urban ruins as having critical potential.

An aspect of contemporary urban ruins that is significant in this regard relates to the notion of ruin porn. Kate Wells (2018: 13–29) discusses the affective quality of such images that have an enigmatic allure, and notes that they evoke a "visual pleasure" as well as a contradictory sense of "ethical guilt". Robert Ginsberg (2004: 285–286), also describes ruins as paradoxical and contradictory, as does Tanya Whitehouse (2018: 13). This perplexing effect on the viewer leads me to think that, even in the most derogatory and seemingly superficial sense, images of ruins may evoke sensations in the viewer that are comparable to those evoked in the apprehension of sublime landscapes.

There is a productive conceptual overlap between the focus on authenticity in nostalgia studies and Lyon's discussion of the notion of authenticity in relation to ruins. For Lyons (2018: 5–6), authenticity is evoked by ruins, in part in response to the hyperreal world in which we now live. Huyssen (2006) also draws links between the notion of authenticity and nostalgia in connection with architectural ruins. Ruins evoke authenticity, he argues, because they relate so specifically to a particular space and time. He contextualises them as part of a contemporary "ruin craze" in both popular and academic discourse that is fixated on notions of trauma and memory (Huyssen 2006: 7–8). For him, much as for scholars interested in analogue nostalgia, it reflects a fear of the loss of authenticity, brought on by the mediated world of contemporary mass culture (Huyssen 2006: 11–12).

2.2 *Formless*

I have discussed the concept of the sublime as historically linked to transcendence, terror and delight (or attraction), which disrupts visual conventions and, in the city context, urban planning rationality. Ultimately it is the contradictory nature of the sublime that interests me – terror and delight, as both unsettling and affirming – and I posit in the case of *District 9* that its idiom similarly functions through both attraction and repulsion. Another concept that displays aspects of the same contradictory effect also enables me to explore the morphology of the landscape endemic to *District 9* and the larger nostalgic dystopian idiom: the formless. The concept of formlessness, as Yves Alain Bois and Rosalind Krauss theorised it in the 1990s, in the exhibition entitled *Formless, A User's Guide* (1997), draws on George Bataille's term *informe* (Arya 2014: 115–120). In the exhibition, Bois and Krauss attempted a radical negation of form, a gesture that perhaps echoes Lyotard's explication of the sublime as a denial of the "solace of good forms" (Lyotard 1984: 81).[13] The notion of the formless enables one to interrogate form and its usefulness in representation. As the antithesis of form, the formless subverts notions of meaning in representation. Such a subversive impulse might therefore be understood along the same lines as the disruptive impulse in formulations of the sublime, such as Lyotard's. But it concerns more than Lyotard's notion of avant-garde art's

---

13 Lyotard derives his view on formlessness from Kant's (2001: 24, §23, 2007: §26) notion that the sublime is "devoid of form" but he develops it further to a conclusion that does not see the sublime as linked to transcendence. Rather it resists rational apprehension or presentation (Shaw 2017). For Lyotard, neither art nor reason can make sense of the limitlessness of the sublime. See also Emily Brady's (2012) discussion of formlessness in Kant's work.

questioning of meaning, in the sense that Dada or postmodern art does. It is a complete subversion of the concept of meaning itself, which takes the notion of disruption further than Lyotard's formulation of the sublime. The work by Bois and Krauss for *Formless, A User's Guide* (1997) demonstrates such thinking. To complement their exhibition, Bois and Krauss created a catalogue with the aim to forge contingent relationships between concepts. And to achieve this effect, they structured the publication into sections that do not necessarily cohere or make rational sense: they attempted to dissolve structure. The same is evident in the works they chose to include in the exhibition (Arya 2014: 120).

Scholars have also argued that the formless, as discussed in this context, is related to the abject (in Julia Kristeva's conception), as that which threatens to subsume the boundaries of the self within the "other" (Arya 2014: 8). The formless is the profound collapse between figure and ground in representation, so that boundaries and structures are undone, and notions of inside and outside disrupted; in the case of the body, anatomical differences disintegrate. It can be argued that this transgression of boundaries finds a counterpart in the postmodern decentering of the subject (Bagnall 1999: 59–63), in which the subject is no longer contained and whole. The experience of the formless is unsettling and discomfiting, and echoes aspects of the aesthetic experience of the sublime. What also makes the formless and the abject so uncomfortable in both art and popular culture is that they depart from the represented as we know it, since the formless and the abject are both defined negatively, by what they are not. The formless is neither subject nor object but exists in an ambivalent state in between. It disrupts containment, in that it is not a form but its negation. The abject likewise disrupts by preventing the subject from being contained and coherent. Both are *beyond representation* and can only be known through their effects (Arya 2014: 125–128).

In discourses on the topic, it is notable that the sublime, the abject and the formless are thought to inspire attraction and repulsion in the viewer at the same time. However, whereas the sublime is associated with transcendence and sublimation, the abject is associated with the opposite, *desublimation*, and a descent into base materiality and horror (Arya 2014: 6). For Rina Arya (2014: 129), the formless concerns a lack of resemblance, in other words, representation that functions beyond the realm of recognition. Significantly, one may note that the abject is more often associated with the body and embodiment than the formless, which lends itself better to understanding the landscape. For this reason, I refer to the formless rather than the abject in my discussion of *District 9*.

•••

To sum up the ideas discussed in Chapters 1 and 2, I ask the question: how do the banners of analogue aesthetics and ruin aesthetics enable us to understand *District 9*'s Johannesburg? The two umbrella terms cast a net over the two main approaches I follow in this book, analysing *District 9* in terms of the media it manipulates to represent Johannesburg (the how), and in terms of which Johannesburg it represents (the what).

Analogue aesthetics points to the role of media technologies in shaping how the city been depicted recently. Analogue nostalgia has been considered internationally in both nostalgia studies and media studies and is useful for contextualising the nostalgic dystopian idiom emerging in the depiction of Johannesburg within the "nostalgia boom" in international popular culture. The boom is tied to recent developments in digital technologies and techniques, and more particularly to the transition from analogue to digital media in photography and filmmaking (Niemeyer 2014: 1–7). Many scholars draw on Benjamin's reflections on authenticity, if somewhat superficially, to interrogate why analogue nostalgia is so prevalent in popular media today. Authenticity is a complex term, as Hansen's (2008, 1987) work on Benjamin demonstrates. But, with regard to its relevance here, it is the evocation of historicity, and its focus on time and space, which is considered the characteristic quality of authenticity and which is transposed onto the scholarly discussion of analogue nostalgia. Although analogue nostalgia is associated predominantly with amateur practices, cinema has embraced the fetishization of analogue processes and technologies in contemporary digital filmmaking. It is clear that moving image media are used to emulate analogue film's qualities, and that visual effects are often employed in contemporary cinema to artificially endow the artefactual characteristics of film to texts that were shot and processed digitally. In the upcoming chapters, this forms the backdrop against which *District 9* is viewed in my argument that Johannesburg may be regarded as an 'analogue landscape'.

Ruin aesthetics relates to my concern with the physical or geographic features of Johannesburg itself (the what), which are characterised by urban ruin. Considering the ways post-industrial ruins have been regarded in recent scholarship as sites of the post-industrial sublime, they can be read as landscapes rather than as urban sites, which allows them to be interpreted through the category of the sublime. These landscapes are then understood to have the effect of being both attractive and repulsive in representations, which in my view accords with how Johannesburg is often depicted. Despite it not being foregrounded or articulated as such in current discourse, depictions of the city demonstrate the contradictory quality of the sublime; they also often employ landscape conventions that evoke sublime landscape depictions. This appears in the sprawling peri-urban character of much of the city of Johannesburg, which includes undeveloped pieces of land; marginalised areas, such as townships and informal settlements; and parts of the landscape that now seem ruinous, such as mine waste areas and inner-city slums.

The concept of the formless lends itself to further understanding how difficult landscapes work visually, especially disintegrating and decaying landscapes. The formless supplements the notion of disruption of form as conceived by Lyotard (1984a) in relation to the sublime; it also complements Trigg's (2006) ideas in the context of post-industrial landscapes, and his argument that the subversion of form acts as a critique of modernist preoccupations with logic and structure. These concepts provide a useful lens through which to view *District 9* in the next chapters.

PART 2

Analogue Aesthetics

∴

CHAPTER 3

Mockumentary: A Fly on the 'Stopnonsense'

1   Skeletons in the Closet[1]

1.1   *Township Planning and Its Discontents: Chiawelo*
Before delving into 'the how' of *District 9*s portrayal of Johannesburg, it is important to consider the setting of the film and Johannesburg's history in the media, because the visual history is so clearly emulated in *District 9*.[2] Chiawelo, where *District 9* was shot, was part of the later development in the greater township of Soweto, between 1955 and 1965. Soweto itself has been the subject of photographic study, as by the well-known struggle photographers Peter Magubane and Sam Nzima, and more recently Jabulani Dhlamini and Jodi Bieber. Many books have also taken Soweto as setting, such as the recent short stories in *Soweto under the Apricot Tree* by Niq Mhlongo (2018), or his earlier novel *After Tears* (2007).

Soweto was established in the 1930s as Orlando, an area for Black residents, and the first houses were built in 1931. It was organised through a grid structure, with wide roads and individual plots of land to be turned into gardens, although this relatively generous allocation of space would not come to fruition. The model for the township was essentially the English Garden Suburb (Foster 2012: 51).[3] Later models included the NE51 housing scheme, first used by the apartheid government's National Building Research Institute to plan the

---

1   A 'stopnonsense' is the vernacular expression used in townships for pre-fabricated boundary walls, which are very common.
2   I cannot do justice to the rich history and the academic discourse around the topic in my brief outline, but further discussion is not within the purview of this book.
3   The notion of the English Garden Suburb was informed by the 1947 Town and Country Planning Act in the UK (Foster 2012: 39–41). This Act envisioned a particular image of a 'good city' as one that was ordered using plans, a technocratic implementation of these plans, and laws that would facilitate further order in how land was designated for use through zones. Aesthetics, efficiency and modernisation were important to this vision. Cities that resulted from this kind of planning were characterised by open green spaces, vertical buildings, traffic efficiency, super-blocks, peripheral suburbs and separation of land use. Additional planning models that influenced township planning in South Africa include modernist movements such as the European association CIAM (*Congrès Internationale d'Architecture Moderne*), influenced by Le Corbusier's universalist views on mass housing (Foster 2012: 39), and models from the US such as the neighbourhood unit, the Radburn layout, and the British Milton Keynes km grid (De Satgé & Watson 2018:42).

township of KwaThemba in the Witwatersrand.[4] Most of the planning took place because colonial, apartheid and, surprisingly, even post-apartheid government structures have sought to "govern and improve" the townships (De Satgé & Watson 2018: 85–94) and planners were often influenced by best practices from the global North. The result was that planning models used in townships often did not connect fundamentally with the people living there (De Satgé & Watson 2018: 1–6).

At the outset, Orlando was located far from Johannesburg, to the south and the west, beyond the mines. Most of the township's inhabitants had been relocated there from inner city slums (Foster 2012: 51). This segregation of the Black population and their removal from the urban fabric embedded segregation in the city's character. The planning agendas employed valued order as the most desirable characteristic of urban space, with informality regarded as undesirable. Slums were often subject to forced removals, and the notion that townships themselves are slums became a substantial part of how townships and informal settlements are depicted in popular discourse in South Africa, as demonstrated in *District 9*'s allegorical portrayal (Wagner 2015: 47).

The squatter movement in Orlando is perhaps one of the earliest prefigurations of the removals allegorised in *District 9*, although the title refers to the forced removals from District Six in the 1980s. Led by James Mpanza, colloquially known as the father of Soweto,[5] the movement was a response to the severe shortage of housing for Black people in Orlando. In 1944 and 1946, Mpanza led people to occupy empty spaces and newly built government houses to draw attention to the problem compellingly, and appeal to the government for sufficient housing provision. Most of the squatters were forcibly removed into camps and shelters (Nieftagodien & Gaule 2012: 10–15).

It is important to note that informal settlements and townships are not the same. Townships have a history of planning, while informal settlements may be regarded as the result of the deficiencies of that planning. Due to insufficient housing in planned townships, almost from their inception, residents often had to resort to unauthorised, informal approaches to housing shortages. The resulting settlements generally abut township areas, so they have become associated with one another, and the appearance of informality has come to characterise the popular image of townships. The various depictions

---

4 'NE51' designates the term "Non-European", and the year this particular model was finalised, 1951 (Le Roux 2019: 274). See Hannah Le Roux's (2019) detailed historical account of the planning models used in this township in 1951 for an explication of the NE51 housing scheme.
5 This history is written about by Noor Nieftagodien & Sally Gaule (2012: 10) and Niq Mhlongo (2010).

of townships in *District 9* show how the appearance of such informal urbanism might seem dystopian. Informal urban practices are often regarded as a failure of planning and government to impose and maintain order (Dovey & King 2011: 22). Land-owning middle classes might furthermore regard land value as threatened by the image of poverty the areas communicate to the outside world.[6] I refer to informal settlements and townships along these lines, in terms of how they have been associated with one another. There are, however, distinctions between these designations, which must be borne in mind. Their association with one another is perhaps the result of the particular place-image of Johannesburg, such as the "township metropolis" that Nuttall and Mbembe (2004: 197) reference.

1.2   Land

Although planning rhetoric espoused utopian egalitarian living conditions, the limitations on land ownership belied such ostensible good intentions on the part of both the colonial and apartheid governments. National Planning law was changed from colonial and apartheid practices only in 1991, and was revised post-apartheid only in 2013 (De Satgé & Watson 2018: 42). As a result, the segregation entrenched in urban planning has only partially been erased and in essence townships have remained untransformed well into the country's democratic era.[7] Part of the problem also relates to land ownership. The Land Act, passed in 1913, limited "native" ownership of land to seven percent of the country's geography, even though Black Africans were the majority of the country's population at the time.[8] This meant that 93% of the land in the country was unavailable for Black ownership.[9] During the inception of the Land Act there was resistance by Black leaders, such as John L. Dube, Dr Walter Rubusana, Saul Msane, Thomas Mapikela and Solomon T. Plaatje, who formed a deputation that travelled to London and presented a petition contesting it to the British Parliament. But this did not prevent the Act from being passed

---

6   See Richard de Satgé & Vanessa Watson (2018: 47) and Marie Huchzermeyer (2011: 71) for more on the image of informal settlements.
7   See Mayekiso (1996) and Myambo (2011, 2018).
8   The Act defined a "native" as "any person, male or female, who is a member of an aboriginal race or tribe of Africa; and shall further include any company or other body of persons, corporate or unincorporate, if the persons who have a controlling interest therein are natives" (The Natives Land Act 2013).
9   Earlier colonial Acts had also laid the foundations for the dispossession of land, and for the control of land by the government. See Vusi Gumede (2015: 87–96), Njabulo Ndebele (2010: IX–XIV) and South African History Online (The Natives Land Act 2013) for a detailed account of these laws and the effects they had on black ownership of land.

FIGURE 1   This image was captured during protests against apartheid in South Africa. Photograph by Paul Weinberg, 1980s.
CC BY-SA 3.0 WIKIMEDIA COMMONS. ANTI-APARTHEID PROTEST. [N.D.].

(Natives Land Act 2013). Land ownership legislation is closely related to the great majority of Black people becoming destitute, according to Sol Plaatjie (1998, Natives Land Act 2013), and it has had long-term effects that are reflected in the prevalence of informal settlements in the country.[10]

1.3   *The States of Emergency*

While townships saw many periods of unrest and resistance to government policies in the 1960s and 1970s, the 1980s in South Africa were marked by extremely violent protests in the townships as residents resisted apartheid laws around education, employment and housing. In 1985, a State of National Emergency was declared. Looking back at news footage of that time now, one sees a country gripped in a state of warfare: media images are marked by depictions of the ubiquitous apartheid police force, recognisable in their

---

10   For further information, see a recent review of spatial inequality produced for parliament entitled *The Role of Land Tenure and Governance in Reproducing and Transforming Spatial Inequality* (De Satgé et al. 2017).

blue uniforms, by military personnel, security police, and armoured vehicles such as Casspirs, as well as burning tyres, thronging masses of *toy-toying* and chanting township residents and political leaders with fists in the air (see Figure 1).[11] Deborah Posel (1990), writing on broadcast news at the time, argues that newsreels during the 1985 State of Emergency became highly stylised, and contributed to a symbolic association between townships and violence. These news items, broadcast by South African Television (SATV) typically used the presence of three motifs: crowds, stone-throwing and fire. The construction of this image of violence associated with the townships at the time allowed the actions of the government through the South African Police (SAP) and the South African Defence Force (SADF) to appear justified, and further served to exacerbate racist stereotypes of Black people, who were presented as acting irrationally, violently, and without a clear political agenda.

The first State of Emergency of the decade was declared on 21 July 1985 and lasted until March 1986, with several to follow, all declared under the Public Safety Act of 1953.[12] In June 1986 a further State of Emergency was instituted, and again in June 1988 (Merrett 1990: 3–12). The Emergency was eventually lifted in June 1990 in three of the four provinces that then constituted the country, and in October 1990 in the remaining province of Natal (now KwaZulu Natal). A final State of Emergency was declared in 1994, when conflict arose in KwaZulu Natal between IFP and ANC factions over the upcoming democratic elections (States of Emergency ... 2019).

Christopher Merrett (1990: 6), writing about the effects of the States of Emergency on censorship in South Africa, discusses them as epitomising the increasing militarisation of South African life. He further discusses one of the most pervasive effects of the Emergencies, namely the number of persons detained under their provision for detention without trial (1990: 13). By 1990, there were over 40 000 (since mid-1985). Even before the Emergencies, the Suppression of Communism Act of 1950 and the Internal Security Act of 1982 legislated many human rights infringements, and restricted individuals from communicating freely and from accessing particular areas; it also permitted the detention of individuals for interrogation, even as a preventive measure on the mere suspicion of wrongdoing (Merrett 1990: 3). In addition, under the Emergencies there was a limitation on liability for the actions of security force

---

11   *Toy-toying* refers to the protest 'dance' performed in townships at the time; see Hilary Sapire's (2013) discussion of resistance to the apartheid regime and the history of the anti-apartheid 'struggle'.
12   See Christopher Merrett (1990: 3) and Deborah Posel (1990: 154) for more on how the States of Emergency affected media representation of these events.

personnel, as long as they were deemed to be acting in the interests of state security (Merrett 1990: 15). This meant that human rights were 'suspended', and there were few consequences for the brutality that agents of the state might inflict on citizens, particularly Black South Africans. This history is relevant to understanding how the township is portrayed in *District 9* as a "zone of indistinction" – an extreme dystopia where "bare life" conditions predominate according to Akpome (2017).

It is also important to note how the States of Emergency affected the country's media at the time. According to Merrett (1990: 14–15), the effect of censorship was to cut the flow of information concerning "conscientious objection, human rights violations (detentions, political trials, assassinations and disappearances), alternative education, and grassroots organisation and methods of resistance in Black townships". The South African media thus portrayed a skewed version of what was happening in the country. Interestingly, between January 1985 and June 1986, there was unusually explicit news coverage of the violence erupting in townships during uprisings. According to Posel (1990: 154–155), it may have been intended to assuage both anti-apartheid critiques and critiques from the right wing in the country against the government's response to township revolts at the time. It was also during this time that the three motifs of rioting crowds, stone-throwing and fires became established as symbolic of township violence. After a brief period, by 1987 news coverage had reverted to its heavily censored mode, however, often without visual accompaniment.

In general, during the Emergencies, many accounts of what was taking place were censored. For example, after rioting broke out in Sebokeng, a report on the protests that unfolded by Johannes Rantete, an amateur journalist living there, was published by Ravan Press in October 1984, but banned shortly thereafter.[13] I refer to this account again below, as it provides an insider view

---

13   Ravan Press was established in the 1970s by Peter Ralph Randall, Danie van Zyl and Beyers Naudé. They published anti-apartheid literature, and later went on to publish Njabulo Ndebele's book *Fools and Other Stories* (1983). They were also known for the *Staffrider* journal series, which published much anti-apartheid literature and also artists' prints (Peffer 2009: XV–XXII). Rantete's account entitled *The Third Day of September* (*The Sebokeng Rebellion of 1984*), was published as a book in the *Storyteller Series* on 14 October, but soon afterwards police raided Sebokeng, and Rantete was detained for some time. Police demanded the colour photographs from Ravan Press, and the book was banned in December. After an appeal on this to the Publications Board, distribution of the book was resumed in January 1985, but it appeared this time with black and white sketches by Goodman Mabote (Rantete 1984, The third day ... 1985: 37–42). These sketches may be less confrontational than the colour photographs but make for interesting comparison with the media images distributed at the time. The illustrations provide detail on the events unfolding, emphasising the role of the police and authorities, often depicting Casspirs

of the unrest in the country and in townships at the time. While *District 9* is not a document of the events in the country, the mockumentary mode in which it constructs Johannesburg conveys a sense of documentary truth or authenticity, which dovetails with the authenticity emulated in analogue nostalgia, discussed in Chapter 2. Furthermore, it draws on media depictions of real events in the country. In these ways it contributes to a particular narrative viewpoint about Johannesburg: that it is dangerous, poverty-ridden and in decay. However, as Kapstein (2014: 172) suggests, it is also an "outsider" or voyeuristic view of township life, with Wikus as a white man venturing into the township from his life outside it. One might even say it is an apartheid view of the township. It is therefore important to consider different points of view such as Rantete's to contextualise the history that *District 9* allegorises.

2 Analogue Landscape: A Parody of Documentary Conventions

2.1 *Low-resolution Realism*

With this brief background on townships and their representation in the media of 1980s, *District 9*'s cinematography and aspects of the production design can be examined in more detail in relation to the analogue effects emulated in the film. Although *District 9* is often described in terms of the science fiction genre,[14] this aspect of the film is to my mind secondary to its mockumentary qualities. Much of the film mimics the appearance of a documentary, direct cinema or *cinéma vérité* (Nel 2012: 552), in which stylistic effects appear to be secondary to visual details, providing realistic evidence of events and spaces (Hight 2008: 205). Such realism is often characterised by an apparent lack of directorial manipulation,[15] and the use of deep focus, which reveals 'real' details in the environment that seem incidental and not included for artistic effect (Mitchell 1992: 23–57). Adele Nel (2012) remarks on the use of such elements in *District 9*, noting that the film conveys an authenticity that enables it to comment on the Johannesburg of the apartheid past, as well as the contemporary city during its production in 2008. Her analysis of the film's formal

---

and police officers surveying the area. Such portrayals of township conflicts appear in documentary photography by well-known photographers in South Africa as well, such as those working under the umbrella of the Afrapix group, but are largely absent from South African media publications at the time, as discussed earlier.

14 See Lorenzo Veracini (2011), Mireille Rosello (2016: 43) and Adele Nel (2012).

15 John Corner (2015) and Stella Bruzzi (2015) provide more insight into the genre's conventions.

features is one of the more detailed, focusing on several aspects of the cinematography and production design, and I refer to it again when discussing the depiction of the landscape.[16]

District 9 mimics many of the documentary conventions thought to be formative in the genre by scholars such as Bill Nichols (2017): the use of location shooting (here Johannesburg), and non-actors, or in this case, the appearance or masquerading of characters as non-actors. The shooting location for *District 9* was important to Blomkamp, to create the feeling of "the real Soweto", and the film was purposely shot during winter (Holben 2009: 26).

Wikus van de Merwe is the quintessential non-actor as he appears as an everyman, who often breaks the fourth wall to address the cameraman and crew directly. Further, *District 9* mimics the documentary genre's extensive use of hand-held camera techniques. In the documentary context, it provides a sense of immediacy, since interviewees and stakeholders are followed on foot and recorded in a candid way. Also, the use of supposed found footage in *District 9*, particularly emulated newsreel footage, is significant. Finally, the appearance of natural lighting foregrounds the airborne pollution so prevalent in Johannesburg's winter landscape (Nichols 2017: XI). *District 9*'s cinematographer, Trent Opaloch, refers to the textures of this location, as well as the quality of the winter light, thick with pollution (Holben 2009: 26).

A significant difference that sets the mockumentary apart from the documentary, however, is its agenda; rather than intending to convey a sense of objective truth or reality, it often aims to satirise or parody (Hight 2008: 205). The element of ironic humour is important in *District 9*, as it contributes to the contradictory experiences it invites viewers to have. It depicts a dystopian landscape, but the use of ironic humour smooths the way to the counterintuitive nostalgia that is conveyed. It is also significant that mockumentary conventions are interspersed with elements of narrative fiction in the film, and that large parts unfold in a narrative rather than a documentary manner – further removing the film from a true documentary context (Bunch in Kapstein 2014: 169). Mockumentary as a genre may also contribute to a pleasurable viewing experience, which is very different from documentary film that primarily aims to educate the viewer. While they may appear at first glance as documentary films, mockumentary films are staged and scripted to implicitly encourage the viewer to find carefully constructed clues to their artifice as one gradually comes to realise their fallaciousness (Nichols 2017: 12).

---

16 It would of course be possible to analyse the film quite closely by looking at generic conventions at work in it, but I have selected to focus on motifs, conventions and structures that contribute to an analogue landscape depiction.

FIGURE 2   Composited newsreel footage from the 1985 state of emergency (Rui (channel), 2008). Still from the video. (South Africa State … 2008).

One of the most important motifs in *District 9* is the television newsreel. In documentary terms, it is common to intersperse interview footage with found footage, and edit them together in an "evidentiary" manner to provide further proof to corroborate a particular argument about an event or place (Nichols 2017: XI–18). In the case of *District 9*, the newsreel footage appears real, though it is completely staged, scripted and performed by actors, not real newsreaders. Blomkamp uses many visual techniques to achieve such a parodic authenticity, and the principle of hypermediacy informs his approach. He does not seek to conceal the artifice of the newsreels, but instead exaggerates their mediatic qualities to draw attention to them as media artefacts of a particular time and place, and products of specific media technologies. Newsreels from the 1980s have a characteristic appearance that is not only due to the media used to record them, but is also attributable to the cathode ray televisions to which they were broadcast. Figure 2 is an example of such newsreel footage, which was broadcast during the 1985 State of Emergency and is now available on YouTube (South Africa State … 2008). One may note its fuzziness, which could be because YouTube videos are often low resolution, but which also evokes

FIGURE 3   An alien levitating a minibus. Still taken from *Alive in Joburg* (Neill Blomkamp, 2006).

the lack of sharpness in images on cathode ray screens (Connolly & Evans 2014: 54). It is further notable that the aspect ratio of the original footage, 4:3, is incompatible with the wider screen format of YouTube, and the image seems to have been horizontally distorted to fit the online format.

The lack of definition is also emulated in *Alive in Joburg* (Figure 3), Blomkamp's short film which preceded *District 9*. It shares a muted palette with the newsreel footage mentioned above. Low-definition sequences abound in *District 9* as well, and in such sequences the quality of analogue footage is evoked in different ways. Figure 4 is a screenshot from the introductory sequence in the film that depicts how the alien ship looked when it first arrived on earth and was stranded above Johannesburg, which imitates 1980s archive footage. Opaloch says that they allowed the focus to "go" when shooting "journalists' material" (Holben 2009: 30), to create an appearance that is "immediate, real and rough around the edges". He also suggests that combining such footage with visual effects created "a kind of reality that's really unique".

In this screenshot, the appearance of analogue media is emulated not only in the fuzziness of the image, or its noise, but also in the text at the bottom of the screen, which recalls the timestamp associated with video footage such as Super8 footage. Archival footage like that in Figure 5 is characterised by the qualities of the film stock and the camera used to shoot it. This screenshot

FIGURE 4   Emulated newsreel footage. Still taken from *District 9* (Neill Blomkamp, 2009).

is from 1974, yet one can see a pronounced resemblance between this historical depiction of Johannesburg and stills from *District 9* (Figures 4 and 6). Giuseppina Sapio (2014) notes that contemporary practitioners working in digital media often emulate the flaws of analogue media to evoke its character. These flaws include low fidelity, noise, motion blur, distorted colour due to ageing film stock, and so on.[17] In cinematography after 2000, computer-generated imagery (CGI) increasingly aimed to emulate the effects of poor craftsmanship in cinematography (Lucas 2014: 149). Writing on the digital turn in cinematography – the transition from analogue to digital cinematography – Christopher Lucas (2014: 149) suggests that such aspects became associated with authenticity, and with a film-look, or photorealism. The aim of the digital film was now to emulate the film medium. The strategy of emulating analogue flaws is used by Blomkamp throughout *District 9*, and was not only implemented in post-production, but also during filming.[18] Along with manipulating camera focus, Opaloch mentions, for example, that they allowed highlighted areas to

---

17   I refer to resolution as the digital equivalent of low fidelity in the case of *District 9*, which is a digital text.
18   The film was shot on digital cameras and printed onto film stock, a process discussed by Kristen Whissel (2007: 2) as commonplace in the era of the digital intermediate.

FIGURE 5   Composited archival footage depicting Johannesburg in 1974.
Still taken from The kinolibrary (channel), 2017. (1974 Johannesburg Street Scenes ... 2017)

become overexposed in shots that were meant to look like 1980s journalistic footage (Holben 2009: 30).

The colour palette remains relatively unchanged throughout the two temporal settings of the film – 1982 and 2010, both past and future – and representations of the contemporary city of 2010 retain the same grading (evident in Figure 6). The Johannesburg of 2010 therefore also appears dated, trapped in the past. Grading has become an established practice in digital filmmaking, allowing cinematographers to colour and digitally alter film text (Lucas 2014: 134–135). Stephen Prince (2011: 65–72) suggests that digital cinematography has become almost akin to painting: digital film can be wholly manipulated to have a particular look, especially for colour and light, and to emulate particular analogue film stock, or evoke it in a more general manner (Prince 2004: 4–5, Lucas 2014: 141–146).[19] More so than chemical processes used for film (such as bleach bypass, flashing, ENR and cross-processing), digital techniques

---

19   Like scholars mentioned earlier, Prince (2004: 80–85) refers to "digital video" when referring to digital filmmaking, and thus uses the term film to imply the use of analogue media technologies in analogue films. I use the term film in relation to both digital and analogue

FIGURE 6   The inner city of Johannesburg. Still taken from *District 9* (Neill Blomkamp, 2009).

make it possible for the cinematographer or visual effects artist to target particular elements in a shot and alter them in isolation. Prince (2004: 27–33) suggests it enables much greater subtlety in how colour effects are achieved, and as a result approaches a more realistic effect.

The ability to finely tune the colour and texture of a digital image in filmmaking is akin to the frequent use of filters by amateur photographers, and even casual users of digital photography on social media platforms like Instagram. Bartholeyns (2014: 51–67) discusses how digital photography emulates analogue characteristics using software applications available to everyday users on their smartphones. For him, smartphones have changed the nature of photography, because they make good-quality cameras available to a vast number of users, including software applications that allow the manipulation of images. Also significant are the social networks where such images may be posted in public forums (Bartholeyns 2014: 54). At the time Bartholeyns wrote, over 7 billion "retro" images were already in circulation via social networks (by now it is presumably far more), images that evoke Polaroid and Kodak camera aesthetics, such as over-exposure and vignetting, which brings to mind

---

media, since I am looking at a cinematic (film) text; moreover, in the context of *District 9*, video would imply VHS video footage, instead of "digital video".

FIGURE 7   Introductory sequence. Still taken from *Gangster's Paradise: Jerusalema* (Ralph Ziman, 2008).

1960–1980s family photography (Bartholeyns 2014:51). Processing photographs in this way enables users to instantly evoke the same nostalgia that family photographs do, often with no real link to the past. In the case of fashion bloggers, such as Khumbula, the Sartists and I See A Different You, there are further implications beyond the evocation of historicity, which I discuss later. Further, the technique is echoed in contemporary filmmaking, with a comparable nostalgic effect. This begs the question: why do users employ filters to age their photographs in the first place? In Chapter 2, I referred to Caorduro (2014) and Niemeyer's (2014) argument that it is to emulate the authenticity associated with analogue media. In *District 9* this takes on another layer of nuance in terms of the mockumentary genre, which already parodies the authenticity of a documentary – itself a questionable notion[20] – while at the same time providing a sense of authenticity by mimicking analogue film to evoke a nostalgic sense of Johannesburg in the 1980s.

Analogue media (instead of digital media) can also be used in a manner which draws attention to the medium itself. One can see a hypermediatic use of analogue technologies in the film *Gangster's Paradise: Jerusalema* (Figure 7).

---

20   See John Corner (2015: 148–149) for a discussion on the veracity of this genre.

Whereas *District 9* was shot digitally, *Gangster's Paradise* was shot entirely on Aaton 16- and 35-mm cameras, and the cinematographer used old film stock, along with Russian Konvas 35 mm cameras with LOMO lenses and a 16-mm Bolex, to shoot the material for the title sequence.[21] The latter is constructed with time-lapse sequences that depict the inner city, focusing on urban decay, against a foreboding cloudy sky. The washed-out colour palette is visible here too, and the time-lapse sequences with their flickering quality result in a look that recalls low-budget amateur filmmaking and photographic techniques such as Lomography, as well as flaws such as frame jitters, overexposure and the like. Budget constraints may have motivated the use of vintage analogue cameras, but they are used to accentuate the gritty appearance of the inner city. Ziman recounts his thoughts at the time: "no cleaning 20 years of grime off the windows or picking up rubbish" (Ziman Steals the Screen 2008).

The use of older model film cameras lends the title sequence a gritty feel, which shares some features with amateur photography such as that of the Lomography movement, popular around the time of the film's making. The movement was already well established by 2006 and embraced "dirty" photography, with imperfections, glitches, defects and the like, valued by the mostly amateur practitioners who enjoyed using it (Minniti 2020: 79–86). The plastic lenses on the toy cameras that sparked the movement and its name – Russian LOMO LC-A cameras from the 1980s – often result in images that lack the crisp and sharply focused appearance of the new digital cameras at the time. The Lomography movement evolved from the early 1990s as a reaction first to the 'serious' practices of amateur photography, and by the late 2000s it opposed the 'cold' and clinical character of digital photography. Users embraced the physicality, unpredictability and imperfections of the photographs produced by analogue cameras. As with analogue nostalgia, the analogue medium was valued for its sense of materiality, and was associated with authenticity. What such a practice represents is not an urge to recoup purely analogue processes and abandon digital media: it was brought about by the advent of the digital turn, and in this way was beholden to digital media's prominence. Sergio Minniti (2020: 90) explains that practitioners often shared their photographs online, scanned into digital format, embracing digital media's ability to be shared widely with ease. He describes it as a new practice, which combines

---

21 Interestingly, the film also opens with a shot of a helicopter over the skyline, like *District 9*. Here the policemen in the helicopter are after the gangster protagonist of the film, Lucky Kunene. The helicopter hovers over Hillbrow, where he is hiding from the police, leading up to the moment where he is shown wounded and bleeding on his bed in a slum building.

older technologies with "new media artifacts, contexts and practices" (Minniti 2020: 90). The title sequence of *Gangster's Paradise: Jerusalema* is a product of its time: although it is produced with analogue technology, it represents a development within the digital context, in which hypermediacy becomes important and emphasises analogue flaws and imperfections, along with an analogue character in general.

Documentary photographic practices at the time make use of a complex interaction between analogue and digital media as well. An analogue colour palette, as evident in the images above, is employed in the widely disseminated photographs taken of Johannesburg between 2008 and 2011 by Mikhael Subotzky and Patrick Waterhouse in their extensive project of photographing Ponte City. Their photographs were taken on medium format film cameras and were then digitally retouched before they were printed onto film negative again. The Mamiya medium format cameras they used have been produced since the 1970s and are thus also historical cameras, prized for their lens quality. The photographers chose to retouch their images digitally, however, so, like *District 9*, they evoke an analogue sensibility that is complicated by digital media processes. Importantly, one cannot equate the myriad ways in which digital and analogue technologies and techniques are used in these diverse instances with any one process. What seems more important is the ethos that informs the outcome: the entanglement of digital and analogue media technologies, techniques of use and processes, which results in an analogue aesthetic. The effect of the analogue aesthetic in *District 9* in particular relates to the documentary qualities it evokes, and the sense of authenticity that results.

Across the contemporary and historical depictions of the city (Figures 4, 5, 6 and 7), the colouring of the images lends them a smoggy, polluted and, most importantly, dated appearance. It is noteworthy that *District 9* does not only use digital media technologies and processes to evoke analogue media, however; it also employs production design and cinematography to emphasise these effects, using the hazy winter light that enhances the washed-out look associated with analogue film. The process to achieve this appearance is thus not purely digital, and visual effects such as digital grading are used in conjunction with what is filmed to create a nostalgic portrayal of the city.

In *District 9* there are many temporal shifts, and it is not always clear which era the film is portraying. For example, the newsreel footage is ambiguous in this regard. In the footage depicted in Figure 8, the low definition of analogue newsreels has been translated differently from that in Figure 4, appearing less fuzzy than the footage of the alien craft. This is a representation of 'current' news footage, in other words, set in 2010, and thus not intended to simulate analogue newsreels, although it is not always entirely clear in the film. Lucas

FIGURE 8   News footage depicting violence in Johannesburg. Still taken from *District 9* (Neill Blomkamp, 2009).

(2014:143–146) notes that, during the early 2000s, filmmakers in Hollywood often experimented with the then new generation of digital cameras to make films. At the time, they were inferior to film cameras, but directors such as Steven Soderbergh used them to make documentary-style films, and to create what Lucas (2014: 141) terms "low-resolution realism".[22] *District 9* follows a similar approach, especially in the constructed newsreel footage. There is, for example, distortion in the image in Figure 8, which makes ghostly outlines visible, particularly in the street pole to the right, and the silhouette of the boy standing to the right of the Casspir; however, the effects could also be interpreted as digital flaws, denoting digital footage. On the other hand, Opaloch (Holben 2009: 26–28) describes the use of earlier generation digital cameras such as the EX1 to shoot footage that represents analogue footage in *District 9*; early digital cameras' shortcomings were used paradoxically to evoke analogue flaws. There is thus a complex relationship between analogue media and digital media in the film, with digital cameras used – though not exclusively – to shoot footage that would eventually appear to be analogue.

---

22   He takes the term from cinematographer M. David Mullen.

The technique of evoking realism through the appearance of low-resolution footage is similar to documentary filmmaking techniques, such as those evident in *The Battle for Johannesburg* (Desai 2010), although the intention was very different because it is a documentary rather than the imitation of one. In this case there are many instances where the camera oscillates in and out of focus, because the camera operator is walking alongside or behind the narrator and interviewees. There are many low-resolution sequences in the film, probably due to budget constraints, and because a small hand-held digital camera seems to have been used at times, as in the shot of Ponte City (Figure 9). Cinematographer Jonathan Kovel (2022) explained that often many different cinematographers work on a documentary film, which is probably why the footage varies so much in technical appearance in this film.[23] The variation as well as the low-resolution sequences convey a sense of grittiness in *The Battle for Johannesburg*, which accentuates the setting of slum buildings in the inner city, where most of the documentary is set. Kovel (2022) recalled that Desai was very clear about wanting to portray the architecture and character of the inner city. There appears to have been little manipulation of the equipment other than to enhance the sense of immediacy and grit, however, which accords with the documentary agenda.

It is clear that in the three films *District 9*, *Gangster's Paradise: Jerusalema* and *The Battle for Johannesburg*, digital and analogue media are often used in conjunction and in ways that emphasise mediatic qualities. As already mentioned, Bolter and Grusin (2000: 48) refer to the process of digital media that references analogue media as remediation. For them, digital media borrow from analogue media, and analogue media in turn incorporate digital media and its functions. This seems typical of the early years of the 2000s, when the transition to digital cinema processes was not yet complete (Whissel 2007: 2–4). But, in fact, the relationship between analogue and digital media has remained reliant on remediation.

In the Hollywood context, many filmmakers still employ the digital intermediate to some degree, and most films are made with references and interactions between the digital and analogue media paradigms. Jamie Clarke

---

23   I interviewed Kovel online in 2022, when he explained in detail his involvement with both *The Battle for Johannesburg* and *Berea*. Interestingly from the point of view of the nostalgic dystopian idiom they share, he was the cinematographer for both these films. Although one would therefore expect his own vision to have translated into the films, Kovel indicated that he was intent on making the two different directors' visions come to life, and that he was following their direction rather than exercising his own creative voice, although his involvement is nonetheless noteworthy.

FIGURE 9   Ponte City visible from the rooftop of San Jose. Still taken from *The Battle for Johannesburg* (Rehad Desai, 2010).

(2017: 105–123), for example, writes about the nostalgia for craftsmanship and shooting strategies associated with analogue media in the 2015 Oscar-nominated films in the cinematography category. He argues that each of the digitally shot films strives for a filmic (analogue) quality, by using on-set techniques to create a sense of "digital realism".

In being shot digitally, but evoking analogue film technologies, *District 9* is situated on the brink of media change between the two paradigms. The temporal context is characterised by a preoccupation with analogue media: the older paradigm is emulated to evoke a sense of authenticity but, as it is a source of cheaper, dated technologies and techniques, it can also lend films and photographs a dated quality. *District 9*, along with film and photography at the time, thus evidences the new ways analogue and digital media become imbricated with each other late in the first decade of the 2000s.

2.2   *The Incidental Landscape*

I now return to the mockumentary qualities of *District 9*, which are characterised by more than the material quality of analogue footage sparked by the analogue renaissance. Apart from newsreel and archive footage, there are also many variations on the interview format in the film, which notably constructs the landscape as incidental and as the 'actual' setting of the film. This contributes to the sense of an authentic Johannesburg landscape in *District 9*, which is similar to the way the city is portrayed in documentary film around the same time, in *The Battle for Johannesburg*, for example, and in documentary photography.

Many of the interviews in *District 9* are staged and include 'expert' interviews at the beginning, similar to those in documentaries, such as the one at the beginning of *The Battle for Johannesburg* (Figure 10). This aspect of the film mimics documentary conventions related to the mode of interactivity that is explained by Hight (2008: 205), and to the evidentiary editing of the expository model that Nichols (2017) identifies. Expert knowledge and institutional discourse are drawn on to establish the supposed truthfulness or authenticity of the information represented. As a documentary, *The Battle for Johannesburg* makes use of interviews with experts such as Lael Bethlehem, the Director of Urban Renewal of the city council (Figure 10), and Nathi Mthethwa, then Director of Inner City Development. Using an observational fly-on-the-wall style, the film also follows stakeholders, such as Shareezah Sibanda from the Centre for Applied Legal Studies, as she liaises with tenants in bad buildings to improve their plight, and Nelson Katame, leader of the Residents Committee of San Jose, one of the bad buildings investigated in the film.[24] Desai's oeuvre is not conventional, and he often adopts a participatory mode of documentary (as Nichols defines it [2017: 132–158]), by inserting himself into scenes as the narrator, and also by positioning himself as someone with a point of view and a stake in the events that unfold throughout his films (Dlamini 2019: 41). In *The Battle for Johannesburg*, he recounts several nostalgic reminiscences of Johannesburg's inner city, specifically Hillbrow, from his younger days, for example. The general tone of the film is often nostalgic and seems to advocate for the revival of Hillbrow, to restore it to its former state. *The Battle for Johannesburg* is thus not a film that provides a text-book comparison with *District 9*'s parody of the documentary genre, since it also seeks to subvert

---

24   Bad buildings are described by Matthew Wilhelm-Solomon (2022) as a designation that became widespread in use by policymakers and journalists during the period leading up to South Africa hosting the 2010 FIFA World Cup. It refers to buildings in a state of decay or dereliction. His book entitled *The Blinded City* (2022) focuses on such occupied buildings and their residents over a roughly ten-year period from 2010. He engages with these buildings through interviews with residents, presenting their stories of hardship and survival.

FIGURE 10　Interview with Lael Bethlehem, director of Urban Renewal. Still taken from *The Battle for Johannesburg* (Rehad Desai, 2010).

some generic conventions, but there are many correspondences that may be productively read side-by-side in the films.

In mockumentary films, documentary techniques are emulated, but with added complexity, since they are also parodic. The conventions applied in *District 9* are typical of the interview format that depicts interviewees as talking heads, and uses text on the screen to emulate documentary conventions, evoking the reportorial model and observational mode, such as those used later by Desai in *The Battle for Johannesburg*.[25] In *District 9*, interviews that recall documentary modes and models serve as mockumentary motifs. In the interview with the character Grey Bradnam (Figure 11), the resolution of the image appears different from that in the newsreel and archive footage (such as Figure 4). Different stylistic devices convey changes in temporal setting, although this

---

25　Nichols (2017: 105–125) identifies various "models" adapted from other media forms, paired with what he calls cinematic "modes", in the articulation of the documentary film genre. I do not consider these distinctions in more detail here, although one could attempt to interpret the films under discussion in such a way. See also John Corner (2015: 147).

FIGURE 11   Interview with Grey Bradnam. Still taken from *District 9* (Neill Blomkamp, 2009).

is complicated by the consistent use of digital cameras to shoot both high- and low-resolution sequences. The news and archive footage discussed above reference the 1980s, and allude to analogue media, or low-resolution realism. Conversely, the interview in Figure 11 is clearly set in 2010 because it emulates digital footage, which is sharper and more defined.

Another style of interview is discernible in the intermittent interviews with Wikus, which is also how the film commences. In one of the first scenes (Figure 12), Wikus attaches a microphone to himself, and addresses the camera directly, apparently speaking to the camera operator or interviewer.[26] The strategy is repeated later in the film as well, which reinforces its generic orientation. The technique suggests that this is not a fiction film; it is a true story. The text at the bottom right of the frame is notable again, indicating the documentary context. Also included in the shot in Figure 12 is the open plan office where Wikus works, which shows many incidental details that emulate *cinéma vérité*. For example, the background includes signage on the wall to the left, hanging askew, and a whiteboard that juts out behind Wikus. Alongside these details, the office employees appear to go about their business unhindered, and the

---

26   In fact, he addresses someone he calls "Trent", which happens to be the first name of the *District 9* cinematographer.

FIGURE 12 Wikus interviewed at MNU headquarters. Still taken from *District 9* (Neill Blomkamp, 2009).

stark fluorescent lighting contributes to the idea that there is no production design and directorial staging in the scene. In *The Battle for Johannesburg*, such incidental details include local children playing outside in the background during the interview with Bethlehem, for example. In *District 9*, the impression created by incidental details is reinforced by the camera's movement, employing a jerky zoom motion that implies the use of a hand-held camera. In shots of Wikus, the documentary mode switches between a 'fly-on-the-wall' style and formal interview strategies. The former observational mode,[27] is often associated with providing an account of events as they unfold for the viewer, with the outcome unknown to the film crew, as is evident in *The Battle for Johannesburg*. This approach conveys a voyeuristic perspective, which in the case of *District 9* has additional significance, since the film is a mock exposé on the apartheid era and its murky history. Viewers may feel as if they are seeing "what really happened" (although of course this is both a parody and allegory of apartheid's history). Such a voyeuristic view of the atrocities committed during the apartheid era, however, would carry the danger of exoticizing or even glamorising

---

27 Nichols' (2017: 132–136) book on documentary is a seminal source on the genre.

the era and its history if it were a documentary film, but the parodic qualities of *District 9* mitigate this to some extent.

Using hand-held cameras to evoke particular effects is not new; since the 1990s with the release of the *Blair Witch Project* (Myrick & Sánchez 1999), it has become a more widely used strategy.[28] In *Gangster's Paradise: Jerusalema* (Ziman 2008) and *The Battle for Johannesburg* (2010), it emphasises the immediacy of the action genre. The latter film uses it in low-resolution sequences when interviewees are tracked as they walk through buildings. At various stages, the director/narrator is shown driving through Johannesburg, as a hand-held camera films him and the surrounding city from inside the car. The strategy establishes the importance of the actual city to the documentary, and also provides a tangible sense of how middle-class citizens, like Desai, traverse the city by car. Viewers witness the problems in the city – and see the city itself – in areas that are perhaps less familiar.[29]

In *District 9* hand-held shots evoke the camera techniques of live news journalism in particular (Nel 2012: 552). Typically, in situations of violent conflict, journalists and camera operators have to be mobile. This is evident in the opening shots of the official *District 9* trailer from the initial scenes, and later when Wikus first visits the alien settlement. In many scenes the camera is operated by someone following a character from behind. Hight (2008: 209) suggests that the hand-held camera, along with grainy footage and other flaws, conveys a sense of amateur video, which, importantly in *District 9*, suggests the authenticity of newsreel footage. The interview in Figure 13 shows Wikus addressing the camera directly again, apparently unaware of conflict erupting behind him, to humorous effect. He admonishes the alien on the left who pushes an MNU officer around,[30] telling him in a rather thick accent to stop "prod[ding]" the officer. Although I do not focus on the film's characters here, it is relevant that the treatment of Wikus is parodic to the point of caricature. He speaks English with an exaggerated Afrikaans accent that plays into stereotypes of Afrikaner identity (Jansen van Veuren 2012: 581–582). He is the butt of the joke, as his surname Van de Merwe indicates: Van der Merwe is a common surname used for the daft everyman Afrikaner character in South African humour.[31]

---

28 Hight (2008: 208–209) and Lucas (2014: 143–146) each discuss this technique in some detail.
29 Desai seems to suggest that viewers would be middle-class citizens, like himself.
30 MNU is an acronym for Multi-National United, a fictional security organization based in South Africa, and responsible for security in the alien camp *District 9* (Brott 2013: 31).
31 The significance of Wikus' name in relation to the well-known jokes is remarked on by Dennis Walder (2014: 151), Adele Nel (2012: 554, 561) and Keith Wagner (2015: 52).

MOCKUMENTARY: A FLY ON THE 'STOPNONSENSE' 95

FIGURE 13 Wikus addresses the camera while a prawn argues with an MNU officer. Still taken from *District 9* (Neill Blomkamp, 2009).

Helen Kapstein (2014: 155) describes Wikus as "a walking Van der Merwe joke" and discusses the use of humour in *District 9* in some detail.

Interestingly, Wikus may be compared with one of the interviewees in *The Battle for Johannesburg*, Gerald Olitzky, a property developer (and owner of Olitzky Property Holdings), who is questioned about his project of rejuvenating San Jose. In one encounter he is shown arguing with building residents who accuse him of taking advantage of them because they are poor. Like Wikus with the aliens in *District 9*, he wants to evict them while trying to avoid conflict, and the encounter serves as an index of the racial tension that underpins land ownership and the history of segregation in Johannesburg, and the country in general.

My interest, however, is in how documentary conventions construct the landscape of Johannesburg as "real" in *District 9*, *The Battle for Johannesburg* and *Gangster's Paradise: Jerusalema*. The landscape shown in the interviews reads as incidental: it is the 'actual' landscape, and just happens to be in the shots with the interviewees. As I have mentioned, Johannesburg's informal settlements and townships are recognisable in *District 9*, even to someone who has not lived in them, and this is equally true for *Gangster's Paradise: Jerusalema* and *The Battle for Johannesburg*. The films thus encourage one to see their portrayal of Johannesburg as credible (Nel 2012: 551). Recognisable elements in the landscape facilitate recognition. In the shot in Figure 13 from *District 9*, for

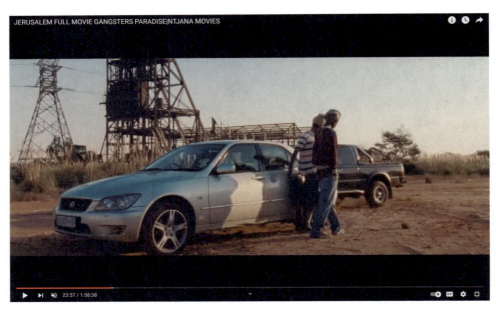

FIGURE 14   Lucky and Zakes near electricity pylons. Still taken from *Gangster's Paradise: Jerusalema* (Ralph Ziman, 2008).

example, electricity pylons are visible behind Wikus. These iconic pylons are familiar motifs in Johannesburg's contemporary landscape, and are also captured in *Gangster's Paradise: Jerusalema* (Figure 14).

Although *Gangster's Paradise: Jerusalema* has a very different generic context, it also relies on the incidental landscape of Johannesburg to establish a sense of recognisable of setting. This is perhaps more in line with how the *film noir* genre came to rely on on-location shooting in Los Angeles in the 1940s and 50s (Olsin-Lent 1987). In *Gangster's Paradise: Jerusalema* the incidental landscape is ubiquitous as the whole film was shot on location, without any sets. The screenshot in Figure 14, for example, shows the pylons alongside abandoned mining headgear. Mine waste areas are in close proximity to Soweto, where the township scenes were shot. The landscape reinforces the element of verité evoked at the beginning of the film, which references true events as the inspiration for the plot. Like *District 9*, *Gangster's Paradise: Jerusalema* appears to have been shot during winter, and the smog and dust in the air make the landscape seem washed-out, while the abandoned structures give it a post-industrial quality.

MOCKUMENTARY: A FLY ON THE 'STOPNONSENSE'

FIGURE 15   *Johannesburg from the Southwest*. Photograph by David Goldblatt, 2003.
Archival pigment inks, 98.5 × 123 cm.
COURTESY THE DAVID GOLDBLATT LEGACY TRUST AND GOODMAN GALLERY

The electricity pylons and other elements in the background of the screenshots in Figures 13 and 14 are also visible in Goldblatt's photograph of mine waste areas alongside the highway that leads into Soweto from the inner city (Figure 15). The reeds (*Phragmites communis*) and Pampas grass (*Cortaderia selloana*) in Figure 14 and Goldblatt's photograph are characteristic of the sparse flora found in mine waste areas, which were planted during the 1950s to curb some of the air and water pollution caused by the mine dumps (Reichardt 2013: 100).

There are many other comparisons one could make between Goldblatt's photograph and the landscape in these shots. One of the most pertinent aspects is not just the motif of the pylons but the analogue language evoked. Goldblatt is known for taking analogue photographs. He experimented with some digital photography toward the end of his life, but he claimed to feel most comfortable with the view camera tripod photography for which he was known (Douglas 2018). He described the camera as one of the most primitive, which requires the photographer to shoot under a black cloth. Furthermore, the chemical process that lends the image such a specific washed-out quality – the bleach bypass process – is particular to analogue developing techniques. This silver retention process used in photography and film creates a pallid, desaturated appearance (Prince 2004: 27). While I have suggested above that *District 9*'s colour palette is based on (or inspired by) analogue film, one may also note a resemblance to analogue photographs of the city and the processes, like bleach bypass, used for analogue photography. I would argue, however, that *District 9*, and portrayals like it, do not aim to faithfully emulate particular kinds of film stock, media or chemical processes. Rather, a generalised analogue character is constructed, one that is not faithful to any specific analogue quality or medium, but serves chiefly to emphasise the nostalgia already implicit in the idiom.

2.3 *Back to the 1980s*

2.3.1 Landmarks

District 9 also makes use of several other techniques to evoke a 1980s feeling. One of the most important is the use of motifs that relate to the period from a cultural perspective. Many of the motifs are iconically South African, which further reinforces a sense of place (Kapstein 2014: 165). Many buildings in Johannesburg's inner city, along with other structures and infrastructure, such as roads, power plants and the mining industry's abandoned equipment, are not only recognisable but now seem arrested in the state they were in before the fall of apartheid.[32] The white flight from the inner city in the 1980s, 1990s and 2000s means that numerous buildings in the city are no longer maintained, and have fallen prey to opportunistic landlords who illegally sublet apartments, in effect giving rise to slums (Beavon 2004: 244–245).[33] In this sense Johannesburg may be thought of as a time capsule, and its depiction in *District 9* evokes the past almost by default. The feeling of nostalgia that has tainted parts of the city is reflected in other films and media representations, as well

---

32 By now I mean the time of writing: 2016–2022. However, this condition has existed in the inner city since the early 1990s (Beavon 2004: 244–245).

33 The term white flight refers to the sudden departure of white residents from an urban area, and is not limited to Johannesburg; the term is also often used in relation to Detroit in the 1950s to 1970s (Jay & Leavell 2017). See also Brodie (2008: 97) and Saks (2010) for more on Johannesburg's white flight.

FIGURE 16   The mothership next to Ponte City as it leaves earth. Still taken from *District 9* (Neill Blomkamp, 2009).

as popular walking tours organised in the city (Joburg Heritage Walking Tour [n.d.]), which focus on the little-known architectural histories of the inner city. They include, for example, the city's Art Deco buildings, and other formerly important buildings, such as the Rissik Street post office, now abandoned and gutted, opposite the languishing Johannesburg city library, itself falling into disrepair.[34]

One of the most important landmarks in *District 9*, which appears in many shots and sequences, is the notorious skyscraper Ponte City (Figure 16). Its principal designers, Mannie Feldman, Manfred Hermer and Rodney Grosskopff, conceived the building, begun in 1975 and finished a few months before the Soweto uprising the next year (Kruger 2006: 150), as a modernist beacon of progress. According to Kruger (2006: 143), the building resembles Betrand Goldberg's Marina City (1967) in Chicago, which she suggests is a city that inspired apartheid architecture; both cities grew from nothing and have an appearance of wealth. Federico Freschi (2019: 67) describes 1960s architecture in South Africa as symbolic of the projected success and progress of the

---

34   The post office was vacated in 1996 and stood empty until it fell victim to a fire in 2009. It is currently under renovation (Joburg's Rissik Street … 2016).

FIGURE 17   *Cleaning the Core (360 Degree Panorama), Ponte City, Johannesburg*. Photograph by Mikhael Subotzky, 2008.
COPYRIGHT MIKHAEL SUBOTZKY AND PATRICK WATERHOUSE, COURTESY GOODMAN GALLERY.

Afrikaner nationalist government and the values of a sophisticated, internationally relevant Afrikaner identity. While the peak of this architectural phenomenon might have been the 1960s, Ponte City espouses many of the modernist preoccupations that the apartheid government expressed in adopting the International Style, which had some references to contemporary Brazilian architecture as well. With its cylindrical design and perched on top of a hill in Berea, next to the neighbourhood of Hillbrow, the 54-story skyscraper was both futuristic and forward-looking, and afforded its well-to-do white residents singularly amazing views of the city (Josephy 2017, Brodie 2008: 161). By 1996, however, the residents of the building were all Black, and many were from other African countries. The demographic change took place from as early as 1976 in the larger area of Hillbrow, a suburb close to the CBD, but only by 1985 was the influx of Africans significant. By 1993 62 percent of the residents in Hillbrow were African (Morris 1999: 53). A similar change had gradually been taking place in adjacent Berea, where Ponte City is located.

As a familiar landmark in the Johannesburg skyline, Ponte City appears repeatedly in *District 9*, and also in *Alive in Joburg* and many other films, such as *The Foreigner* (Maseko 1997), *Gangster's Paradise: Jerusalema* and *The Battle for Johannesburg*. Ponte City fell into decay in the 1980s and 1990s and has since seen several waves of renovation that have met with limited success (Josephy 2017: 67–85, Ponte City 2022). Around the same time that *District 9* was being shot, photographers Subotzky and Waterhouse were documenting the building, which coincided with a project to clear its atrium, where enormous heaps of rubble and garbage had accumulated, as is visible in Subotzky and Waterhouse's images from the time (Figure 17).[35] Svea Josephy (2017), who

---

35   See also *South Africa's Tower of Trouble* (2014), for an independent short documentary on the revival of the building, as well as Subotzky's website for a text on the building by writer Ivan Vladislavić (2014).

analyses this project in some detail, proposes that it represents a "portrait" of Johannesburg.

The building is a dubious beacon of progress. If anything, it represents the ambiguity of Johannesburg itself, as a place that is home to many people, but also has substantial problems that most citizens are aware of, even if they are not directly affected by them. Josephy (2017: 70) argues that Subotzky and Waterhouse's project captures both the positive mythology of the building as envisioned in its planning, and the negative mythology around its demise, as well as the sense of homeliness and mundanity of the everyday lives of its residents. Such a building probably evokes mixed feelings of both belonging and shame in South African viewers who see it in representations. In the title of her article on the building, Josephy describes the building as "Acropolis now", ominously evoking the film *Apocalypse Now* (Coppola 1979). The title of course also evokes the Acropolis in Athens, an iconic and classical urban landmark on a hill, which is now a ruin. In *Gangster's Paradise: Jerusalema*, as Ziman explains in an interview, the building is compared with the Biblical Jerusalem, a shining city on a hill, which the character Lucky ironically calls a *new* Jerusalem (that never comes to fruition) (Lehman 2011: 114, 123; Mututa 2020: 211). In 2010, in a socio-medical research project entitled "Visual Hillbrow", Emilie Venables (2011: 124–143) interviewed HIV-positive men who lived in Hillbrow. They were asked to take photographs and make cognitive maps, as well as narrate their feelings about living in the area. Many of them conveyed mixed feelings, regarding the neighbourhood as unsafe, unhealthy and rife with social problems, while at the same time being proud of its landmarks (the Hillbrow Tower, for example) and thinking of it as home. Ponte City might evoke comparable mixed responses from residents of the building and citizens of Johannesburg in general. Ponte could be interpreted as a symbol of the apartheid regime, evoking negative connotations, and it could also be regarded negatively because of its sordid afterlife in post-apartheid Johannesburg. As one of the most iconic buildings affected by white flight, it might furthermore be seen as symbolic of white anxiety, symbolising a white fear of the loss of hegemonic supremacy (Gabay 2018: 1–45), which I consider later in relation to the mining landscape.

Discussed at length in Venables' research, the Hillbrow Tower also recurs as a landmark in *District 9*, *Gangster's Paradise: Jerusalema* and *The Battle for Johannesburg*. Originally called the J.G. Strijdom tower, after a Nationalist Prime Minister of the 1950s, it is one of the most recognisable buildings in the city, visible to the left of Ponte City in Figure 16. Completed in 1971, it was built by the Post Office as a telecommunications signal tower. Like Ponte, it was an engineering feat, with its ambitious 270m height, and it cost R2 million to erect this landmark (Brodie 2008: 161). The building was initially open to the public,

FIGURE 18   The MNU headquarters with mine dumps in the background. Still taken from *District 9* (Neill Blomkamp, 2009).

and even had a revolving restaurant at the top, but it was closed to visitors for security reasons in 1981. As early as 1982, Paddi Clay and Glynn Griffieth had already described it as a drop-off point for prostitutes in their book *Hillbrow* (1982). Josephy (2017: 68) describes Hillbrow in the 1980s as a "grey area" of interracial mixing, with a growing reputation for prostitution, gangsterism and crime in general. I have mentioned the link between white flight and inner-city decay in the 1990s, but the crime rate in the CBD and adjoining areas was already high in the 1980s, and Hillbrow is invariably presented as having a tarnished reputation related to social ills and moral decay – a testament to the persistence of social reputations of place, or indeed place-images.

Another recognisable building in *District 9* is the Carlton Centre, constructed through a partnership between Chicago architects Skidmore, Owings and Merrill and local firm Rhodes, Harrison and Hoffe, to echo the First National Bank building in Chicago by Perkins and Wills (Kruger 2006: 143) – another instance of apartheid architecture drawing inspiration from Chicago. In the film it serves as the MNU headquarters (Figure 18). Wagner (2015: 57–58) describes how it rises above the camp (or township) and serves as a symbol of the bureaucratic control of the apartheid regime. In the background of Figure 18, one can see mine dumps, a reminder of the financial underpinnings of buildings such as the Carlton Centre, which was once the tallest building in Africa.

2.3.2 Militarisation

In Figure 8, a still image from *District 9*, one can see the emphasis on militarisation and the security police presence, which in *District 9* (and *Alive in Joburg* in Figure 4) resembles the actual vehicles and police in 1980s media. A similar police vehicle also appears in *Gangster's Paradise*. The Casspirs, security vehicles used by the police during the historical States of Emergency, were ubiquitous at the time, and also appear in historical documentary photographs and newsreel footage, as well as in Goodman Mabote's illustrations for Rantete's 1984 account of the Sebokeng rebellion.[36]

The vehicles, omnipresent in 1980s imagery of Johannesburg, are emulated in the 2010 MNU vehicles in *District 9* (Figure 19). The effect is a conflation of past, present and future. Blomkamp may thus be said to amplify the analogue nostalgia in *District 9*, the "nostalgising" (Niemeyer 2014: 10) of the present, in the content of the film as well as its visual effects. Similar to Instagram filters that endow contemporary photographs with a sense of historicity and create an "instant past" (Bartholeyns 2014: 51–69), Johannesburg, depicted here as the science fiction city of the future, is simultaneously the city of the apartheid past. Temporality collapses in the analogue aesthetics at work here, rendering the future *as* the past, which casts the present in a nostalgic light and also suggests that not much has changed from the country's past to the present. Many scholars that have written about the city have made the point that there are disturbing parallels between the geopolitics of apartheid Johannesburg and democratic Johannesburg.[37]

A militarised quality is also emphasised in *Gangster's Paradise: Jerusalema* and *The Battle for Johannesburg*, in the latter through the opening scenes where the eviction agents known as Red Ants[38] are clearing a slum building with military fervour. In *Gangster's Paradise: Jerusalema*, there are numerous portrayals of the security measures that abound in *District 9* as well: barbed wire, security gates, militarised vehicles, uniformed security guards and police, and so forth. All three films seem to reference the carceral character of the city, which has engaged the attention of scholars interested in the city. It is

---

36   Visual artist William Kentridge also produced an etching in 1989 entitled *Casspirs Full of Love*, commenting on the States of Emergency and the political tensions in the country at the time.

37   Scholars such as Mellissa Thandiwe Myambo (2011), Mzwanele Mayekiso (1996: 13), Aghogho Akpome (2017), Martin Murray (2011), Jayne Poyner (2011) and Jennifer Robinson (2010) have considered the lack of geopolitical transformation in the city.

38   The Red Ant Security, Eviction and Relocation Services are known for enforcing evictions in the country. They are often associated with the terrorisation of residents (Neille 2020).

FIGURE 19   MNU vehicles that resemble Casspirs. Still taken from *District 9*
(Neill Blomkamp, 2009).

also evident in other representations produced at the time. An example is the artwork entitled *Rewind: A Cantata For Voice, Tape and Testimony*, an interactive video directed by Gerhard and Maja Marx (2007), and with music by Philip Miller in 2007. In the video (see Figure 20) countless images of township houses emphasise doors, windows and security measures, such as burglar bars, barbed wire and security gates. The images highlight township planning in the uniformity of the design of the houses, but also how the plans have been subverted by residents and homeowners, who closed doors and windows, and made other alterations to suit their needs.

2.4   *What can Mockumentary Poetics Do?*

What does the landscape constructed through *District 9*'s mockumentary poetics look like? This landscape is recognisable mostly for its quality of being under siege and in decay. It is a landscape marked by barriers, military technologies, and general signs of deterioration and destruction. Opaloch describes the landscape of Chiawelo looking like a war zone (Holben 2009:26), and Blomkamp affirms this in a 2012 interview, saying that the environment was difficult to shoot in, with pollution, broken glass and rusted barbed wire everywhere (Smith in Nel 2012: 552). In *District 9* there are ubiquitous references to newsreel footage from the States of Emergency, with recognisable aspects of the infamous landscape depicted in the media from the 1980s. One thinks of

MOCKUMENTARY: A FLY ON THE 'STOPNONSENSE' 105

FIGURE 20   Still taken from *Rewind: A Cantata for Voice, Tape and Testimony* (Gerhard and Maja Marx, 2007).
IMAGE COURTESY OF GERHARD MARX

FIGURE 21   Wikus addresses the camera while an informal structure burns behind him. Still taken from *District 9* (Neill Blomkamp, 2009).

scenes of destruction, such as in the screenshot in Figure 21, that depicts raging fires, pervasive dust, brown polluted skies and a washed-out appearance that echoes the ominous tone of the news itself. The landscape is characterised by watchtowers, surveillance and other forms of militarisation. Nel (2012: 552) describes it as an "African ghetto" that is claustrophobic and dirty, characterised by informal housing and "nightmarish labyrinths and alleys", with the filthiness exacerbated by repulsive unhygienic cattle carcasses for sale. It truly is an "abject cityscape" (Nel 2012 550). While it has the feeling of reality, it is important to note that this is a reductive distortion, which may contribute to a false portrayal of townships as remorselessly hellish.

It is part of the complexity of depictions like *District 9* that they may contribute to damaging stereotypes of South African cities. As with any representation, this is a particular view of what townships are like. This landscape of siege depicts Johannesburg as trapped in a state of crisis, a living dystopia or zone of indistinction, a landscape utterly broken. An important aspect of the mockumentary genre is that it complicates the sense of realism. This realism is important in the broader idiom, reinforced in the use of documentary techniques in *Gangster's Paradise: Jerusalema* and *The Battle for Johannesburg*, in which the actual setting of the city lends the depictions a sense of the "real" city. They also focus on the dystopian qualities of the city, however, and portray the contemporary demise of Hillbrow and the bleak future of the city: from both a fictionalised and a documentary perspective *District 9* provides a more complicated portrayal, due to the ironic and self-reflexive qualities of the mockumentary genre.

To *what end* does *District 9* employ mockumentary techniques then? How does this relate to nostalgic dystopia more generally? One of the most obvious answers to these questions is that the documentary qualities of the mockumentary genre dovetail with the fetishization of authenticity that analogue nostalgia is known for. The genre allows the film to simulate a documentary of apartheid Johannesburg, in a depiction that resembles many of the contemporary portrayals of the city in film, photography and popular media. In other words, it constructs a war-torn dystopian city that closely resembles aspects of the actual city, a quality shared by the other films discussed, as well as by the documentary photography and archival footage that *District 9* evokes. The use of humour inherent in the mockumentary genre makes *District 9*'s landscape visually palatable and it is instrumental in the film's ironic reflective nostalgia. Although the city depicted in the film is dystopian, it is also the childhood home of many South Africans of a certain generation, such as Blomkamp, and Moloi who grew up in Soweto (Vundla 2017), along with authors Jacob Dlamini and Niq Mhlongo, who both grew up in townships – and probably like many who watch the film. In *District 9* the look of analogue media enables one to engage nostalgically with the landscape despite its dystopian qualities. The film can be forgiven for foregrounding the problems of this difficult landscape, because it is not actually a documentary. It sparkles with false historicity and simulated authenticity through digital visual effects. The simulated element is not hidden from view but flaunted through hypermediacy, made apparent in the digital emulation of analogue qualities in the film.

Craig Hight (2008: 209) suggests that the mockumentary genre contributes to the complexity in the exchange "between analogue and digital forms of mediated reality" in contemporary filmmaking. In *District 9* specifically, the mockumentary qualities enable the viewer to engage less with an ethical consideration of apartheid (the film's allegorical content), than to savour its humour and nostalgia. Hight argues that mockumentary replaces the documentary genre's call to action with a *"call to play"* (Hight 2008: 211, emphasis in original text). While I would not suggest that *District 9* is easy to watch or even enjoyable, or that play is a viable ethical response to apartheid's history, the call to play seems blatant in the film. I would argue that the mockumentary qualities of *District 9* enable the contradictory aspects at work in the idiom to come to the fore and, what is more, makes it possible for them to coexist. If not for the humour brought to the film by its mockumentary conventions, it might be far more difficult to digest any of the nostalgia it evokes.

Johannesburg as mockumentary city can thus more easily be tolerated for its dystopian character, so that one may think of it nostalgically, or even with a touch of ironic humour. To me, this is most emphatic in relation to the landscape rather than to apartheid history as such. An aspect of *District 9* which is also interesting in terms of the mockumentary genre, is that the site of the most violent encounter is also the site of redemption or transformation. The township landscape, here depicted as washed-out (in colour) and ruinous, also becomes the site where Wikus ultimately finds a reluctant belonging and redemption. In this way, the film permits the township setting to be recast as the site of salvation. This is significant from an allegorical point of view. While scholars have suggested that the alien character Christopher Johnson has Christ-like attributes, or that Wikus attains a form of redemption through his bodily suffering, the landscape has not often been considered in this light. I argue that the redemptive aspect here is more than just a white Afrikaner man being cast as an anti-hero who eventually gives up his status as white man, to be saved by the 'other', the alien Christopher. The landscape is integral to situating redemption and transformation in a complex contradictory context. It contributes crucially to the "rewriting" of post-apartheid history that Blomkamp attempts in *District 9* (even though it should be approached with scepticism and critique). The landscape is infused with elements that make it unbearable to look at – violence, destruction, poverty, abject suffering and decay – but incongruously it evokes feelings of familiarity and nostalgia and finally transformation through Wikus' dubious redemption.

CHAPTER 4

Township Nostalgia

1   Analogue Nostalgia

1.1   *Subversive Resistance*
While *District 9* used digital cameras but manipulated the film to achieve the effects of analogue nostalgia, the broader idiom evokes analogue nostalgia in diverse ways. As previously discussed, *Gangster's Paradise: Jerusalema* is shot entirely on analogue cameras with old film stock, and Goldblatt is known for only working with analogue photography. The preference for analogue cameras is perhaps indicative of the valorisation of analogue media since the inception of digital media, paralleling the kind of reaction that filmmakers, such as Spielberg, and cinematographers, such as Christopher Doyle (Clarke 2017: 105–106) and Wally Pfister (Mateer 2014: 6), had (and still have) to digital cameras being used in the film industry (Lucas 2014). Although digitally retouching their work, younger photographers such as Subotzky and Waterhouse also use analogue cameras, such as the Mamiya medium-format camera. The valorisation of analogue media conveys a sense of authenticity and historicity in *District 9*, as in the other instances mentioned above.

In South Africa, there are numerous examples of Instagram photographers and fashion bloggers using similar techniques to represent Johannesburg in a manner that constructs a feeling of historicity. They include the aforementioned collectives Khumbula, the Sartists and I See A Different You. The Instagram bloggers' photographs of Johannesburg and its surrounds are nostalgic and yet – like *District 9*'s evocation of the past – ironic. I See A Different You, in their photographs in Figures 22 and 23, portray some of the grittier neighbourhoods in the city, such as Hillbrow and industrial parts of Soweto. They are accompanied by fond hashtags connoting belonging – "hood", "home" and "kasilami" (a vernacular word for "location", which is what the townships were often called in apartheid's institutional language). The colouring of these images resembles photographs of the city by Subotzky and Waterhouse, Tillim and Goldblatt. In *Power Park//Soweto* (Figure 22), which depicts the abandoned power station at the foot of the surviving towers, the ruins of the structure are juxtaposed with glowing cloud formations; in *Johannesburg//Home* (Figure 23), which depicts the inner city of Johannesburg and Hillbrow, the historical high-rise architecture is limned by the sunset, giving the buildings a rosy halo. In both images there is evidence of a manipulated colour palette that

FIGURE 22   *Power Park//Soweto*. Photograph by I See A Different You, 2016.
COURTESY OF ISEEADIFFERENTYOU 2016

echoes the backward-looking cinematographic agenda of *District 9* and recalls aged analogue photography such as Polaroid prints and family photographs from the 1980s. The colours are warm and dusty, with even the sky a dusky blue. *Johannesburg//Home* glows with such deep browns that it reminds one of faded film photographs from the 1960s to the 1980s that often become more brown and red in tone as they age.

In an article on the practices of collectives such as I See A Different You, Khumbula, and the Sartists, Leora Farber (2015) argues that the practice of depicting the present in a nostalgic register, and the use of a dated visual language, signifies how these collectives grapple with the apartheid and colonial past of South Africa. They reimagine the past as they wish it to appear. Even though the past is not a pleasant place or time, romanticising it gives these photographers some agency over it: in a sense, they re-write history and create it differently. The past about which they feel nostalgia is not the actual past, but an imagined past in the manner of reflective nostalgia. In Harness Hamese's photograph of three young men in a township context (Figure 24), they appear to be on the street, but are pouring tea and drinking it from teacups. They are dressed in vaguely old-fashioned attire, all three in suits and one wearing a 1920s-style boater. According to Farber, they are performing

FIGURE 23   *Johannesburg//Home*. Photograph by I See A Different You, 2016.
COURTESY OF ISEEADIFFERENTYOU 2016

one of the identities (almost like personas) that these collectives employ to counter historical stereotypes of Black men as uneducated layabouts and criminals: they portray themselves as perfect gentlemen. They counter apartheid-era perceptions of Black men living in townships, and reimage that past by projecting the present onto a nostalgic past of their own making. The nostalgic quality is heightened by the sun appearing to set in the smoggy surroundings, one of the few touches of colour in a largely monochrome photograph. Farber (2015: 114) refers to this practice as "subversive resistance",[1] but one may also understand it in terms of Lees' (2004: 24) "freedom to" shape the city and their own identities along with it. The landscape of Johannesburg is steeped in a history they should not celebrate, and yet these photographs present the city nostalgically, reclaiming the past despite its sordid character. The bloggers recast the city of the past as a city they feel fond of, one that bears the historical traces with which they choose to imbue it.

---

[1] Leora Farber borrows this term from Deborah Willis (2003) to describe the strategies that Black people employ to resist racist stereotypes in representations.

FIGURE 24   *The Three Stages of Preparing Tea.* Photograph by Harness Hamese, 2014. Digital print.
COURTESY OF THE PHOTOGRAPHER

1.2   'Native Nostalgia'

It is crucial to consider the significance of nostalgia in the larger South African context when examining analogue nostalgia in these representations. As with all forms of visual representation, *District 9* does not exist in a visual vacuum, but within the context of nostalgic portrayals of South Africa's past in other forms and expressions, such as literature and popular media. The broader context also points to the fact that the idiom and its nostalgic impulses are not the preserve of a white view of Johannesburg and its townships alone, as my previous examples might suggest.

The way the photographers discussed above depict the townships in their work brings to mind one of the most influential accounts of township life of recent years: novelist Dlamini's book *Native Nostalgia* (2009), published in the same year as *District 9*'s release. Dlamini's account of his childhood in the township of Katlehong near Johannesburg elicited harsh criticism from fellow author Eric Myeni and journalist Andile Mngxitama, who accused Dlamini of an apologist depiction of apartheid (Jones 2014: 110). It has also, however, been described as brave and daring, since he refutes the master narrative of Black suffering under apartheid (Akpome 2018: 105–115). Although Dlamini makes it clear that his intention is not to pardon the atrocities of apartheid or to imply that it was positive in any manner, in *Native Nostalgia* he asserts that poverty, crime and degradation did not determine Black life under apartheid in its totality. Instead, he seeks to complicate how townships and Black life are understood in contemporary South Africa (Dlamini 2009: 1–19). This seems especially important when looking at seemingly stereotypical depictions of townships exemplified in nostalgic dystopian depictions.

Dlamini's description of Katlehong is invaluable as a register of the complexity of an individual's lived experience of township life. The nostalgia he professes to feel comes from his childhood in a specific place, and from the viewpoint of having lived there. While he describes his particular feeling as reflective by referring to Boym's discussion of nostalgia (Dlamini 2009: 17), as I do with reference to *District 9*, his view of the township is distinctively different from the perspective of a white person visiting the township, such as the character of Wikus – or the experience of director Blomkamp, a white middle-class man who grew up in suburban Johannesburg, and indeed my own experiences as a white middle-class woman living in a Johannesburg suburb today. Dlamini's view is from inside a township, and thus his use of nostalgia is situated differently to *District 9*'s portrayal of the city as nostalgic, or films such as *Gangster's Paradise: Jerusalema* and *The Battle for Johannesburg*, made by directors who portray parts of the city from outsider perspectives to at least some degree. Dlamini (2009: 65–76) admits that some readers may regard him as a traitor of sorts, a "rat", for undermining the master narrative of Black struggle under apartheid, but he maintains that his depiction of township life aims to generate a complexity which counters the notion that Black life is homogenous. His more recent book, *Askari* (2014), is an equally daring investigation, in this case of the Black enforcers of apartheid who worked with the government, and hence against the Black population of South Africa who suffered under its laws.

Dlamini describes *Native Nostalgia* as neither memoir nor cultural biography, but a combination of both in a narrative of fragmented memories. He explains that townships may have been planned to impose racial and ethnic or tribal segregation, but that his lived experience was in some ways very different (Dlamini 2009: 45). Like the photographers discussed in this chapter, his view of township life is infused with acts of resistance to the apartheid regime. While townships such as Katlehong were part of the reformist or scientific "new" townships planned after the advent of apartheid policy in 1948, the planning agendas they represented were often undermined in residents' lived practices. Dlamini mentions, for example, how Katlehong was planned using a grid system, alongside a railway running its length, and divided into rectangular sections with numbered houses. Yards or plots were allocated to houses, and he describes his own home as having an L-shaped lawn, with a peach tree planted in the front of the house with its *stoep*, or veranda. There was an outdoor toilet, a coal shed and a fence, with two separate gates for pedestrians and cars to enter the property. Amidst all this pretence of suburban structures, essentially planned by the government, he recounts how people would erect fences and subdivide their plots according to agreements between neighbours. In this way, residents asserted agency and laid claim to the space in seemingly prosaic ways. One might compare it with how fashion bloggers reclaim the township landscape and its past to bend it to their own narratives.

Niq Mhlongo (2010: 11–15), who grew up in Chiawelo in Soweto, has similar fond memories of that township. In an essay for photographer Jodi Bieber's photo essay book entitled *Soweto* (2010), he describes the township of his childhood in terms of how people lived ordinary lives there, despite facing severe challenges. He remembers the township with nostalgia, recalling social events: watching "Chinese movies" at the nearby bioscope, places such as *shishanyamas* (barbeque or *braai* restaurants), soccer games, *stokvel* (informal saving schemes), gatherings, and so forth. He describes how his family of eleven people lived in a two-bedroom house, and how the owning of a television was a measure of wealth. He recounts the prevalence of gangs and violent crime, but he describes how Soweto, or *Msawawa* as he refers to it colloquially, became the symbol of democracy and the "New South Africa" (Mhlongo 2010: 14). As with the fashion bloggers, the townships represent home to Mhlongo and, although his account may be considered romanticised, it also serves as a counterpoint to what he calls the "nuisance questions about crime, unemployment, or how it is to live in a place of poor shanty dwellings where people die of violence and disease every day" (Mhlongo 2010: 11). The Chiawelo he describes is not by any means the same place depicted in *District 9*, despite his acknowledging the same circumstances: poverty, unemployment, violence and segregation.

1.3 *Constructed History*

As discussed in the previous chapter, Caoduro (2014) suggests that the visual style of analogue photography emulated in digital photography indicates a yearning for authenticity in amateur photographic practices like those on Instagram. Authenticity is rootedness in a particular history, which gives it a fixed quality. One of the significant aspects in the depiction of decay in Instagram photography is the focus on tactility: texture in the landscape and environment. Such texture and tactility is equally evident in *District 9,* and reflects the larger media trend of analogue nostalgia at work in a nostalgic visual language.

In a photograph in the *Black History Tribute* series, by Anthony Bila (2014) for the collective Khumbula, tactile elements are visible in both the subject matter and the treatment of the image.[2] In the township setting (in this case Alexandra in Johannesburg), there is evidence of much decay, from the disintegrating paving in the foreground to the textures on the walls of the structures, and the worn patches of grass near the feet of the two men who pose for the photograph in the foreground. There are miscellaneous abandoned architectural elements and scattered rubble, and the door behind the figures seems battered and peeling. Razor wire (ubiquitous in *District 9*) tops the walls, and an oil drum serves as a chair. The formality of the men's appearance contrasts sharply with their environment, dressed as they are in a vintage style, with jackets made of heavily textured fabrics that evoke tweed and houndstooth. The photograph itself seems to have been digitally altered, as if treated to look like an aged Van Dyck print, with sepia colouring, and scratches on the surface of the image – digital filters that add further texture to the image.

Writing about home movies and nostalgia, Giuseppina Sapio (2014: 44) considers the yearning for tactility in analogue nostalgia with reference to Benjamin's discussion of the loss of tactility in daily life. In the 1930s, in *The Writer of Modern Life*, Benjamin (2006) suggested that the use of rich fabrics such as velvet in interiors in Paris was an attempt to bring back a sense of touch to modern life. Sapio (2014) argues that by using analogue effects such as the application of filters, users bring back tactility to their digital home videos. In other words, the flaws of analogue video in old home movies, such as noise, poor focus, and decay in colour and film quality, have become associated with the time when they were made, and stand in for the authenticity associated with that time.

Sapio (2014: 39–50) discusses "hipster" culture as a search for tactility and authenticity in "vintage" products such as clothing and accessories.[3] Pam Cook (2005) also refers to this desire for authenticity, which is apparent in the evocation of nostalgia in consumer capitalism. The work of South African bloggers can be contextualised within this wider analogue nostalgia boom. But, although the way they imbue their work with an appearance that evokes the past is not unique to South Africa, the way they apply it is unique to the local context. They make use of digital media's propensity for recreating analogue

---

2   See the Khumbula website at https://khumbula.files.wordpress.com/2014/07/bila.jpg.
3   See Marilyn DeLong, Barbara Heinemann and Kathryn Reiley (2005) who write on hipster culture in the fashion context.

effects to evoke and reconstruct South Africa's racialised past of trauma and violence, which allows them to control the historical narrative of race to some extent. While *District 9* seeks to transform the township (perhaps questionably) into an unlikely site of redemption for an Afrikaner man, the work of the bloggers I've been discussing unearths a different fictional version of a past Johannesburg, where the townships are inhabited by gentlemen who appear educated, dignified and refined against all odds. The feeling of historicity and authenticity in their photographs affords their constructed version of history more nuance and value.

CHAPTER 5

Sci-fi City

1 Science Fiction Poetics

1.1 Retrofuturism and 'New Bad Future'

While the mockumentary genre is predominant in the poetics of *District 9*, especially in terms of its cinematography, it is not the only genre at work in the film. Many scholars have regarded it primarily as a science fiction film, although I find it more productive to interpret *District 9* as a mockumentary film that draws on the science fiction genre. Discussing *District 9* as a science fiction film using the conventions of the documentary form, Mireille Rosello (2016: 43) discusses how these genres relate to each other. She points out that, while science fiction often asks the viewer to suspend disbelief in order to follow a story about aliens, for example, a documentary seeks to furnish the viewer with truthful information. Mockumentary simulates or parodies the pursuit of truthful information, complicating the notion of documentary. According to Geoff King and Tanya Krzywinska (2006:11), science fiction is an intertextual genre that defies clear definition, as mockumentary does. Along the same lines, Vivian Sobchack (1998: 63), in her seminal book on the science fiction genre, describes it as less clearly defined than is often thought. She suggests that science fiction cinema engages both with science and its empirical methods, and with more cultural motifs related to the transcendentalism associated with magic and religion. Drawing on Sobchack, one may infer that an underpinning of science fiction with its own inherent complexity contributes to the complexity of how *District 9* portrays nostalgic dystopia. *District 9* reflects elements that recur in the science fiction genre in predictable ways. These include prevalent utopian or dystopian settings (Williams 1978) and the manipulation of temporality, which renders the past and present as unstable categories.[1] The latter is uniquely pertinent in the case of *District 9*, which conflates aspects of two periods of time, the 1980s and the 2000s. The analogue nostalgia used in the cinematography is further enhanced by the temporal quality of the science fiction genre in the film, reinforcing its nostalgic effect.

---

1 King & Krzywinska (2006: 54–55), Nel (2012) and Sobchack (1998: 254) all consider temporality in the science fiction genre, indicating its typical complexity.

© LANDI RAUBENHEIMER, 2025 | DOI:10.1163/9789004710955_007
This is an open access chapter distributed under the terms of the CC BY-NC-ND 4.0 license.

King and Krzywinska (2006) also discuss several design styles that have influenced the look of science fiction films, such as futurism, gothic and post-apocalyptic design, and retrofuturism. In *District 9* much of the alien technology is retrofuturist, which recalls visions of the future that were popular in the 1980s. Showing those as fallible and dated is in a sense allegorical of apartheid itself. The Johannesburg landscape depicted in the film echoes this retrofuturist design sensibility, focusing on buildings that, in the futuristic depiction of 2010, are seen as past their prime, and degenerating into slums. This, in turn, prompts the view that the city itself is in decline. As such, it may imply to even the sceptical viewer that in the past the city was 'better'. Takayuki Tatsumi (2015: 139) describes how the depiction of the city and the spaceship in *District 9* differentiates it from other science fiction films. It portrays a uniquely South African science fiction aesthetic, a "dirty, almost steampunk look" that reminds him of Hayao Miyazaki's anime films, as well as the cyberpunk subgenre (Tatsumi 2015: 138–139).

Dystopian depictions of the future, particularly of the cyberpunk subgenre, are not uncommon in contemporary science fiction cinema, and were prominent in the Hollywood films in the 1980s and 1990s that Sobchack (2008: 271–272) describes in her "third map" of the genre of science fiction in American cinema. Films such as *Blade Runner* (Scott 1982), *The Terminator* (Cameron 1984), *Robocop* (Verhoeven 1987) and *Total Recall* (Verhoeven 1990) are marked by a paranoid, anxious outlook on urban life. Often, they both critique and eroticise the ills associated with dystopian urbanism.[2] They depict garbage, decay and industrialisation as aestheticised, and Sobchack (2008: 262, 271) argues that the city becomes exoticised as a setting, depicting "excess scenography". In *Screening Space: The American Science Fiction Film* (1998), Sobchack bases an earlier iteration of this argument on Fredric Jameson's *Postmodernism, or the Cultural Logic of Late Capitalism* (1984). She contends that science fiction films of the 1980s frequently emphasise the mediated qualities of postmodern society (Sobchack 1998: 229–262), and proposes that Jameson's discussion of postmodernism could be employed to interpret the science fiction genre in

---

2 Janet Staiger's (1988: 20–40) discussion of the *future noir* genre is also pertinent in some respects. She discusses *Blade Runner* and its cityscape in some detail, referring particularly to the links between urban architecture and class in this dystopian depiction of Los Angeles. As with *District 9*'s Johannesburg, the city is depicted as a failure, with only the privileged – mostly those occupying top positions in corporate business – residing in skyscrapers that overlook the squalor of the future city. As discussed in the previous section, landmark buildings such as Ponte City and the Carlton Centre play such a role in *District 9*, indicating a skewed balance of power.

1980s cinema. Such films are postmodern in many ways: simulation and the real are often portrayed as intertwined, and immediate and mediated hyper-real experiences are seen as interchangeable, reflecting Jameson's notion of "depthlessness" in postmodern society (Sobchack 1998: 254). In other words, these films problematise and romanticise the increasingly mediated quality of postmodern life. One may conclude that dystopian depictions of the future are endemic to this particular period of science fiction cinema, at least in Hollywood. The films are also known for how they conflate temporality (Sobchack 1998: 272–281), reflecting the collapse of history that Jameson theorises as uniquely postmodern.

What is intriguing with regard to *District 9* is Sobchack's argument that 1980s science fiction films are often fundamentally nostalgic (1998: 229, 274–281). She writes about how this nostalgia is constructed in a manner strikingly comparable to the analogue nostalgia employed in *District 9* and by the fashion bloggers I described earlier. In films from the 1980s, such as *Back to the Future* (Zemeckis 1985), not to mention television series of the time, there is an intertextual approach to constructing temporality as fundamentally backward-looking and nostalgic for the 1950s. According to Sobchack (1998: 274), films like this exude a "pseudo-historical depth", a term she takes from Jameson: history appears not as a realised temporal setting, but a set of aesthetic styles to be emulated at random. In essence, these films embody a kind of simulacrum of history. She further argues that history here is not so much remembered directly as it is remembered from popular media (Sobchack 1998: 274–276). I argued earlier that Blomkamp may have been influenced by popular science fiction depictions from television and cinema in South Africa during his childhood in the 1980s. Insofar as *District 9* references newsreel footage from the 1980s, as well as several science fiction motifs of the time, it follows that the film shares some of the dominant motifs and themes of 1980s science fiction films, rather than the cyberpunk references Tatsumi suggests.

One 1980s subgenre that Fred Glass (1989: 7) identifies as "new bad future" resonates strongly with aspects of *District 9*. Glass identifies several codes of the subgenre that find their way into *District 9*. A standout element in new bad future films is the setting, which, in the films Sobchack (1998: 255–272) discusses, typically depicts the decay of modernist progress in future society. According to Glass (1989: 10–11), this bleak, dystopian vision is the product of pessimism about the transformation of technologies in contemporary society and their ability to bring about positive transformation. It also conveys cynicism about the political and cultural implications and power relations embedded in how such technologies are disseminated and used. In films such as *Blade Runner*, *Robocop*, *The Terminator* and *Aliens*, he identifies the premise that future society is considerably worse off than current society. Very often, such fictional societies are not set in the distant future but seem to be on the not-too-distant horizon, as fantastical yet plausible visions of what is to come (Glass 1989: 12).

While *District 9* is not set only in the 1980s, the influence of media from that time has been acknowledged by Blomkamp (2020) and Opaloch (Holben 2009).[3] One may therefore surmise that the film's visual design draws on science fiction films from the 1980s: the dystopian setting of near-future Johannesburg certainly seems reminiscent of the post-apocalyptic settings of *Blade Runner* and *The Terminator*. The figure of the cyborg in such films was very relevant to the socio-political concerns of western societies in the 1980s, which subscribed to the values that Hollywood films unconsciously espoused, such as neoliberal capitalist thinking.[4] In *District 9* the cyborg is an essential motif that informs the body armour Wikus dons towards the end, representative of change or transition in society. Glass argues that the cyborg motif represents a transitional object in new bad future films, enabling the audience to make sense of the changing world in which they are living (Glass 1989: 26). The motif works almost like a fetish, assuaging anxiety.[5] The cyborg in *Robocop*, for example, alleviates anxieties around dehumanisation in late capitalist society's valorisation of instrumental reason, and serves to reassure audiences that urban decay can be curbed, and that humans and technology can coexist (Glass 1989: 39–40). These concerns remain relevant in society at the time of writing (especially South African society), where the so-called Fourth Industrial Revolution is a driving force in much academic debate concerning the future of the world, industry and academia.[6]

---

3 In his interview with me, Blomkamp mentioned how important it was for him to use older, earlier generation digital cameras such as the EX1, to achieve an unpolished look, which he describes as "washed-out" and "burnt out".
4 An interesting point here is a debate in 2012 around the relevance of science fiction to Africa. Author Nnedi Okorafor (in Kapstein 2014: 158) quotes Professor Naunihal Singh as saying that, if *The Terminator* were to screen in West Africa, it would not be popular at all: it might not speak to people who are grappling with poverty, and who do not have the luxury of imagining the future and technology. Implied here is the mismatch between neoliberal ideas of progress and the reality of people living in impoverished societies. On the other hand, the recent popularity and topicality of Afrofuturism, which imagines Africa as the epicentre of human development within the context of technology, speaks to a different impulse in relation to science fiction (Womack 2013).
5 See Glass' (1989: 26–33) discussion of Peter Fuller's work on object relations.
6 See Klaus Schwab's (2016) seminal book on the topic, Bryan Edward Penprase (2018: 207–228) and Michael A. Peters (2017: 1–6) for the impact on the Fourth Industrial Revolution on education.

Another motif Glass (1989: 12–14) identifies is the use of television within the films themselves. *District 9* makes extensive use of television formats such as interviews and newsreel footage, and even portrays old cathode ray television sets as signifiers of the decay in the township setting of the camp. Glass (1989: 14) argues that, within the subgenre of new bad future films, there is a suggested symbiosis between social decay and television as a medium, but ironically these films employ the aesthetics of television formats despite their conceptual contempt for its effects on audiences.

The last and one of the most crucial elements of the subgenre, which is echoed in *District 9*, is the presence of extreme violence. Such violence is prevalent in the new bad future films that Glass discusses. He points out that extreme violence is often in tension with the seemingly leftist political messages of the films, which are, broadly speaking, critical depictions of capitalist society. He suggests that this incongruous element allowed the genre to attract varied audiences, including viewers who watch films for the entertainment of spectacle alone. In many films, the violence appears justified through audience identification with the reasons for it. In *Robocop*, for example, the violent cyborg figure of Murphy has the righteousness of the law behind him. Glass argues that audience identification with the cyborg's power (which he refers to as phallic) even allows the violence to take on a redemptive tone. *District 9* is surprisingly violent, given its salvific plot and Wikus's character arc. Yet audiences can still see the film as redemptive as well as an indictment of apartheid and its concomitant violence (Wagner 2015). The violence is a deeply constitutive element of the contradictory nature of nostalgic dystopia at work in *District 9*. Although it might seem incongruous with critical outcomes, it is commensurate with the dystopian picture of Johannesburg in the film and reinforces Wikus's need for redemption. The landscape, itself ravaged by violence, needs to be redeemed just as much as Wikus.

1.2 *Spaceship/Township*

An important aspect of the production design in the film, often overlooked in relation to the notion of landscape, is the depiction of the spaceship or alien mothership. The ship, pictured in the screenshot in Figure 25, hovers above the city but is not merely its allegorical antithesis. Rather, it acts as a mirror image to the camp and the actual township of Chiawelo. It represents the same concept the township does in the film: a space of abjection humans find repulsive. The spaceship can be read as representative of the township in terms of its design, with the ship's decaying and rusted exterior reminiscent of the rusted corrugated iron sheets in the informal settlement of the camp. There

FIGURE 25 The mothership hovering over the township. Still taken from *District 9* (Neill Blomkamp, 2009).

are suggestions in the film that the spaceship could represent a dystopian view of the mining industry in Johannesburg as well.

Blomkamp describes the aliens' presence on earth as motivated by illness: they had no choice but to "land" in earth's atmosphere and so are not conquerors but, as Rosello (2016: 36) suggests, more like migrants. This is evocative of the mining industry's historical reliance on migrant labour.[7] When the ailing creatures are finally broken out of the ship, the humans quarantine them in what is intended to be a refugee camp (Woerner 2009). However, the quarantine may also be seen as an allegorical reference to the historical States of Emergency, and how they impacted the townships in South Africa in the 1980s, as the camp rapidly becomes a prison of sorts (Rosello 2016: 38). The climate of surveillance and militarisation during the States of Emergency created a "state of exception" in many of the townships, which became isolated, and concentration-camp-like. Johannes Rantete (1984), for example, describes how, after the third of September 1984 (the first day of the so-called Vaal uprisings), people could not get food in Sebokeng, and how difficult it was to leave the township since the buses had been burned. In effect, the township became quarantined, not unlike the camp in *District 9*.

---

7 See Philip Harrison & Tanya Zack (2012: 555).

What can we learn by looking at the spaceship design in *District 9*? The ship is like a flying saucer, which has a particular history in western science fiction. Pilot Kenneth Arnold was the first to use the term "flying saucer" in June 1947 to describe unidentified flying objects he saw near Mount Rainier in Washington State in the US (Kinnear 2010: 85). The flying saucer became entrenched in popular discourse around the imagining of spaceships after the advent of the launch of Sputnik by the Soviet Union in 1957, and the dawn of the Space Age. The 'saucer style' of spaceship has consistently had a connotation of alien life, along with negative aspects, such as alien invasions or abductions (Clute et al. [n.d.] spaceships). Kate Kinnear (2010: 35–36) explains that science fiction representations of alien spacecraft are often designed to appear as foreign as possible, and the fact that a saucer has no clear indications of windows, a cockpit, or other directional indicators supports this.[8] The round shape is disorientating to humans in that existing aircraft have less symmetrical structures, instead having a front-back and top-bottom asymmetry that connotes direction. The ship in *District 9* is not just a saucer, however: although its horizontal contour is rounded, it has a particularly angular appearance in its structural details, reminiscent of 1980s military technology. The Lockheed F-117A stealth fighter aircraft (Figure 26), developed in the 1980s and test flown in the US is a good example. In fact, people who believed they had spotted UFOs at the time are thought to have seen one of these aircraft from a particular angle, and mistaken it for a flying saucer (May 2018: 173–174). The angular and symmetrical details on the Lockheed F-117A aircraft resemble the design sensibility of *District 9*'s mothership.

The angular shapes of parts of the ship also recall the octagonal watchtowers erected on the borders of townships during apartheid, which appear in some scenes in *District 9* (Figure 27). The panoptic structures embody the surveillance character of the apartheid regime, and the policing of the boundaries of the townships, suburbs and inner cities that occurred in South Africa in the wake of the pass laws and the Group Areas Act of 1950 (Jansen van Veuren 2012: 576).[9] Rantete (1984) mentions several instances of security police closely observing township residents in Sebokeng during the unrest preceding the States of Emergency; the presence of police or security police is ubiquitous

---

[8] In her Masters degree study on the aesthetics of spaceship design in science fiction film and television, Kate Kinnear (2010: 39) examines how flying saucers became the most common shape for alien spaceships in western science fiction.

[9] The pass laws required all Black people to carry a passbook or '*dompas*', which recorded where they were allowed to reside and could be used to track their whereabouts (Peffer 2009: XVI).

FIGURE 26   The Lockheed F-117 Nighthawk Low-Observable / Stealth Strike Aircraft, first airborne in 1981. (Lockheed 2019).

in newsreel footage from the time. In addition to the Lockheed aircraft and township watchtowers, the spaceship resembles apartheid-era floodlights, like those visible in Mofokeng's photograph of Diepkloof (Figure 28). Many are still found in townships and along some highways, casting a characteristic yellow light.

Even though the ship is alien and its design emphasises how "other" it is, many aspects of its appearance and style relate to the landscape over which it hovers, mirroring it rather than differentiating the craft from it. The textures on spacecraft in science fiction films – what Kinnear (2010: 3) calls "nurnies" and "greebles", serve to indicate technological complexity (Figure 29). Kinnear refers to this style specifically as "used future", where many details, which would commonly indicate complexity and technological advancement, suggest wear and tear, rather than the sleek appearance in the human space station in Blomkamp's subsequent film *Elysium* (2013), for example. The surface details in the *District 9* spaceship reinforce how dated the ship looks, in addition to conveying the ship's scale and providing a visual resonance with the township landscape below. There is even evidence of grease, dirt build-up and rust

FIGURE 27   Apartheid-era watch towers. Still taken from *District 9* (Neill Blomkamp, 2009).

FIGURE 28   *A Taste for Life, Baragwanath Terminus, Diepkloof.* Photograph by Santu Mofokeng, 1985. Silverprint, 30 × 45 cm, edition of 5.
© SANTU MOFOKENG FOUNDATION. IMAGE COURTESY LUNETTA BARTZ, MAKER, JOHANNESBURG

FIGURE 29　The mothership from below, with the command module beaming up. Still taken from *District 9* (Neill Blomkamp, 2009).

(Tatsumi 2015: 139), correlating with the appearance of townships, where they result from the informal building methods of accretion that residents employ (Dovey & King 2011: 13). Corrugated iron is the most common material used to construct dwellings, and it is often old, corroded material recycled from previous structures. The *District 9* ship might not be made of sheets of corrugated iron, but its rusted and dirty metal surface, with many parts hanging from it like entrails, is still reminiscent of township structures (Figure 29). Its mechanical shape and character seem to reiterate a nostalgic view of technologies, rather than a futuristic one. It is in keeping with the backward-looking visual character of the film with its dated appearance evident in visual effects and the overall visual design.

Another reference to dated technology is the ruined alien body armour that Wikus can use because of his now mixed DNA. Such mechanical armour was a topical motif in science fiction films such as *Robocop* and *The Terminator*, and also in an animated Japanese television series, *Robotech* (Maceck 1985), which aired on children's television in South Africa (Figure 30). Takayuki Tatsumi (2015: 130–142) suggests that Blomkamp's influences may include references to several anime films and television series from the cyberpunk genre in the late 1980s and the 1990s, and that the body armour also resembles giant robots in the *Gundam* (Tomino & Yatate 1979) and the *Neon Genesis Evangelion* (Anno 1995) series (Tatsumi 2015: 133).

FIGURE 30   The mechanical robot from the series *Robotech* (produced by Carl Maceck, 1985). Still from video (Robotech-Intro … 2011, screenshot by author).

Like the ship, the body armour in *District 9*, as seen in Figure 31, evokes retrofuturist notions of space travel and warfare prevalent in the 1980s. It appears rusted and in disrepair, having languished in the camp for many years. Mechanical armour like this might have seemed highly futuristic in the 1980s, conjuring cyborg visions that would enhance human physicality and power, as in the film *Robocop*. However, here there is little to show for such notions of progress, as the body armour seems unimpressive and defeated, a thwarted futuristic dream. Once again, it is symbolic of the failure of the rationalist modernism espoused by apartheid South Africa (Gaule 2005: 2338–2339). When the body armour is understood within the rubric of used future and draws on the new bad future subgenre of the 1980s, it indicates several things: it could signal a collapse of faith in technology, which is typical of the genre (Glass 1989: 11), as well as indicating the transitional potential of the cyborg identity that Wikus is assigned near the end of *District 9*.

What Wikus represents might also be said of the landscape as well: it reflects the unrealised transformation that Wikus embodies. Wikus has been interpreted in terms of his allegorical representation of hegemonic apartheid-era

FIGURE 31 Wikus in the mechanical body armour suit. Still taken from *District 9* (Neill Blomkamp, 2009).

whiteness, or his Afrikaner identity.[10] As he transforms into an 'other', he is rejected by his own people, even though his transformation into an alien is still not complete. I interpret this incomplete transformation as symbolic of whiteness in contemporary South Africa; he is in a state of unrealised metamorphosis, but also of becoming alien to the place where he grew up. The landscape echoes this uncertainty. It is neither urban nor rural, and it seems decayed and beyond hope, yet there is also evidence of everyday lives lived in the dwellings. Townships persist in the democratic life of contemporary South Africa, despite being the conceptions of colonial and apartheid agendas of racial dehumanisation.

The ship represents many of the same things as the body armour; it is also, in some senses, the landscape's 'other'. It is the dark side of the city, the city's "upside down", as the phrase is used in the recent retro science fiction television series *Stranger Things* (Duffer & Duffer 2016).[11]

---

10   Wikus is written about by Jansen van Veuren (2012), Nel (2012), Walder (2014), Wagner (2015) and Brott (2013).
11   In this series the 'upside down' is depicted as the underworld and is the shadow side of the 'real' world. It shares the same geographic location, but is a site of distortion and abject horror, just as the townships are when they are depicted as zones of indistinction.

FIGURE 32   Humans break into the alien mothership to rescue the sick creatures. Still taken from *District 9* (Neill Blomkamp, 2009).

Notably, some of the introductory sequences in *District 9* portray the spaceship in a manner that recalls mining, as in the screenshot in Figure 32. The aliens had to be broken out of the ship, and they are depicted as starving in the dark, like trapped mineworkers after a mining accident. The rescue teams look remarkably like workers descending into a mine. I consider the history of mining in the area later, but it is pertinent here that the mining industry in South Africa was from its inception marked by racial inequality. Most of the workers were from the African continent, exploited as cheap labour, while the mines were run by the so-called Randlords, chiefly English settlers who had the capital to invest in the industry (Harrison & Zack 2012: 554). There is a long history of labour disputes around conditions in the mines, the safety of mineworkers, and the abhorrent compounds where they were housed. Such a state of bare life existence is echoed in the spaceship's interior, where the aliens are trapped, warming themselves at fires made in large oil cans – like those commonly used in the townships for warmth and cooking. Iconically South African, the brazier motif appears in contemporary artworks by Kagiso Pat Mautloa and William Kentridge, as well as photographs by Andrew Tshabangu. Tshabangu's photograph *Brazier – Joubert Park I* (Figure 33) depicts homeless people living in Joubert Park in the inner city of Johannesburg. The dense smog

FIGURE 33   *Brazier, Joubert Park I – City in Transition Series*. Photograph by Andrew Tshabangu, 1994. Archival print. 120 × 84cm.
FROM THE IMAGO MUNDI COLLECTION "ART THEOREMA #2"

from the fires gives the park an otherworldly character that invites comparison with the set of a science fiction film.

Blomkamp also refers overtly to this motif in *Alive in Joburg*, depicting the aliens using such cans to make fires (Figure 34). The brazier is another feature contributing to the allegory of apartheid racism constructed in *District 9*, and equates the aliens to Black people during apartheid, as discussed in considerable detail in research on the film.

The spaceship is not entirely dystopian and ruinous. It is the key to the future and the liberation of the aliens. In this sense it becomes almost like an archaeological site to be excavated, one that holds the promise of treasure to be unearthed. Unlike an archaeological site, however, the spaceship points to the future, not the past. The treasure here is the liquid, an alien substance essential to their survival, unrecognised by Wikus when he accidentally sprays himself with it.[12] In an interview, Blomkamp described the mothership as a

---

12   In the recent film *Black Panther* (Coogler 2018), there is also reference to such a mineral resource, vibranium, as the key to freedom from colonial rule.

FIGURE 34   Aliens huddle over braziers. Still taken from *Alive in Joburg* (Neill Blomkamp, 2006).

vessel where the aliens could live for thousands of years (Woerner 2009). One might note that, in the science fiction genre around the 1960s and 70s, spaceships often came to signify permanent escape (Clute et al. [n.d.] spaceships). The notion is especially pertinent to *District 9*, where the alien ship is not only the means for the aliens to escape from their capture in Johannesburg, but also the only hope for Wikus's escape from his mutated alien body.

Near the opening of *District 9* something is shown falling from the ship; a "command module", which is visible in Figure 35. Experts in the mock interviews at the beginning of the film surmise that the loss of the module is why the alien ship became inoperative and could not return whence it came. However, the module is not lost: the alien Christopher lives in it, buried underground, with a shack built on top of it that looks like every other cheaply constructed dwelling in the camp. Only towards the end of the film is the command module revealed as the basement of his shack. When Christopher can return the module to the mothership, the ship itself can leave (Figure 36).

The scene in Figure 36, taking place near the end of the film, depicts the command module being beamed up, to the accompaniment of an ethereal soundtrack. Biblical associations with such an ascension into the sky, and the attainment of freedom in this manner, are commonplace in science fiction

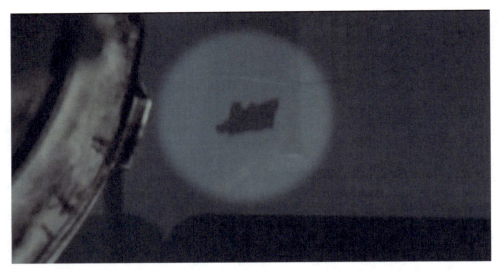

FIGURE 35   The command module drops from the mothership. Still taken from *District 9* (Neill Blomkamp, 2009).

FIGURE 36   The command module rises from the ground. Still taken from *District 9* (Neill Blomkamp, 2009).

with its pervasive religious motifs.[13] Sobchack (1998: 55–63) devotes a section of her book to exploring how magic, religion and science interact in the genre: religion in fact serves as the only "answer" in many science fiction film plots, where the unexplained or forces beyond human control (such as aliens) affect human fate. In *District 9*, the township is the unlikely setting where this almost religious redemption of the aliens and the humans is set in motion.

• • •

Focusing on 'the how' over the last three chapters makes it clear that *District 9* employs analogue nostalgia to construct its vision of Johannesburg, as do *Gangster's Paradise: Jerusalema* and *The Battle for Johannesburg*, and the work done by photographers such as Goldblatt, and Subotzky and Waterhouse, as well as amateur fashion bloggers I See A Different You, Khumbula and the Sartists. It is significant how the interplay between digital and analogue media technologies has shaped this emerging idiom in depictions of Johannesburg across these diverse examples, where practitioners represent very different social contexts. In many respects, Johannesburg has become visually defined by the analogue aesthetics and analogue nostalgia of these portrayals. This implicates media technologies and practices *of the time* in the nostalgic dystopian image of the city. The change from analogue to digital technologies impacts professional and amateur practices alike, in both film and photography. It has far-reaching and diverse implications, which cannot be understood solely as the product of particular technologies or media forms. More than a mere technological development or media practice, analogue aesthetics is ultimately decisive in how the idiom of nostalgic dystopia is shaped. The coherence of the visual vocabulary across diverse examples lies in the result rather than the individual processes or techniques employed.

Along with analogue nostalgia, two sets of generic underpinnings characterise how *District 9* portrays the analogue landscape: the mockumentary and science fiction genres. In the mockumentary genre, *District 9* emulates 1980s documentary and newsreel conventions to construct an analogue landscape that imitates the actual apartheid past of Johannesburg, including the violence in the townships during the 1980s. By mimicking analogue newsreel footage, as well as using digital grading and cinematographic techniques to emulate analogue flaws and achieve a "low-resolution realism" (Lucas 2014:143–146), a depiction of the 'real' Johannesburg landscape is constructed.

---

13   John Clute et al. ([n.d.] Religion) and Sobchack (1998: 288–289) spend considerable time on this topic.

It is no accident that the photographs and films I have analysed share a visual vocabulary on so many levels: they draw on the idiom to capture the realities of the city, reflecting a concern with (historical) actuality or authenticity. In Goldblatt's depiction of Johannesburg's mine dumps, and in Subotzky and Waterhouse's project documenting the landmark building Ponte City, there is a particular poignancy in the depiction of a 'document' of Johannesburg, and in capturing it with analogue cameras, an element which the films also flirt with in different ways. However, in *District 9*, the mockumentary genre lends additional complexity to the depiction of Johannesburg, undermining the sense of documentary fidelity in its humour and hypermediacy, which emphasise the mediatic qualities of the film. The constructed media quality of the depiction of Johannesburg is flaunted, imbuing it with an analogue character that suggests authenticity. But it also creates an artificiality that ambiguously softens some of the gravity of the allegorical content of the film. The humour inherent in the mockumentary genre allows the film to construct the apartheid past as nostalgic, despite this being preposterous. By relying on media nostalgia to reiterate the reflective nostalgia, the film permits viewers to indulge in the visual aspects of nostalgia without focusing on the allegorical politics that are depicted as if they represent a documentary truth.

The softening of the allegorical content through the mockumentary genre might further be argued to lend credence to the redemption afforded to the film's main character, Wikus. In a sense, he can 'rewrite' apartheid history in a manner that redeems him, and releases white Afrikaner masculinity from the shame of the atrocities that the regime committed. Such redemption has justifiably been argued to be deeply gratuitous. Yet the mockumentary genre employed by Blomkamp is instrumental in enabling the dystopian landscape of the township under siege to attain a redemptive quality. The dystopia of the township becomes the site of hope for the aliens and of allegorical redemption for white South Africans in the figure of Wikus.

As is the case in *District 9*, popular photography for Instagram and fashion blogs by the collectives I See A Different You, Khumbula and the Sartists does not emulate particular film stocks or cameras faithfully, but rather seeks to convey a 'feel' of historicity and authenticity in their portrayal of Johannesburg as nostalgic dystopia. This strategy allows them to recreate the apartheid past as a place they can reminisce about, re-casting themselves and the landscape in a hopeful light. Referred to as "subversive resistance" by Farber (2015), this approach can be understood as fundamentally critical, enabling the "freedom to" reimagine the city and the townships in new ways (Lees 2004: 24). The Black photographers present a significant counterpoint to the supposition that nostalgia creates a white perspective on the city; they employ nostalgia in ways that articulate their own senses of identity and belonging in the context of South African history.[14]

The second generic underpinning of *District 9* is 1980s science fiction and retrofuturist production design that romanticise the city's decay, which can further be related to the new bad future subgenre. In the 1980s, Hollywood science fiction cinema was itself characteristically nostalgic, according to Sobchack (1998: 229), and *District 9* shares several motifs with these films: a dystopian setting; the figure of the cyborg; the portrayal of historical television forms and technologies within the films; and the depiction of extreme violence – all reflected in *District 9*'s Johannesburg landscapes. The power of Blomkamp's science fiction poetics doubles nostalgia by recalling both 1980s visions of the future as well as 1980s Johannesburg.

The spaceship in *District 9* is portrayed as a dated and decaying technology and, like the apartheid township in contemporary portrayals, as a failure that haunts Johannesburg. But although the ship is depicted as a site of abjection, it transforms into a 'way out' for the aliens when Christopher finally manages to repair the command module and ascend to the mothership. By implication, the township too, although embodying apartheid's historical urban segregation, becomes a symbol of redemption or escape from the city's history. The city's portrayal is far from simple, however.

What the analogue nostalgia and the analogue aesthetics in *District 9* and related depictions ultimately point to is that nostalgia can be geared towards divergent and complex outcomes. In this way, Johannesburg incongruously becomes a place to be nostalgic about, a place where history is rewritten and where the victims and perpetrators of apartheid may gain the unlikely "freedom to" shape the representation of the landscape in new ways (Lees 2004: 24). This contradictory dynamic characterises many of the aspects of Johannesburg as nostalgic dystopia. It is both in decay and vibrantly alive, both shocking and arresting to look at, and both repulses and fascinates the viewer. In all this, it offers a unique aesthetic possibility of transformation that would not occur in beautiful, untroubled depictions of place.

---

14 As with Wikus's redemption discussed above, one might again question the implications of this strategy.

PART 3

Ruin Aesthetics

∴

CHAPTER 6

Mining Landscapes

1 A History of Mining

Having considered how media technologies have contributed to *District 9*'s iconic representation of Johannesburg, I now arrive at the content of this portrayal: the city itself. The city as it appears in the film favours particular locations within the landscape. In the following chapters, I excavate these, drawing on the popular archive alongside the film's portrayal of the city. What these settings seem to have in common as axiomatic representations of nostalgic dystopia is that they are all in some way derelict, which is fundamental to *District 9*'s ruin aesthetics.

The first of these settings is the mining landscape, which persists as abandoned mines and mine dumps around the city. They are prominent in the establishing sequence of *District 9* (Figure 37), where Johannesburg is shown by an aerial shot approaching the city from a distance. With interspersed 'expert interviews', the sequence establishes the story of when and how the aliens came to park their ship above Johannesburg. At the same time, it introduces viewers to the visual qualities and textures of Johannesburg. Blomkamp (2020) described how the mine dumps are etched into his childhood memory of Johannesburg; for him, they shape the city's character, and the dominance of the mining landscape in this sequence is deliberate and significant. Large mine dumps loom in front of the familiar skyline of the city, with suburban settlements dotting the foreground. Johannesburg is a landscape haunted by industry, which is also seen in a project entitled *After the Mines* (Figure 38) by British photojournalist Jason Larkin, which eloquently captures the significance of the dumps. Johannesburg is, in effect, a post-industrial city.

Johannesburg was founded in 1886 upon the discovery of gold in the area that came to be known as the Witwatersrand. The gold reef is situated in an east-to-west direction and transmuted the area's farmland into a bustling town within a matter of months after its discovery.[1] The industry did not lend itself to artisanal small-scale mining, because most of the gold was too deep underground. As a result, a small group of mining magnates from the Kimberley diamond fields, subsequently known as the Randlords (Harrison & Zack 2012: 554), who

---

[1] Refer to Clive Chipkin (1993), Guy Trangos & Kerry Bobbins (2015: sp) and Lucia Saks (2010).

FIGURE 37   The spaceship and mine dumps. Still taken from *District 9* (Neill Blomkamp, 2009).

FIGURE 38   *After the Mines*. Jason Larkin, 2013.
COURTESY OF THE PHOTOGRAPHER

FIGURE 39 Johannesburg's mining waste belt (Trangos & Bobbins, 2015).
COURTESY OF THE AUTHORS

had the funds to invest in the necessary machinery, dominated gold mining there. The mining town that resulted from this enterprise was marked by social and racial segregation from the outset, with the Randlords setting themselves apart by building homes in suburbs to the north of the town.[2] Black migrant labourers from rural areas lived in the central city, and poor white labourers (mostly Afrikaner 'boers' or farmers who had left their farms) settled in areas like Brickfields and Burghersdorp.[3] Most of the mining activity took place to the south of the town, and the mine dumps and slimes dams that resulted are still to be found along the southern edge of the city (see Figure 39).[4]

The dumps that resulted from mining were not necessarily coordinated with the planning of the city Johannesburg, and they abut residential areas to

---

2 See Clive Chipkin (1993) and Sally Gaule (2005: 2337–2338).
3 See Clive Chipkin (1993) and Sally Gaule (2005: 2339–2340).
4 These terms can become confusing as they are often used interchangeably. I refer to mine dumps, tailings dumps, slimes dams, tailings and other varieties of mine waste sites in general as mine waste areas (MWAS), in the same way as Tahira Toffa (2013: 24–31).

the south, such as Soweto, and are intersected by highways (Trangos & Bobbins 2015). To the northern side of this informal boundary, many dumps are adjacent to the central business district (CBD) and industrial areas.

In 1921, when the gold price dropped significantly, mine owners replaced expensive white labour with Black African labour, sparking a white miners' rebellion and a march under the banner "Workers of the World Unite for a White South Africa". Racial segregation in the mines and in the city was entrenched by legislation such as the colonial colour bar that prevented Black Africans from attaining higher-level jobs in the mines (Harrison & Zack 2012: 554).

During the early mining period until 1928, many Black African labourers came from the Portuguese East Coast (Mozambique). Their recruitment took place through the Witwatersrand Native Labour Association (WNLA), and some argue that recruiting Black labourers from across southern Africa was the only reason deep-level gold mining was economically viable.[5] Migrant labourers were housed in men-only compounds for limited-period contracts and were permitted to return to their families in rural areas only once these had expired, essentially fracturing family structures. Socio-political and socio-economic concerns are integral to understanding Johannesburg's mining history. Such concerns are thoroughly covered in historical, geographic and wider cultural discourses, however, so are not repeated at length here.[6]

Although mine dumps are shifting landscapes and change rapidly in geographic terms, at the time of writing (2022), the cluster of mine dumps depicted in *District 9* still exists. It is situated to the southwest of Johannesburg, at the intersection between the so-called Soweto highway and the N1 Western bypass (visible running behind and in front of the dump in the foreground of Figure 37). The cluster is in an area known as Mooifontein 225-Iq, and forms part of the Central Rand Goldfields (CRG) mines that have declined drastically in production since the 1970s: all the large mines operating there shut down by the late 1970s (Harrison & Zack 2012). The Mooifontein dumps are just three of about 270 tailings dumps in the Witwatersrand area (Figure 40). Some 70 of them were re-treated to recover further gold in the 1990s, but they remain as dubious monuments to the mining industry. The mines here are often described in geographic discourse as abandoned because many have not been

---

[5] See Harrison & Zack (2012: 555), for example, who cite Jonathan Crush, Alan Jeeves & David Yudelman.
[6] Philip Harrison & Tanya Zack (2012), Clive Chipkin (1993), Phefumula Nyoni (2017: 133–154) and Janet Munakamwe (2017: 155–186) all write about the history of mining and the effect the industry had on particularly Black labourers and their family lives.

FIGURE 40   A google maps rendition of the three Mooifontein mine dumps west of the city (on the left) (Mooifontein 225-IQ 2018).

rehabilitated and still have adverse health, environmental and socio-economic impacts (Mhlongo & Amponsah-Dacosta 2016: 279–294).

2   Post-landscape

2.1   *The Poison Belt*

The mine dumps are challenging not only in terms of how they have altered the landscape's image but also, as mentioned above, how they pose several health and environmental risks to communities living in their proximity. These landscapes are poisoned and poisonous. Before 1991, mines were abandoned when they became unprofitable. Due to a lack of legislation, many of them left corresponding waste sites untreated and the landscape unrehabilitated, the burden of maintenance falling to the government (Mhlongo & Amponsah-Dacosta 2016: 280). The around 6000 abandoned mines across the country would cost up to R30 billion to rehabilitate and maintain.[7] Gold waste that dates to before 1952 (directly after the period of high productivity in the CRG, 1886–1948) tends to be high in uranium and thus has levels of radioactivity that can cause radiotoxicity. Main Reef Road, for example, which was built on mine tailings and traverses the inner city of Johannesburg, is in fact radioactive (Liefferink [n.d.]).

Another side effect of the abandoned mines is acid mine drainage. Water permeates the old mines and, as it rises to the surface, its acidity contaminates the groundwater (Trangos & Bobbins 2015). In addition to acid mine drainage, many of the mine dumps are sources of airborne pollution when toxic dust, classified as PM10,[8] is blown across the city (Milaras et al. 2014: 1). This occurs especially from July to October, when the dumps are dry (Cukrowska et al. 2017). A case where mine dumps posed a substantial threat to residents' health is in the informal settlement of Tudor Shaft, its name related to the old mine, where about 1800 people were living.[9] The settlement established in 1996, was built on top of mine tailings, and the adjacent natural water source had high levels of uranium, which reportedly exceed those that residents of the Chernobyl area experienced after the nuclear reactor meltdown there in 1986 (Stassen 2015, Li 2013), making the area utterly uninhabitable. Eventually, in 2017, after many years, residents of Tudor Shaft[10] were relocated to "Reconstruction and Development Programme" houses in Kagiso Ext 13.[11] This not-uncommon situation highlights the implications of toxicity in the environment, and demonstrates that the mining belt is a problem-ridden artificial landscape that will

---

7   For more on the rehabilitation of South African mines, see Milton Milaras et al. (2014: 2), Guy Trangos & Kerry Bobbins (2015) and Sphiwe Emmanuel Mhlongo & Francis Amponsah-Dacosta (2016: 283).
8   This refers to particulate matter with size less than 10 μm in diameter, which humans can inhale due to its small size (Nkosi, Wichmann & Voyi 2017).
9   This informal settlement also captured the imagination of authors interested in Johannesburg. Mark Gevisser writes about the informal settlement as abject, dystopian and radioactive in his memoir, *Lost and Found in Johannesburg* (2014: 176–184). He also draws on the science-fiction novel by Lauren Beukes entitled *Zoo City* (2010) to discuss the mining landscape around the city in general.
10 Tudor Shaft was created when the government forcibly removed residents from another informal settlement a short distance away. Since that time many studies were undertaken on the toxicity of the mine waste at Tudor Shaft, although residents were only moved in 2017 (Decommissioning Projects … 2021).
11 This was government subsidy housing as part of the Reconstruction and Development Programme (RDP) instituted by the African National Congress in 1994 to address housing shortages in the country, in particular for people living in informal settlements (Everything you need … 2017).

have effects on natural life and humans for hundreds of years to come (Coetzee et al. 2003).[12]

Goldblatt's photograph, *Johannesburg from the Southwest* (Figure 15), referred to earlier, shows what would be hidden from inside the city: a few isolated shacks standing behind mine waste, underneath towering electricity pylons, seemingly surrounded by mine dumps. The inhabitants look like ants, lost in this ruinous landscape that resembles a scene from a post-apocalyptic film. As well as the drabness of the washed-out sky and desaturated landscape, there is a focus on decaying materials: the rusted corrugated iron of the shacks, and the erosion of the pale dust of the mine dump in the background. The landscape seems barren and uninviting: even the plants here lack colour and vigour. While the electricity pylons are iconic in the Johannesburg landscape, they also echo the headgear that would have been visible when the mines in this area were active. In Figure 41, a remarkably similar post-mining landscape is captured by photojournalist Larkin, although the bright green of the foreground plants lends more colour to the scene.

Goldblatt's and Larkin's photographs demonstrate the industrialisation of the landscape around Johannesburg. In both photographs, the contrast between the yellow dust of the mine dumps and the adjacent soil is marked, making the mine dust seem even more alien. The lack of figures or dwellings and the presence of the electricity pylons and the railway line and train alongside the mine dump in Larkin's photograph make his a more overtly industrialised scene and imply the far-reaching significance of the mining industry in Johannesburg. Railways were historically important to mining development, as transporting ore and other valued materials such as coal was essential to the mining process (Francaviglia 1997: 55, Foster 2003). In Johannesburg the railway lines traverse the city in a course parallel to the mine waste areas to transport materials along that route. These structures fundamentally altered the landscape and remain part of it, just as the mine waste areas do, thus rendering it a post-industrial landscape.

---

12   In May 2016, Water and Sanitation Minister, Nomvula Mokonyane, directed the State-owned Trans-Caledon Tunnel Authority to implement a so-called 'long-term ACID MINE DRAINAGE solution' in the Witwatersrand. The estimated date for implementation of the plan was 2021 (Solomons 2017). It aims to supply fully rehabilitated water fit for human consumption to the area, alleviating the province's need to rely on the Vaal Dam and the Lesotho Highland Water Project.

FIGURE 41   Image 4/39 from *After the Mines*. Photograph by Jason Larkin, 2013.
COURTESY OF THE PHOTOGRAPHER

2.2   *Sublime and Formless Landscapes*

As Monika Läuferts and Judith Mavunganidze (2009) assert in their discussion of post-industrial heritage in Johannesburg, the mine dumps around the city are unlikely to be seen as valuable parts of history to be preserved, due to their adverse effects on the environment and citizens. Richard V. Francaviglia (1997), who discusses mining landscapes from a historical and cultural perspective, describes them as "hard places", but thinks of them as having historical value. Writing about mining in California in the US (which coincided with the gold rush in Johannesburg), he argues that mines and the landscapes they shaped are historically significant and even didactic cultural documents. These sites may reveal much about the socio-political character of the times when they were in high production. He also suggests that the mining apparatus creates its own kind of landscape and alters the topography of a mining settlement in ways specific to the kind of mining undertaken. Coalmines, for example, are frequently open pit mines, leaving large open cavities in the landscape. These mines also often have leach dumps and tailings ponds (comparable to the mine waste areas produced in gold mining: slimes dams and dry tailings dumps) (Francaviglia 1997: 1–24). Francaviglia mentions that certain kinds of flora can flourish in mining landscapes, and numerous eucalyptus trees in the Johannesburg area, planted for their wood to be used as props in the mines, seem to be a testament to this. There has been some planting on mine dumps, but many are barren of any vegetation. In line with such changes, geographers note that mining influences the visual aesthetic of a landscape, affecting the sense of place.[13] What is notable about the mine dumps of Johannesburg is their proximity to residential areas. Despite their harmful effects, they are now topographically iconic to parts of Johannesburg, such as Florida and Soweto, because mine dumps are almost always visible in these areas.

The way that the dumps frame the city in the screenshot from *District 9* (Figure 37) suggests the impact of the declining mining legacy on the city. It is this focus on decline and decay that marks the landscape itself as one of ruins. Francaviglia (1997: 215) suggests that, while such industrially ruined landscapes are now regarded negatively, industrial landscapes were often valorised as symbols of progress in the Victorian era, when they were even depicted alongside pastoral landscapes. Nye (1994: 36–43) writes about this phenomenon and notes how in the 1800s Jacksonian era in the US, industry and nature were not seen as opposed to each other. The progress that technological advancement symbolised was linked to the nation's moral health: natural wonders were celebrated alongside manufactured wonders that transformed nature into something even more remarkable. Later examples of this valorisation of technological progress are evident in South African Moses Tladi's painting, *Mine scene*,[14] and J. H. Pierneef's Johannesburg Railway Station panel series (1929–1932). Tladi portrays a mine dump with industrial buildings to the left of his painting, the dump, structures and natural landscape features blending seamlessly. The golden light that bathes the scene is echoed in the golden colour of

---

13   Geographical studies such as Milaras et al. (2014: 9) and Mhlongo and Amponsah-Dacosta (2016: 280) consider the appearance of the landscape as altered by mining.
14   Refer to Angela Caccia's (2016) article on Tladi. The date of the painting seems unknown, but he was active around the same time as Pierneef.

the large dump. Pierneef's thirty-two panels were commissioned by the South African Railways and Harbours for the newly built Johannesburg Park Station in 1929 and installed in 1932 (Coetzee 1992). In them, the artist represented different landscapes of South Africa that were considered iconic, including scenic mountain vistas. Amongst these scenic panels are two that, perhaps unexpectedly to contemporary viewers, depict mining landscapes.

In these paintings, the mining apparatus and its effects on the topography are completely integrated with the landscape. Pierneef's depictions are quite unlike those in *District 9*, where the landscape seems polluted and washed out. In *Rand Gold Mine*, his painting of the City Deep gold mine located near Johannesburg, the mining equipment suggests its own beauty, as the smoke from the smokestacks mingles with majestic cloud formations above the mine, and their curving forms contrast with the geometry of the large, formally centred mine dump. *Premier Mine* portrays a diamond mine in Cullinan outside Tshwane, where the famous Cullinan diamond, the largest diamond of gem quality ever found, was discovered (Cullinan [n.d.]). The raw red earth of the open mine in the foreground dominates the scene, its enormous scale creating a sense of splendour that belies its scarring of the natural landscape. Pierneef's heroic depictions of diamond and gold mines represent the importance of South Africa's mineral wealth to the country's socio-economic history.[15]

Pierneef sets up these compositions in much the same way as he portrays sublime natural landscapes in other paintings such as *Rustenburg Kloof* or *Mont-aux-Sources*. In these paintings, the landscape is constructed to display grandeur and overwhelming scale in the towering mountain ranges, sheer cliffs and imposing cloud formations (Schön 1973). Everything here points to the natural world's scale, bounty and beauty, underpinned by a natural order. In applying similar compositional strategies to his paintings of mines, Pierneef undermines the binary of nature against the rationality of human endeavour, instead seeing an order in nature that seems equally mathematical and systematic (Bouman 1955).[16] N. J. Coetzee (1992:21) argues that Pierneef sees both nature and culture as emanations of a divine will, and therefore does not distinguish between the beauty of scenes depicting industry and those depicting the natural world. Lize van Robbroeck (2019: 51–52) suggests that Pierneef's

---

15   Coetzee (1992: 39).
16   Dylan Trigg (2006: 147–148) suggests that historically the sublime was framed within an opposition between nature and human reason, since in the Kantian sublime, for example, human reason allows the viewer of the sublime in nature to experience a sense of triumphant survival in the face of nature's forces.

station panels, and much of his other work, were influenced by the Northern Romantic tradition of landscape representation, evoking the immanence of God in nature.

There has been much debate around Pierneef's significance in the South African canon: those critical of his work cast him as an Afrikaner nationalist proponent of white supremacist notions of ownership of the South African landscape. His landscapes rarely allude to human interventions, apart from the two mining paintings and the occasional farmhouse or small town, and are devoid of people. The absence of so-called native peoples and their dwellings is particularly conspicuous, implying that the land was originally empty of human influence. Known for his Afrikaner nationalist sentiments, Pierneef advocated for an ostensibly unique African art, uninfluenced by European conventions, yet paradoxically presented an exclusively white view of the South African landscape. Van Robbroeck suggests that his landscapes exemplify settler landscapes, which purported to be 'empty' before white settlers arrived, and that Pierneef saw Afrikaners as bound up with the land and thus with an implicit claim to belonging (Van Robbroeck 2019: 51–54). Such a view of white belonging in the South African landscape is problematised in contemporary depictions such as *District 9*, where whiteness is depicted as in a state of anxiety and non-belonging.

Mining was primarily a colonial project at the outset, the industry 'claimed' by Afrikaner nationalism only later. But the mining landscape throughout its history can be seen as a 'white blight', leaving a poisoned landscape in its wake. Contemporary depictions of the mine dumps imply awareness of this taint as opposed to the favourable light in which Pierneef painted them. Yet the sublime remains relevant when attempting to comprehend these landscapes.

The mining landscape has caught the attention of recent photographers. Two years after Larkin's photo essay *After the Mines* (2013), a comparable visual document of the landscape of mine dumps around Johannesburg was published – Johannesburg-based photojournalist Jansson's 2015 book on acid mine drainage called *An Acid River Runs through It*. While the photographs in these projects seem documentary in nature, and focus on an ecological agenda, one cannot but be entranced by the aesthetic qualities of these dystopian images. In the photographs by Jansson and Larkin, the latter in Figure 42, the landscape seems impossibly vast, with little to indicate the scale of the dumps they capture. Pierneef's depictions celebrated the power of industry in the landscape through scale, but these images depict the aftermath, as signalled in the title of Larkin's photographs; all that remains of the now defunct mining industry is the poisoned land and waterways, the "acid river" of Jansson's title. These

FIGURE 42 Image 28/39 from *After the Mines*. Photograph by Jason Larkin, 2013.
IMAGE COURTESY OF THE PHOTOGRAPHER

arresting landscapes are wholly sublime landscapes, immense and incomprehensible, and eerily devoid of humans.

Larkin's and Jansson's photographs are reminiscent of Edward Burtynsky's well-known photographs of industrially poisoned landscapes (Figure 43 was taken by him in Johannesburg). Often described as sublime[17] because of the

---

17   See, for example, Amanda Boetzkes (2010) and Jennifer Peeples (2011), who write on post-industrial landscapes.

FIGURE 43   Gold Tailings #1, Doornkop Gold Mine, Johannesburg, South Africa. Photograph by Edward Burtynsky, 2018. Pigment inkjet print on Kodak Professional Photo Paper, 121.9 × 162.6 cm. Toronto: Nicholas Metivier Gallery.
PHOTO: © EDWARD BURTYNSKY, COURTESY NICHOLAS METIVIER GALLERY, TORONTO

sheer incomprehensibility of the scale they depict, Burtynsky's photographs are notable for their bird's-eye-view presentations of the landscape. Neither Larkin nor Jansson use this pictorial device, but the opening sequence in *District 9* is filmed from a helicopter, creating a high and distant observation point for the viewer. Notably, *District 9*'s opening shots lack human figures, like all the images of mining landscapes discussed here. The removal of the human subject from the surveyed physical landscape is typical of the sublime landscape in terms of its conventions, going as far back as Burke's and Kant's formulations.[18] When viewers are at a safe remove from the forces of nature, they can find aesthetic satisfaction or even a sense of transcendence, overcoming

---

18   Both Boetzkes (2010: 23–26) and Meghan Kirkwood (2019: 436–438) consider Burke's and Kant's ideas around human subjects and their relation to sublime landscapes.

their physical limitations, made apparent by the vast scale of the landscape (Boetzkes 2010: 23–26).

Writing about photography of mining landscapes, Meghan Kirkwood (2019) suggests that removing people from such landscapes gives them a sublime quality. She writes, quoting Giblett, that Burtynsky's work removes context and social consequence from the image, rendering an abstract sense of landscape that allows "the viewer to more freely ponder the relationship between beauty and decay" (Kirkwood 2019: 437). Such a distancing effect does not leave room for the critical potential I detect in post-industrial landscapes.

An alternative interpretation is proposed in Kirkwood's subsequent discussion of *Legacy of the Mine* (2013), a monograph on mining by South African-born photographer Ilan Godfrey. Regarding Godfrey's depiction of a mine dump near Soweto (Figure 44), she argues that the presence of people prompts the viewer to move beyond an abstract contemplation of scale. To see children in this landscape, with no indication of where the landscape begins or ends, may prompt practical questions such as why they are there, and how they got there to begin with (Kirkwood 2019: 438). Yet, at the same time, sublime elements are present, and even heightened by the small figures. This landscape is vast compared to the children, and its topography is unfamiliar, uncanny, and alien. The relationship between humans and the landscape depicted here, indeed nature itself, is perhaps precisely what we should focus on.

Gangster's Paradise: Jerusalema likewise depicts children playing on a mine dump in Soweto. In the scene, they slide down its slopes on pieces of cardboard, while Lucky and Zakes run a car washing business at the dump's foot. The children seem to have claimed the site for recreation and are oblivious to its dangers. Although the depiction is very different from Godfrey's, there is a sense of danger and foreboding, since film audiences would be aware of the site's toxicity and risks. The scene perhaps highlights the fraught conditions of childhood in this context, emphasised when it ends with a panning shot revealing from a high angle how close the dump is to houses: they appear just across from it with only a road separating the two areas. The sequence may leave the viewer with a sense of unease and foreboding, despite the commonplace appearance of children at play and teenagers trying to earn pocket money by washing cars, activities associated with suburban life.

In the case of Burtynsky's photographs, which omit human presence, Amanda Boetzkes (2010) considers that they often show nature as something beyond representational grasp. The landscapes he depicts evoke nature but are entirely man-made. Boetzkes (2010: 29) uses Jean Luc Nancy's term "ecotechnological" to describe them. In other words, nature itself is produced or determined entirely by humanity's technological relationship to it, whether through

FIGURE 44　*Legacy of the Mine. Riverlea Mine Dump, Main Reef Road, Johannesburg, Gauteng.*
Photograph by Ilan Godfrey, 2011.
IMAGE COURTESY OF THE PHOTOGRAPHER

industrial incursions and adverse consequences, such as global warming and other effects of climate change, or attempts to set things right, as in conservation, resource management, sustainability, or other means. Whereas transcendence over the sensorial was the focus of the Kantian sublime, Boetzkes (2010) argues that contemporary sublime landscapes, like those depicted by Burtynsky, completely reconsider how the sublime operates. Earlier, I referred to a post-colonial reframing of the sublime, which here can be extended to a reconsideration of the sublime in terms of post-industrial landscapes. Post-industrial waste sites or mine waste areas reassert humankind's inability to comprehend and grasp nature. Boetzkes (2010) argues that post-industrial landscapes also articulate a new contact with nature, which will reconfigure how humans regard it. Her contention recalls media philosopher Mark Hansen's (2015) theory that, in the post-human world of the Anthropocene, humankind is no longer central to even its own view of the world, but is nonetheless implicated everywhere.[19] In these terms, it might seem that humankind is under threat of being subsumed by such toxic landscapes. These vistas represent nature's reconstruction by humans: they are thus implicated within the landscapes, related to the forces of nature, both destroying and recreating it.

The most important element, comparable to earlier formulations of the sublime, is the notion that these landscapes, and photographs of them, are both attractive and repulsive; for Boetzkes (2010: 27), this dynamic evokes Kant's description of the oscillation as a vibration, in which the opposing responses alternate. Boetzkes suggests that Burtynsky's work represents landscapes that simultaneously evoke nature and convey anxieties around large-scale environmental crises (2010: 30), which would indeed have dystopian implications. The photographs in Figures 42, 43 and 44 are compelling in this regard. They present landscapes that seem otherworldly, made of matter that is unnatural and strangely coloured. Nothing here comes across as soil, and the bleached yellows and ochre colours of the dust evoke the toxic mineral content of the sulphides, such as cadmium and pyrite, in Johannesburg's mine waste areas. The sludge around the dump structures in Larkin's and Burtynsky's photographs likewise conveys a sense of toxicity (Figures 42 and 43). The bodies of liquid do not look like water and appear to be highly saturated with coloured matter, dyed to the point of being paint-like.

The dumps have a very particular materiality. I would suggest that they may be interpreted as an instance of the formless, theorised by Bois and Krauss in the 1990s. The formless, like the abject, is about a collapsing of boundaries between things – between figure and ground (in a pictorial sense), and between subject and object. In these landscapes one can see several aspects of such transgressions. Mine waste areas seem inside-out: what should be buried underneath the landscape now becomes the landscape itself, a monstrous inversion. Mine dumps furthermore lack structure and definition – not only in their physicality as structureless "dumps", but also in their identity as non-landscapes. They are a prime example of the "base material[ity]" that Bois and Krauss (1997: 29) refer to as formless. In this sense, they are not so much unnatural as primordial. None of the terms that describe clearly defined landscape features apply here: neither landforms such as mountains and

---

19   Hansen does not make use of the term Anthropocene, but his writing focuses on the relationship between humans and technology that has shifted society from the centre of its own worldview, in other words, as post-human.

valleys, nor bodies of water such as rivers and lakes (Brook 2012: 114). As waste products, mine waste areas litter the landscape, creating a negative topography, a non-topography of sorts. Although they seem monolithic, they are also transient; they have been reprocessed through leaching, for example, or are blown around the city as toxic dust. They may best be understood as objects that escape fixity and definition as landscape, even though they are granted seeming permanence in representations. They do not represent the rationality of modern urban planning,[20] because they are waste products,[21] nor do they represent the supposed chaos of nature in Enlightenment thinking. Rather, they denote something more ominous, a kind of entropy towards decay. These landscapes are akin to some of Robert Smithson's land art, such as *Asphalt Rundown*, made in the late 1960s on the outskirts of Rome.

Smithson is known for his work with post-industrial sites such as mine dumps. In an interview with Moira Roth in 1973, he suggested that there is often an urge to return industrial landscapes to a supposed previously pure natural state. To him, this did not seem possible: instead, his work can be understood as a series of aesthetic interventions with post-industrial landscapes that allow one to see them afresh – as artworks rather than as wasted sites (Ryan 2007: 95–116). For Smithson, such sites are evidence of the traces of time, and the marks of entropic change on the landscape. The urge to explore entropy may be compared with how the formless disrupts rational categories of aesthetic experience and landscape. Writing about Smithson's work in the context of environmental aesthetics, Maskit (2007: 323–337) suggests that categories for landscape, such as the beautiful and even the sublime, fail to allow for an appreciation of post-industrial landscapes, such as abandoned mine sites, because they apply only to so-called natural landscapes. I would argue

---

20   When I refer to urban planning in Johannesburg, this implies both colonial and apartheid planning regimes, which conceived of planning based on models from the global North (De Satgé & Watson 2018).

21   The notion of waste is itself interesting in relation to mine waste areas, as it bears similarities to the formless. Waste, that has recently come to be of interest across disciplines such as cultural studies and media studies (Schneider & Strauven 2013: 412–414), is often understood to have a spatial quality, as wasted space, or spaces that are seen as wastelands, idle spaces or dangerous spaces because they do not function as (middle-class) society would have them (Scanlan 2005). Objects that are considered rubbish, garbage or waste are seen as detached from their social context and function (Edensor 2005: 108–117), and as something that is to be separated and removed or which has become devalued (Scanlan 2005: 10). See Walter Moser (2002), Mary Douglas (2002) and Kirsten Seale & Caroline Hamilton (2010) for notable discussions on the significance of the concept as one that has a subversive potential to challenge the rationality associated with modernist and Enlightenment ideas of urban planning and landscape.

that, while post-industrial landscapes defy neat categorisation, the sublime is the only category by which we can attempt to apprehend them. Since the sublime has already been explored in relation to artificial or technological landscapes,[22] I consider it a useful lens to scrutinise how mine dumps establish a post-industrial place-image of Johannesburg. Brook (2012) suggests that, over time, many kinds of industrial landscapes may be regarded aesthetically. Of course, this does not mean that they are ecologically sound or desirable, only that a person may experience them as sublime by looking at or interacting with them. While the sublime is most often associated with more scenic motivations in looking, Brook (2012: 111) suggests that aesthetics can itself be a far more embodied practice. We should therefore keep in mind that landscapes are typically inhabited by experiencing bodies, and that *living* in a place affords aesthetic experiences different from just looking at it in a picture, or from a distance.[23]

There is an unsettling tension here between thinking of post-industrial landscapes as aesthetic objects and as sites of human activity. Aside from such sites being poisoned and dangerous, because they no longer fulfil their original function, they are also unregulated spaces (Edensor 2005). In some ways, therefore, such places afford a degree of freedom to those who choose to interact with them. And the negative effects of illicit activities afforded by that freedom are clear. A recent example is the case of a music video crew who were viciously attacked on a mine dump outside Krugersdorp. The suspects are illegal miners (colloquially called *zama zamas*), reported to habitually hide in tall grass in the area with the intent to commit crimes (Masweneng 2022, Steyn 2022).[24] On

---

22 The sublime has been applied in the context of the artificial environment, such as industrial landscapes, by David Nye (1994), and more recently has been considered in terms of the Anthropocene by Amanda Boetzkes (2010) Isis Brook (2012) and Dylan Trigg (2006).

23 According to Brook (2011: 111) participatory aesthetics is a relatively new field within aesthetics that pursues exactly this: the lived aspect of a landscape as part of its aesthetic character. In short, what is at stake in the field of participatory aesthetics is a complication of the academic understanding of the relationship between aesthetics and the lived (and by extension embodied) world, countering the critique that aesthetics is scopic in orientation, and that it neglects the socio-political aspects of landscapes. Brook (2012: 113) suggests, for example, that a farmer, working on and living in a landscape, might have a deeper investment in aesthetic appreciation of the landscape than an artist may have, because the farmer has a physical relationship with the landscape. Farmers regarding land as practical and necessary to their survival would not necessarily preclude them from regarding the land aesthetically.

24 This upsetting crime led to xenophobic backlashes, as members of the public in the area urged police and the military to take action against illegal aliens in the country (Phooko 2022, Mob attacks … 2022, Magome 2022).

the other hand, these sites may become more productive spaces of freedom, of children's play, for instance, something that is nostalgically depicted or romanticised as innocent and pure, as in *Gangster's Paradise: Jerusalema* or Godfrey's photograph (Figure 44). And, not least, these sites may be subject to a nostalgic urge to restore them to a "pre-industrial" state.

In *District 9* the mine dumps of Mooifontein are nostalgic objects because they bear the physical traces of the city's history. This nostalgia is not only for the untouched natural landscape before Johannesburg existed, but an ironic nostalgia that looks back on the history of mining in the area that led to the city's founding, including its unsavoury aspects, now so recognisably present in the waste that remains. The mine dumps also constitute landscapes that offer aesthetic potential. Despite their real physical threat to humans and the ecology around Johannesburg, one may still legitimately consider what they offer from an aesthetic point of view. Maskit (2007) suggests that such localities may have the potential to transform the way we regard or "see" post-industrial sites, which echoes Brook's (2012: 115–116) suggestion that the aesthetic appreciation of landscapes may stimulate or require one to regard the same site from different perspectives. Johannesburg's landscapes are sites of change and metamorphosis in themselves, in flux and unresolved. They embody change materially, geographically, pragmatically and visually. This embodiment of change impacts our very notions of landscape and place as such.

CHAPTER 7

Urban Ruins

> Though one of Africa's most urbanized settings, [Johannesburg] is also seen as a place of ruins – of ruined urbanization, the ruining of Africa by urbanization. But in these ruins, something else besides decay might be happening.
> SIMONE 2004: 407[1]

1 A Sublime Johannesburg?

Along with mine waste areas, one of the most significant aspects of Johannesburg in *District 9* is the presence of urban ruins or decay. The city is frequently portrayed as if having stopped its development at some point in the 1980s. Although this is a distinct point of view and even an exaggeration, as Blomkamp admits (2020), it is not an unrealistic depiction of Johannesburg, and many scholars have engaged with the issue of the city's stasis and decay.[2] Urban decay is not typically formulated in terms of "ruins", so why use the concept here? Before considering its relevance in this context, the meaning and implications of ruins first need to be clarified. According to Robert Ginsberg (2004: 285–286), who writes on the aesthetics of ruins, a ruin constitutes the remains of a human-made construction in a state that is beyond repair due to a process of decay or destruction. The ruin no longer displays its original unity of form, yet offers new possibilities for aesthetic enjoyment. Because the original structure is absent, ruins are furthermore marked by a sense of loss. However, what is absent or lost remains implicit in the ruin itself. This understanding of ruins recalls how photography functions

---

1 Simone does not intend quite the same as I argue in terms of what decay and ruins offer. He suggests that the decay in the city is belied by complex infrastructures constituted by social relations, which he terms "people as infrastructure" (Simone 2004: 407). His point on the ruinous image of Johannesburg is pertinent, however, and illustrates that 'place-images' are complex and can offer more than is immediately apparent.
2 See Kruger (2013, 2006), Nuttall & Mbembe (2004), Robinson (2010), Bremner (2010), Bunn (2008), Poyner (2011), Murray (2011) and Parker (2016, 2014).

© LANDI RAUBENHEIMER, 2025 | DOI:10.1163/9789004710955_009
This is an open access chapter distributed under the terms of the CC BY-NC-ND 4.0 license.

FIGURE 45A Koobus approaches Wikus from behind. Still taken from *District 9* (Neill Blomkamp, 2009).

as *memento mori* (Woods 1984, Sontag 1977), capturing the past in a seemingly frozen moment.

Beyond this, ruins can be approached in a more extended sense with reference to landscape. For example, they are not just evident as derelict structures in the inner city, but also in the generally ruinous character of much of the landscape of Johannesburg in the depictions I consider here. In many cases, rather than depicting particular buildings as ruins, depictions show the ubiquitous rubble that pervades the urban landscape. Considering the urban decay prevalent in these depictions as ruin rather than simply decay evokes the affinity between ruins and the sublime. It invites a deeper consideration of the peculiarly contradictory responses they seem to invite, such as attraction and repulsion as well as nostalgia, despite their dystopian character.

One of *District 9*'s most emblematic sequences featuring ruins is set in the camp itself, and warrants a closer look. The sequence of about 30 seconds takes place towards the end of the film, in the third act, immediately after Wikus offers himself up to allow Christopher Johnson's escape. It is set amongst ruined buildings and rubble, and opens with a full shot of Wikus wearing the alien mechanised suit discussed previously in relation to science fiction. About three seconds into the sequence, Koobus, a violent, militant mercenary for the MNU, enters the shot from the left and delivers a fatal blow to the suit with a giant cannon he carries on his shoulder while chasing Wikus who is in the right

FIGURE 45B Wikus falls out of the alien mechanical suit. Still taken from *District 9* (Neill Blomkamp, 2009).

FIGURE 45C Wikus crawling from the wreckage of the alien mechanical suit. Still taken from *District 9* (Neill Blomkamp, 2009).

half of the frame (Figure 45a). The sequence has a hand-held feel, perhaps shot with a camera in the same position as the cannon on Koobus' shoulder. After being hit, the suit 'vomits' black fluid, falling to its knees. The next shot is a close-up of Koobus laughing gleefully, followed by one of Wikus inside the suit, looking wide-eyed and feverish. The brackets inside the suit around Wikus's face release him as the suit powers down, and the image cuts to a long shot of Wikus in profile, collapsing out of the suit (Figure 45b). The horizon is now visible, and Wikus slowly drags his body from the remains of the suit on the left of the screen (Figure 45c).

In the middle foreground in the screenshot taken from the end of the sequence, Wikus appears, dragging himself by his arms in the dust. To his left are the remains of the body armour, and beyond him, further away, is a structure that looks like a ruined dwelling. It is unclear whether it has been composited into the shot, or is physically part of the setting. The structure has no roof, no doors or windowpanes and consists only of bricks and some remaining wall coverings such as tiles, plaster and paint, much of it covered in graffiti. Around this abandoned ruin is rubble, some of it probably from the building itself. There is also other miscellaneous debris that alludes to the remains of a domestic environment, such as pieces of fabric, ruined pillows, plastic food and drink containers, cardboard packaging for household items, and other unidentifiable objects that contribute to the overall accumulation of rubble.

To the right are some shacks, and some mattress springs leaning against a fence. The shacks are informal domestic structures made of sheets of corrugated iron, stones and other found materials that could be used to fashion walls or a roof. A few straggling weeds are growing to the right and behind the structure, the only plant life. The notable aspects of the landscape here are the blue sky, dotted with white clouds, the bright sunlight, and the dust in the foreground. The colours in the scene are washed out, and this emphasises the worn-out and decayed textures of the structure, the refuse and rubble. The only colour amongst the muted tones of the buildings and rubble is a portion of a blue wall in the centre of the ruined landscape, which forms a focal point and echoes the blue of the sky beyond. The protagonist himself is barely differentiated from the setting and his body armour blends seamlessly with the rest of the rubble. The ruined landscape seems as much the subject of this sequence as the characters within it.

Before considering *District 9*'s climactic scenery from the point of view of the post-industrial sublime, it is helpful to make a comparison with a photograph by David Goldblatt (Figure 46) documenting the historic District Six, the area copiously evoked in allegorical readings of *District 9*. District Six in Cape Town was declared a "white group area" in 1966, and over the following

FIGURE 46 *The Destruction of District Six under the Group Areas Act, Cape Town 5 May 1982.* Photograph by David Goldblatt, 1982. Gelatin silver print, 27.9 × 34.8 cm. Manhattan: Museum of Modern Art.
COURTESY THE DAVID GOLDBLATT LEGACY TRUST AND GOODMAN GALLERY

fifteen years 60 000 people were forcibly removed, chiefly to the area known as the Cape Flats (Hallet & McKenzie 2007:19). Goldblatt's photograph was taken in 1982, the year when the most aggressive forced removals took place there (Wagner 2015: 47). The date corresponds to the temporal setting for the 'historical' parts of *District 9*, when the aliens arrived over Johannesburg.

The visual correspondences between Goldblatt's photograph in Figure 46 and the scene I've been discussing in *District 9*'s third act are striking. The deep foreground, as well as the ruin in the centre of the image even makes one wonder whether Blomkamp saw this photograph and had it in mind when planning this crucial scene in which Wikus turns a corner in his metamorphosis and sides with the aliens rather than the humans. Goldblatt's view of District Six is unusual in that it is dominated by undeveloped (stripped) land, bearing only the tracks of heavy vehicles.[3] Though some of the structures in the area remain, they blend in with the city of Cape Town in the background, and one is left with the impression that District Six is nothing but a ruined structure at the edge of the city. The raw, unstructured land – soil, dust, dirt, rocks – appears to be waiting to reclaim its territory from the jaws of urban development.

1.1   *More than a Feeling*

How can ruins such as those in *District 9* and in District Six in Goldblatt's photograph be understood as landscapes? And could these be interpreted as sublime landscapes of some kind? Trigg (2006: 95–118) writes about post-industrial ruins in relation to traditions of apprehending ruination in aesthetics. He refers to the history of the representation of ruins in art, and post-industrial ruins in relation to this tradition, situating ruins in opposition to the development of rational thinking and the importance of reason in western urban planning from the Enlightenment onwards.[4] For him, ruination and ruins subvert the role of reason in society, and thus serve a critical purpose.

Although some of the spaces I look at are urban or peri-urban rather than strictly post-industrial, I use the term post-industrial ruins throughout this chapter. The implicit umbrella of post-apartheid ruins applies to them all, since these urban landscapes have their foundations in apartheid spatial planning, which espoused modernist planning ideals, as did industrial architecture. These spaces have in common a collapse of such ordering principles because of their ruination. Urban ruins share much with scholars' descriptions of post-industrial ruins. These spaces are in the process of decay: they are not resolved and they do not lend themselves to a classical interpretation of ruination.

---

3   One might compare it with photographs by George Hallet, Clarence Coulson, Jackie Heyns, Gavin Jantjes and Wilfred Paulse. These photographers tend to focus more on the people living in the area, even during times of forced removals. The book *District Six Revisited* (Hallet & McKenzie 2007) is a collection of some of the work of these photographers.

4   See, for example, Richard de Satgé & Vanessa Watson's (2018) and Sally Gaule's (2005) discussions of how townships were planned to impose a western sense of order on the African landscape based on urban planning models from the global North. Saks (2010: 154) refers to spatial planning in this sense as based on "rationality, fixity and a homogenous view of race". Charles Gabay (2018) discusses how whiteness has been associated with notions of order and the ordering of society. Edensor (2005: 85), writing about western urban landscapes, discusses how in contemporary society such landscapes are marked by a sense of blandness, to be relatively soothing and present few physical impediments to human movement in cities. Edensor (2005: 86) suggests that there is an agenda in ordering, which masquerades as a universal set of values or common sense, and Gabay's discussion of whiteness in relation to rationally ordered space implies that such a sense of ostensibly universal values is also what underpins whiteness as a set of values and behaviours.

For Trigg, post-industrial ruins are useful in an aesthetic sense, not because they will further decay, but because they are complete in their incompleteness (Trigg 2006: XXI–XXIX). Andreas Huyssen (2006: 15) refers to a sense of a lack of closure or wholeness in some representations of ruins. This lack of closure is what interests me in the prevalence of images of ruins and ruination in Johannesburg's contemporary place-image. What is the aesthetic usefulness or critical potential of this seemingly unresolved image of the city?

Leading up to his discussion of the post-industrial sublime, Trigg cites examples of ruins that function in a relatively straightforward manner. These are historical portrayals of classical ruins, such as the ancient Roman theatre of Marcellus, and the village of Ninfa in Italy, examples that provide the viewer or visitor with a pleasurable aesthetic experience (Trigg 2006: 144–145). Because the ruins are so ancient and seem stagnant in time, they have an air of finality and closure, and therefore can be apprehended coherently and understood as unchanging. This is the kind of depiction of ruins that Huyssen (2006: 14) describes as picturesque in character, while Joanna Zylinska (2017: 86) refers to it as romantic. Such representations are in the tradition of ruins in a landscape that probably dates back to a woodcut from 1499 entitled the *Hypnerotomachia Poliphili* (Murray 1971: 17). These representations inspired the *vedute* etchings made famous by Giovanni Battista Piranesi in the eighteenth century, depicting the ruins of Rome for tourist souvenirs.[5]

In their romantic approach to ruins, portrayals like these may evoke a sense of nostalgia in the viewer, which may not be productive because they do not encourage a critical interpretation. Trigg (2006: 53–65) is doubtful about the aesthetic usefulness of nostalgia in the context of ruins, arguing that longing for the past is often related to the uncritical valorisation of progress. For Trigg, this is not a contradiction: our reliance on memory of the past is related to considering time and progress as linear and necessarily progressive; such reliance relates to the Enlightenment notion that remembering the past will allow one to develop and improve upon it, and thus supports modernist notions of progress. Nostalgia is often understood as a longing for a return to past order or reason perceived to have been lost. In these portrayals, it may point to a valorisation of ancient civilisations such as the Roman Empire. Nostalgia is also a function of a site becoming a place, when people confer meaning on it over time, creating a place-image (Shields 1991). When such a past becomes a fixed point of reference, it loses its potential to destabilise the narrative of reason,

---

5 *Vedute* paintings or etchings typically represent landscapes with pleasing views of ruins, created for tourists. Peter Murray (1971) provides a useful overview of the influential artists in this tradition in his book *Piranesi and the Grandeur of Rome*.

because it becomes static, quantifiable, and part of the narrative. As with the *vedute* etchings, this may lead to a complacent viewing experience. However, Boym (2001), discussed earlier, offers a more complex interpretation of nostalgia than Trigg, and I too would argue that not all forms of nostalgia are as simple as a longing for the past. Huyssen's (2006: 12–13) discussion of nostalgia in relation to the notion of authenticity is instructive in this regard. For him, nostalgia as brought about by images of ruins, such as those of past empires, does more than express fantasies of domination and of power. Rather, ruins serve to articulate an awareness of the transitory character of human power, and the Enlightenment fear that all human history might ultimately be wiped out by nature. An uneasy experience of urban ruins does not preclude nostalgia, which can be more complex than a simple valorisation of an edified past.

Piranesi's work did not only depict static and pleasing ruins; he later moved beyond such popular conventions when he produced the series *Antichità Romane* in 1756. In these etchings, his depictions become very dramatic and romantic, and can indeed be termed sublime, as in his etching of the *Foundations of the Mausoleum of Hadrian*.

In this work, tiny figures in the foreground convey the immensity of the ruins and, even though the masonry is decaying, it seems impressive, sturdy and monumental because of the low viewpoint and strong chiaroscuro (Murray 1971: 46–47). There is something seemingly eternal about these ruins. Human time seems folly by comparison, as is emphasised by the ant-like figures in the image. The apparent stability of these monumental ruins engenders a pleasurable sensation in the viewer, although there is also threat embodied in their scale. Huyssen (2006) discusses Piranesi's *Carceri d'Invenzione* (imaginary prisons) as depictions that further defy picturesque interpretations, and push the notion of unpresentableness even further than his sublime Roman ruins.[6] Huyssen (2006: 13–20) proposes that they share some conceptual underpinnings with Adorno's interpretation of avant-garde art, such as a denial of cohesion and wholeness, which can nudge the spectator to a place of critical contemplation rather than mere visual consumption or pleasure.

One might recall Goldblatt's photograph of tiny figures inhabiting shacks on a mine dump (Figure 15) in relation to Piranesi's depictions. But Goldblatt's landscape evokes no sense of grandeur. Rather, the setting seems unremarkable and mundane, capturing the matter-of-fact existence of people who appear to be making do with what little they have in an unforgiving context.

---

6 I discuss the notion of the unpresentable later in this chapter. Here Huyssen uses it in the context of avant-garde art, which sought to resist recognisable form in representation, often opting for abstraction instead.

Like the *Carceri* in Huyssen's interpretation, however, post-industrial ruins such as the mine dumps in Goldblatt's photograph have a destabilising effect on the viewer in Trigg's estimation. Rather than presenting a sense of human grandeur and power, they evoke a sense of the folly of modernity's exploits. Post-industrial sites are often still undergoing decay, and thus seem ambiguous in temporal terms. There is no sense of closure for the viewer, as such ruins point to transience rather than a sense of arrested time. As a result, they may inspire repulsion instead of pleasure; in Trigg's view, they are more ontologically significant than classical ruins. He sees post-industrial ruins as more akin to the sublime, and classical ruins to the beautiful, following Burke's formulation (Trigg 2006: 147–148). He goes on to describe how the Kantian triumph of reason over the senses often cannot take place, as the indeterminacy of time, sense of place and form in such ruins precludes such resolution. For him, much as for Brook (2012), such ruins are uncanny rather than only sublime, in the sense that nature is no longer under control of the senses of the observer. Nature returns as a familiar yet unfamiliar entity in the fauna and flora that reclaim these sites, asserting its dominance over human reason. There is thus an unsettling yet affirming aesthetic effect in such ruins. In terms of their affective qualities, post-industrial images such as Goldblatt's seem to represent "cultural pessimism", or a contemporary condition of apathy and disillusionment brought on by a loss of faith in the narrative of progress (Trigg 2006: 116).[7] This pessimism is often linked to gratuitous consumption in post-capitalist society, which may indicate a culture in decline (Trigg 2006: 119–125).

Post-industrial ruins may also relate to urban anxiety due to the collapse of "platial" boundaries, which Paul Virilio discusses in relation to contemporary urban space (in Trigg 2006: 126).[8] This is because capitalism bestows sameness and uniformity upon all places, an aspect exacerbated by digital media and its cultures.[9] The city becomes a place of desolation, indeterminacy and ambiguity (Trigg 2006: 131) when it is abandoned or ruined, and the order that was imposed by it is erased.

---

7 See also Miles Orvell's (2013: 647) discussion of urban ruins and the notion that globally there is a culture of mourning and a "narrative of decline", embodied in the photography of urban decline. Huyssen (2006: 8) identifies a comparable nostalgia at work in the Northern transatlantic, considering industrial decay in Europe, the former Soviet Union and in the US.
8 "Platial" may be understood as the place-based equivalent of "spatial" (Westerholt et al. 2018: 1).
9 See Gaule (2005) for a discussion on how such planning regimes sought to bestow a sense of structure and uniformity on townships to allow the government to exert power and control over them.

With regard to Johannesburg, anxiety takes on additional meaning because of the city's politically volatile history. Here ruination is often related to the collapse of apartheid, as the former regime's physical and institutional edifices collapse. During the 1980s, Johannesburg was already moving towards decentralisation, with the inner city in decline and the development of shopping malls and business districts outside this area (Brodie 2008). By the 1990s, many buildings were unoccupied and beginning to be reclaimed by the poor. Nechama Brodie (2008:97) explains how opportunistic landlords would illegally rent out space in buildings, taking advantage of desperate tenants, and creating slums in buildings that had not been maintained for many years and were unsafe to inhabit. Since the early 2000s, the Johannesburg City Council has been working with the Johannesburg Development Agency to turn this situation around and renew the decaying CBD, but this has resulted in other challenges, such as pockets of gentrified developments amid very poor and decayed parts of the city. One such area is the notorious Hillbrow, which was once the pinnacle of the apartheid-era's aspirational inner-city architecture. After the end of the apartheid-era it changed radically, as white residents and businesses abandoned the area.

1.2   Hillbrow: A New Jerusalem

The phenomenon of white flight, along with the growing incidence of slums in Hillbrow, is central to the film *Gangster's Paradise: Jerusalema*. The film is discussed with reference to how it portrays this part of the city by many scholars. Alexandra Parker (2018) refers to how Hillbrow may be compared to an American gangster film "ghetto", or seen as a "fallen city on a hill" (Lehman 2011: 113). Although he takes a more optimistic view, Addamms Mututa (2020) describes its urban qualities as errant, referring to dilapidation and trash. In *Gangster's Paradise: Jerusalema*, the protagonist, taxi-driver Lucky Kunene, starts a business run through the Hillbrow People's Housing Trust, which in his words would "take [...] back the streets, building by building". The scheme involves tenants taking over the rent in bad buildings and holding landlords – the building owners – to ransom, on conditions such as improving the facilities. This premise is not pure fiction. Ziman attests to how reading about such events inspired the plot of the film (Ziman Steals the Screen 2008). Such reported practices are what Mututa (2020: 218) refers to as "errant" gentrification, where (often white) landlords are in effect circumvented, and residents take control of buildings by means that are legally dubious, but which may ultimately lead to an improvement of living conditions.

By these means, Lucky soon becomes very wealthy, and the plot develops further from that basis. But what is of interest here is how *Gangster's*

FIGURE 47   Lucky's taxi in front of Dunvista Mansions. Still taken from *Gangster's Paradise: Jerusalema* (Ralph Ziman, 2008).

Paradise: Jerusalema depicts Hillbrow itself. Like *District 9* and many related portrayals of Johannesburg as nostalgic dystopia, the film constructs its portrayal of urban slums in a manner that evokes documentary films, such as *The Battle for Johannesburg*, and documentary photography of the time.

In the screenshot in Figure 47, a sequence in the second act that Mututa (2020) also writes about, Ziman has selected a low-angle shot, to give prominence to the garbage accumulated outside Lucky's Hillbrow abode (a building called Dunvista Mansions) throughout the film. There are signs of urban decay in the peeling paint on the building on the left, and the minibus taxi is itself the worse for wear. The Hillbrow Tower lurks in the background, becoming a minor character in the film, stepping in as a point of reference, but also appearing in moments of crisis, when Lucky stares out of his window at the view of this once impressive structure (Figure 48).

The feeling of grime is tangible, and pervades the Hillbrow setting of *Gangster's Paradise: Jerusalema*, which, corresponding to its generic agenda as a gangster film, foregrounds the dystopian qualities of Dunvista Mansions and its surrounds. Johannesburg takes on a noir quality in many shots of the cityscape which emphasise darkness, smog and the spectre of lawlessness hanging

FIGURE 48   Lucky staring out of the window. Still taken from *Gangster's Paradise: Jerusalema* (Ralph Ziman, 2008).

over it. In the screenshot in Figure 48 one can see the glow on the horizon as the city lights are reflected in the urban pollution. Lucky gazes through the open windows, which have not been cleaned in a long time, and the inside frames are grimy, as if the pollution has permeated the inner spaces of the building. Shots like this, which occur several times throughout the film, suggest that Lucky is not beyond hope, however. When he stares up at the Hillbrow Tower there is the suggestion that he still dreams of bigger things, despite his gloomy circumstances. Hillbrow, though dystopian, is the setting of Lucky's success and his transformation into a middle-class citizen.

In some sequences, there is a focus on the decay, perhaps the errancy that Mututa (2020) refers to in his discussion of the film. Shots such as the one showing a police vehicle parked beyond a pile of trash (Figure 49) emphasise the dire state of Hillbrow, with the armoured vehicle implying how rife violent crime is. The garbage in the foreground seems to be growing out of control, and the asphalt is falling apart. The scene depicts an urban landscape of ruination, no longer resembling anything functional. In places, the plastic debris, unidentifiable for the most part, has melted into the remains of the road, as if fires had been burning here, outside in the street. Opposite are buildings that appear to

FIGURE 49 Trash and a police vehicle. Still taken from *Gangster's Paradise: Jerusalema* (Ralph Ziman, 2008).

be residences, which point to a time when this locale functioned as a suburban street and was not an unconstrained site of litter and fires in makeshift braziers. The blurring of boundaries between activities indicates the collapse of order ubiquitous in the Hillbrow of *Gangster's Paradise: Jerusalema*. Informal trade and private activities, such as cooking dinner or socialising, all merge in spaces not designed for these activities, which Abdoumaliq Simone (2004: 1) suggests is characteristic of African cities, where improvisation and seizing unplanned opportunities is critical to survival in the urban context.[10] In effect,

---

10 Simone (2010: 263–334) is interested in understanding forms of urbanism prevalent in contemporary African cities, which he terms "black urbanism", often maligned and misunderstood from a western perspective. For him, informality is related to the presence of the market or informal economy and a 'making do' mentality. He looks at various cities in the world where Black people have settled, including Johannesburg, Dubai, Bangkok and Douala in Cameroon. He argues that it is essential to acknowledge alternative notions of urbanism from the modernist western norm. Black urbanism is one such alternative, structured around informality for historical and economic reasons. Rather than focusing only on the problems of such urbanity, he strongly proposes that it is important to consider the creativity and improvisation of people in such communities, who face extreme

this changes the urban landscape and breaks it down into more fundamental elements from a material point of view. The breakdown and decay of both architectural structures and domestic waste seem to be part of this process.

In Emilie Venables' (2011: 133) socio-medical research on Hillbrow, there are photographs taken by the participants in her study that draw attention to the lack of waste removal services in the area. In them, men can be seen ankle-deep in garbage bags during a municipal strike, and they narrate how service delivery is an ongoing problem in the neighbourhood. Documentation of such waste is also prominent in photographs by Jono Wood and Guy Tillim, as well as documentary photography that engages with waste removers themselves, such as Sabelo Mlangeni's *Invisible Women*, 2007 series and photographs by Mark Lewis (2015) who documented waste recyclers working in Johannesburg.

1.3   Ponte City

The physical decay of Johannesburg and its apartheid legacy is ironic, as the collapse of apartheid should have resulted in citizens' freedoms and a more egalitarian social structure. Instead, it has resulted in abandoned sections of the city, where those in poverty live in urban ruins.[11] As in many such spaces in the world, in the town of Nala Sopara in Mumbai (see Mukherjee 2017: 287–309), Douala in Cameroon, or Bangkok in Thailand (see Simone 2010: 263–334), for example, many buildings in the inner city of Johannesburg are collapsing but are not empty. As depicted in *Gangster's Paradise: Jerusalema*, there is vibrant life often invisible to middle-class citizens. Such resilient life is laid bare in Subotzky and Waterhouse's project documenting Ponte City. Instead of only showing it as a landmark on the Johannesburg skyline, the two photographers documented people's windows and television screens, and took many portraits of the building's residents over several years, capturing a human angle of the building. However, they devote considerable attention to ruined structures and debris in the atrium of the building as well.

---

constraints politically, economically, practically and socially, and yet develop highly flexible systems of complex exchange and interaction to survive. He also emphasises how customary practices are interwoven with informal adaptations of official governing systems and the market, allowing people to benefit maximally from the few available resources. Although it may appear messy, the environment here necessitates temporary solutions and flexibility, and for him residents of informal urban environments actively shape their surroundings (Simone 2010: 282) in innovative non-western ways (Simone 2010: 286).

11   See Kruger (2013, 2006,) Nuttall and Mbembe (2004), Robinson (2010), Bremner (2010), Bunn (2008), Poyner (2011), Murray (2011), Parker (2016, 2014) and Saks (2010: 155–156), as well as Desai (2010).

Subotsky's photograph in Figure 17, though documentary in approach, is notable for capturing the scale of the rubble in this building, and presents a different view of Ponte. Although the building is still impressive on the contemporary Johannesburg skyline, on closer viewing, the scale of its decay overshadows its presence there. Although Subotzky and Waterhouse's project focused on the resilience and humanity of residents, the attributes of the building itself feature just as much. The project points to the post-apartheid built environment of Johannesburg more generally, with its qualities of urban ruin, which in Figure 17 seem to dwarf the human workers engaged in cleaning Ponte. When considering this photograph from the point of view of the site, perhaps as a landscape of sorts, its imbrication with the post-industrial sublime can be supplemented by what Miles Orvell terms the "destructive sublime" (2013: 647–671). He discusses this concept in relation to photography of sites of urban destruction in the United States. These include Detroit, an industrial city that has been decaying over time,[12] as well as sites of natural destruction, such as New Orleans, which was devastated by Hurricane Katrina, and of politically motivated destruction, such as New York in the wake of the attack on the World Trade Centre in 2001.

In the destructive sublime, decay itself becomes a decisive factor in how the sublime manifests through representations. Orvell (2013: 647) focuses particularly on the contradictory affects that such photographs may elicit in the viewer, namely, feelings of grief and loss, but also an aesthetic pleasure, which may in turn be unsettling. Orvell (2013: 670) suggests that there is an aspect of fascination for viewers in photographs that one could label "ruin porn". The discomfort that sites of urban disaster in the United States may hold for viewers could be akin to what viewers of dystopian depictions of Johannesburg experience. In beholding a moment of decay and devastation related to the city's political circumstance, they experience ambiguities of place such as a nostalgic dystopia. Ponte City may evoke such contradictory responses.

The socio-political position of viewers is formative in how they experience such portrayals. Who would experience nostalgia in seeing these images, for example? Desai, director of *The Battle for Johannesburg* – who overtly positions

---

12   Detroit's 'demise' was due to race riots resisting racist economic and geographic structures in the city in the 1960s, and a resulting economic disinvestment or 'white flight' (Steinmetz 2008). Between 1964 and 1972 there were many racial uprisings across American cities. One of the largest, in Detroit in 1967, took place against the backdrop of years of discrimination against Black citizens working in the factories in the city, fuelled by racial tensions. For a nuanced discussion on this fraught history, see Mark Jay and Virgina Leavell's (2017) article, Material Conditions of Detroit's Great Rebellion.

himself as a middle-class citizen and an outsider to spaces of urban ruination such as these – reminisces about how Hillbrow used to look when he was younger. He states in his film that it has "gone downhill". His racial heritage complicates Desai's position: as an Indian man who grew up in exile, he would only have known Hillbrow during the demise of apartheid, shortly after his return to South Africa in the 1990s, and his feelings of nostalgia must be based on that. His parents, on the other hand, who would not have frequented Hillbrow at night in their youth, as it was off-limits to Indian people under apartheid law,[13] would be unlikely to view it nostalgically, in the way white citizens of that generation might feel.

Ruined or decaying buildings such as Ponte City are also complicated by another factor, which Orvell (2013: 648) relates to Alois Riegl's 1903 discussion of monuments – what he calls "age value" in ruined or decaying buildings. Riegl argues that, within the cultural understanding of ruins in Europe in the early twentieth century, "age value" is ascribed to things that deteriorate slowly, at a pace that aligns with "nature" (Riegl 1996: 73), and not those that are subject to violent and sudden destruction. For him, age value lies in imperfections that creep in over time, making the structure seem incomplete or fragmented. Such a notion of ruins resembles how scholars discuss analogue nostalgia as a valorisation of the imperfections of ageing analogue media recouped in digital media.[14] It may also recall Benjamin's notion of the aura of authenticity, which regards historicity, the passing of time and the distance from an object as contributing to its sense of authenticity. Huyssen (2006) relates this to ruins.

Age value, in a way similar to Trigg's (2006) view of classical ruins, accrues when decay takes place slowly. There is a point, however, when total decay undermines the pleasure of age value, when a ruin becomes unintelligible: structure has given way to chaos or formlessness. Riegl (1996: 74) points out that a mere pile of stones will no longer afford aesthetic pleasure. The post-industrial sublime functions more effectively in this register, where urban structure surrenders to the "chaos" of nature (Trigg 2006). The post-industrial sublime can only truly unfold when one can no longer romanticise a ruin. In photographs of Ponte City (Figure 17), architectural reason is no longer at work but is completely subverted. The mountain of debris epitomises a descent into chaos: it looks more like a (mining) landscape than the interior of an atrium or any other architectural form. In 1903, Riegl (1996: 74) used the word "formless"

---

13   Zola Maseko's (2002) film *A Drink in the Passage* is a short reflection on 'white' Hillbrow in the 1960s; it tells the story of a Black sculptor, and his encounter with a white man who invites him for a drink at his home in the city one evening.
14   See Schrey (2014), Bartholeyns (2014) and Sapio (2014).

to describe such decay, prefiguring Bois and Krauss' (1997) use of the term. I consider this an important guiding principle when exploring the sublime in depictions of Johannesburg. It lurks not only in shapeless mine waste areas, but also – perhaps surprisingly – in the city's decaying buildings, which threaten to undermine the urban fabric of historic Johannesburg.

Victor Burgin (1991: 22–23) discusses Julia Kristeva's concept of the abject in relation to the sublime, proposing that the way the female body is seen as abject could sometimes be projected onto sublime landscapes.[15] Burgin argues that the affective response to fearsome landscapes conceals the fear of extinction of identity in the loss of the boundaries of subjectivity. He quotes Klaus Theweleit, who talks about the landscape subsuming one's body, dissolving it, until one is "in a state where everything is the same, inextricably mixed together" (Burgin 1991: 22). In the screenshot of Wikus crawling in the dust in *District 9* (Figure 45c), it is precisely such a dissolution that occurs. His body is disintegrating and re-forming itself as an alien body, but at that point he is neither one nor the other. In the disintegrating landscape, he almost looks like another piece of rubble. Burgin suggests that the force at work in such a dynamic is entropy – a topic covered also by a chapter in Bois and Krauss' (1997) book. While the grotesque, the abject, the *informe* or formless and the sublime are distinct categories of aesthetic experience that could be analysed theoretically in considerably more detail than I can here, it is worth noting where they overlap, and where they inform each other in *District 9*.[16] If the

---

15 Norman Bryson's (1993: 216–223) discussion of the abject body in *House of Wax* is also relevant here. He argues that the *informe* (Bataille's famous notion) is that which can only be approximated in representation, because it lies beyond representability. For him, monsters are already within the safe space of the representable, and as such are only indicators of what cannot be understood. This is comparable to how representation of landscape functions in relation to the sublime. The latter cannot 'reside' in representation, since it is incommensurate with representation (Brook 2012).

16 In recent studies of the grotesque, it has been argued that the effect that grotesque images have on viewers may be compared with the effect the sublime, when "the categories of our understanding suddenly and momentarily fail" (Van den Oever 2011: 111). Both the sublime and the grotesque (along with the formless) may simultaneously elicit attraction and repulsion in viewers. It is important to note that these effects are described in studies of both the sublime and the grotesque, though the differences between the grotesque and the sublime regarding their formal features are clear and pronounced. Following up on Noël Carroll's 2003 argument that the grotesque is much more prominent in contemporary film than it was in earlier decades, Van den Oever (2013, 2011) argues that the current prominence of the grotesque in film cannot merely be ascribed to the increasing demands of the entertainment industry, as Carroll claimed. She asserts that many of the distortions he discusses are technology-induced, accidental side effects of new technologies, which happen to leap into the grotesque, yet are not consciously created by the entertainment

landscape in the film is formless, evoking the sublime of post-industrial decay and destruction, then the abject and grotesque qualities of the characters in the film, like the 'prawns' and Wikus's mutating body, are fitting inhabitants.[17]

The concept of the formless is the collapse of dichotomies, the collapse of figure and ground.[18] In the photograph of Ponte City, the 'figure' (form) of the building has been slowly collapsing into the 'ground', subsumed in decay and uniformity, until things approximate the inextricably mixed matrix that Burgin (1991: 22) refers to: it seems as if trash and the building may become indistinguishable at some point. Arya (2014: 7) suggests that if the sublime is an experience that leads to a transcendence of the body and the senses, then the abject casts one down into horror and disgust in a process of desublimation. The formless could also work in this manner, since it shares with the abject a collapse of boundaries and a devolution into homogenising chaos, no longer distinguishing different forms of materiality. The horror and disgust one may feel in response to these images has the added aspect of moral concern (Orvell 2013: 647–671). One may simultaneously feel empathy for people who live in such appalling conditions and experience a morbid fascination because such photographs are so compelling to look at.

1.4 Considering Entropy

What is the significance of the fascination of these places? Clearly they deny the viewer the sense of triumph articulated in theories of classical ruins as sublime. These images are simply too *real* to allow one to have such an abstract response. Does the formless quality of these cityscapes then allow the viewer some sense of agency or transformation in response to these depictions? The collapse of order and form runs contrary to modernist urban planning and the sameness imprinted upon much modernist urban space under capitalist

---

industry. She writes that "the experience of the grotesque, [...] is not merely or exclusively a perceptual experience of grotesque (fused, hybrid, monstrous) beings; it is, more fundamentally, an experience of the distorting powers of the new technologies themselves effectively 'working' on the percipients in the perceptual process and destabilising their notion of images, representations, beings and meanings" (Van den Oever 2011: 101–102).

17 Many scholars discuss the 'prawns' as abject (see Nel [2012] and Jansen van Veuren [2012]), and the term grotesque is also used by some. The characters of the film are not my focus, but they may be seen as metaphorical of the landscape itself, which, like abject or grotesque figures, is in a state of transformation, and so between two fully formed states. Wikus's own transformation is thus interesting here insofar as it points to the landscape and its transformation (or lack thereof).

18 Rosalind Krauss (1999: 73–73) and Rina Arya (2014: 120–125) both discuss this collapse with reference to the notion of the abject.

regimes, as is evident in mass housing, for example.[19] In the South African context, although these sites are negative in terms of extreme decay, filth and poverty, they also represent the decay of an oppressive political regime of separation and modernist urban hegemony. In writing about such decay in the film *Gangster's Paradise: Jerusalema*, Mututa (2020: 212) argues that this errancy, which I call entropy, is a form of "aggressive customization". For him, the city is continuously unfolding in the present, its future uncertain; the city is "emblematic of hope, yet experienced as gloom" (216). In this sense, these spaces may hold an element of critical potential, however unlikely it may seem at face value. Of course, a difficult yet prudent question to ask is *for whom* that freedom is available. In *Gangster's Paradise: Jerusalema*, it is the residents themselves who turn this state of decay around and to their advantage (such as it is) through the customisation of how their buildings are run. Parker (2018: 66) points out, however, that the film could be seen as an outsider perspective on inner-city life in Johannesburg, made by a white filmmaker, who portrays Hillbrow from his perspective. The same may be said of *District 9*. The reality portrayed in the documentary *The Battle for Johannesburg* is bleaker: only a handful of residents of a bad building secure better accommodation from the city council, when their original residence (San Jose) is renovated for higher income tenants. They seem to remain at the mercy of this entropic process rather than at the helm of it.

Then again, one might think of these depictions as portraying a radical reversion to organic disorder. While the images are often shocking, inspiring repulsion, they demonstrate human survival against the odds. A viewer might not be able to imagine living in such conditions, but some people do so daily, as is portrayed in *The Battle for Johannesburg*. In South Africa, the realisation that this is not as far removed (geographically speaking) from a middle-class life as some might think brings home the reality of social stratification and poverty in the country. It also serves to highlight the position of the viewer. Repulsion as an affect can be useful in this context. Such a response could be more productive for the viewer than pleasant feelings of delight evoked by ruins presented as picturesque landscapes of past grandeur (Trigg 2006: 146–148). A feeling of

---

19   The notion of sameness referred to here is not to be confused with the homogeneity engendered by entropy in the formless. The latter is a dissolution of boundaries, and results in the loss of subjectivity in a way that resists and dissolves the structures that allowed modernist sameness to develop in the first place. The sameness of mass housing or modernist urban planning is discussed as oppressive by Adorno & Horkheimer (1993: 32); Trigg (2006) is interested in how such planning regimes could be undermined by their physical decay in post-industrial ruins.

repulsion is closer to an experience of space as sublime, where the viewer is challenged rather than placated. This sublime signifies a rupture with reason and structure, where progress itself is questioned, and space becomes contingent (or indeed formless) rather than rational. This is the unpresentable, the denial of "good forms" (Lyotard 1984b: 81).[20]

One might further speculate that such a rupture would constitute a shock, or a form of violence exerted through or upon the viewer, as Lyotard (1984a) formulated in his theory of the avant-garde and the sublime. Although Lyotard was writing about art, in the context of urban landscape one might consider that this contradictory affective aesthetic approximates a truer version of such a rupture than artworks ever could. This undoubtedly has ethical implications, especially since the photographs depict actual living conditions that people contend with. The problematic nature of this critical or aesthetic potential should be interrogated, but its character should first be thoroughly probed.

As Trigg (2006: 95) suggests, decay in the post-industrial context seems to have ontological significance, indicating the loss of a bygone worldview, that no longer aligns with lived experience. This could not be more obviously the case than in the post-apartheid context of Johannesburg depicted in *District 9*, especially for the figure of Wikus. As a white Afrikaner, he finds himself irrelevant and having to metamorphose into something he considers monstrous, within a setting that seems an uncanny parody of western urban planning. This brings to mind the anxiety that Trigg (2006: 130) discusses, relating to being displaced from rational modernist space, generally considered to be a "native form of dwelling" where humans "naturally" belong. In the context of urban ruination, this anxiety is related to the loss of the ostensibly utopian future of the city – a "retroactive causality" in which the now ruined city signifies a rupture in how the future would have been conceived within apartheid rhetoric (Hook 2014: 186–190, 2012: 232). From the perspective of apartheid's white identity, the presence and activities of Black residents signify the loss of the "white vestiges" of the city (Mututa 2020: 216). The associated anxiety is also related to the threat of the abject and of subsumption into the undefined (Burgin 1991: 22); it is made more intense by the fear of the 'other', those on the

---

20   The unpresentable refers to Lyotard's interpretation of the sublime and is premised on the fundamental grappling with presentation or form, which is inherent in post-modern or avant-garde art. Simon Malpas (2002) engages with this in depth in examining Lyotard's understanding of the sublime in relation to abstract art. Philip Shaw (2017: 170) refers to this version of the sublime as one that approaches a point of "self-cancellation", facilitated by the denial of form inherent in abstraction. Elsewhere I also refer to Crowther (1996) and Carroll (2008), who engage with Lyotard's argument.

margins of society (Arya 2014:7). The camp that houses the prawns in *District 9* epitomises this allegorically, as an area where the other is quarantined, expelled from the city, unable to contaminate the humans, and where Wikus mutates into the abject as a result of such contamination.[21] It is clear then that the sublime qualities of this 'post-landscape', which is post-apartheid, post-colonial, post-industrial, and perhaps post-sublime, is bound up with white anxiety, and has particular implications from this point of view.

---

21 Kapstein (2014: 159–161) discusses how Wikus becomes contaminated through a process that clearly aligns with notions of abjection, where his body is compromised, he is 'infected' with alien DNA and his very DNA is altered. She refers to a scene in the film where a television broadcast explains that Wikus is contagious after being infected through sexual intercourse with aliens. This is obviously a false report, but it emphasises how aliens are seen as other, and how, through a process of abject transformation, Wikus loses his sense of human identity and his human body. The false report is also an allegorical reference to South African legislation under apartheid that prohibited inter-racial marriages, the Prohibition of Mixed Marriages Act of 1949 and the Immorality Act of 1927. These Acts served the racist agenda of preventing miscegenation, which had been common in early settler society (see Mandaza 1997: 157–181, Kapstein 2014: 160).

CHAPTER 8

White Anxiety

1   Hegemony in Ruins

Having earlier examined the work of Instagram photographers who employ nostalgia to negotiate "subversive resistance" to racial stereotypes, I now turn to another stratum of racialised affect within the sediment of the represented Johannesburg landscape: white anxiety.

The landscape in *District 9* and related depictions represent two urban topographies that can be linked to white anxiety: the mining landscape and the ruins of colonial and apartheid urban planning in the inner city and the townships. Both these enterprises are in decay in the city as depicted in these representations, resulting in the associated qualities of the nostalgic dystopian idiom, inviting nostalgia for a time before their demise.

In historical Johannesburg, those who owned land were generally white and of settler descent, and those who worked in the mines were generally Black. This history reveals a tension that runs through *District 9* and other depictions in the idiom of nostalgic dystopia. In particular, the tension is indicative of Johannesburg's history as a former 'white city', and here I am referring particularly to the CBD and the mining industry, the (former) centres of commerce in the city. The changing character of the city, and the decay of its apartheid vestiges is linked to white anxiety.

Before considering *District 9*'s engagement with white anxiety as it shapes the Johannesburg landscape, I would like to reflect on Vincent Moloi's short film *Berea*. The film is premised entirely on the demise of the elderly character, Aaron Zukerman, who appears marooned in his apartment in Berea in the inner city, the same area as Ponte City. The film opens with shots of urban decay in shabby facades and informal trade on the streets below. A Jewish widower, Zukerman lives alone and seems only to interact with a prostitute who comes to see him every week. He is depicted as decrepit and dithering, keeping his curtains drawn against the harsh Johannesburg sun, and nostalgically clinging to family rituals even without family. In one scene (Figure 50), he finds himself on the street below his apartment where he is a fish out of water. The only white man in sight, he is overwhelmed by the bustling noise of minibus taxis and fumbles confusedly with a baby bootie he picks up. The bootie belongs to a Black prostitute he rejected earlier – not the same (implicitly white) woman he sees weekly. Perhaps remorseful for how harshly he ejected

FIGURE 50 Zukerman out of place in the street below his apartment. Still taken from *Berea* (Vincent Moloi, 2013).

her from his apartment, he has gone downstairs to pick it up. She is less than grateful when he does find her on his second outing downstairs, telling him to save himself instead of trying to save her. In this scenario, he comes to realise that he is not a hero but a minor character, an outsider in the lives of the Black citizens who now reside in the area alongside him. Zukerman portrays the lack of belonging and disorientation that whites may feel in post-apartheid South Africa, and especially in its changing urban character. There are some suggestive shots of changed street names and former buildings that have been appropriated, such as a Hebrew High School that is now an informal supermarket. Zukerman is captured from a very low angle (reminiscent of the shot from *Gangster's Paradise: Jerusalema* in Figure 47), which reveals urban decay and garbage bins as they compete with him for the focal point of the shot. In the inner city, Zukerman is out of place, and out of touch with the changing environment. Ultimately, however, Zukerman is not portrayed as irredeemable, although he must undergo a transformation to acclimatise himself to the post-apartheid city. Towards the end of the film, he opens his heavy curtains, perhaps in a gesture of acceptance of the city he now lives in, no longer the white Johannesburg in which he had made his life.

District 9's portrayal of Wikus could be considered equally emblematic of the white anxiety that *Berea* portrays.[1] Like Zukerman, Wikus is presented in relation to the landscape on several occasions in the film. The scene from Act Three (Figures 45a, 45b and 45c) is especially significant, as it evokes several aspects of white anxiety. Like Zukerman, who is out of place in the inner city, Wikus, as a white man, is allegorically out of place in the township, where he finds himself in a climactic violent confrontation. Townships were originally designed to segregate Black people from the urban centres of cities (De Satgé & Watson 2018). *District 9*'s fictional camp and the South African township are presented in symbolic connection with each other, and Wikus accordingly only seeks refuge there when he has no other choice. In terms of the allegorical significance of the film, the aliens represent the otherness of Black people constructed by apartheid. Wikus here is becoming such an 'other' and is in a state of as yet unrealised transformation. Crawling in the dust of the township, it is as if his human self is becoming dust; in the process he relinquishes his whiteness and transforms into the other he fears so much.

One may argue that the presence of nostalgia in *District 9* and other depictions indicates white anxiety about the future of the city and South Africa, but what exactly is the phenomenon of white anxiety? It may be premised on latent forms of racism, such as a belief in the basic incompetence of Black leadership, and the collapse of structures and institutions under its rule (Straker 2013: 91–100). Whiteness is often associated with the fallacious belief that white people are superior to other races (Freschi 2019: 68) because of an inherent ability to order the world successfully, and their faith in the institutions that edify this ordering (Gabay 2018). In the South African context, and particularly in urban architecture, it is further historically characterised by an "embrace of modernity", a depiction of progress and success, which was adopted as symbolic of Afrikaner nationhood (Freschi 2019: 67). The fear of the loss of this supposed superiority is what Charles Gabay (2018) describes as white anxiety. For both Zukerman and Wikus, this fear has already materialised. Zukerman is disorientated and lost – not recognising the city he lives in. Wikus' lack of belonging is reflected in the landscape's topography. Urban order has collapsed just as apartheid has. Like Wikus himself, the landscape is in a state of incomplete transformation, it is formless, and as such defies apprehension and comprehension.

---

1 Although in this film, a Black filmmaker is portraying white anxiety, and the city, from his point of view.

Gillian Straker (2013), participating in a psychosociological research project entitled the "Apartheid Archives Project", sees white anxiety as indicative of a reassertion of a belief in white supremacy. She suggests that whites may feel a sense of vulnerability related to the loss of privilege and the implications of guilt that linger in post-apartheid society (Straker 2013: 84). Melancholia could result from such a lingering sadness because overt mourning cannot take place, as whites face their relative powerlessness in the new political climate. They may also suffer from feelings of betrayal by their own group and its former ideals, which were revealed to be false and even villainous. Melancholia is contextualised here in terms of complex emotional responses in the transition from loving something to rejecting it or hating it unconsciously. In other words, white people must reject the actions of apartheid and related nationalism, which, during apartheid, they might well have identified with, and even have thought of themselves as patriotic for doing so. When such a reversal cannot be processed openly, and previous beliefs have to be denied, they can become "entombed", haunting the subject (Straker 2013: 96). Because people cannot openly mourn the loss of such sentiments of belonging or identification, there is a residual grief that cannot be processed or assuaged. Apartheid and its contradictory after-effects seem to defy understanding, and the scale of the atrocities of that era can itself be regarded as unpresentable, further stalling the process of transformation towards new political persuasions.

Another aspect that feeds into white anxiety is the perception of crime in the country. Gary Kynoch (2013), writing on literary depictions of crime as racialised, argues that in post-apartheid South Africa crime is often perceived and portrayed by white citizens as racially motivated. For Black citizens, however, violent crime does not seem to have this racialised character, but is thought of as more commonplace, as crime was already rife in the apartheid era due to poor conditions, and concomitant with the poor policing of segregated townships. Kynoch refers to various literary texts that portray the white fear of violent crime perpetrated by Black people, such as *Cry the Beloved Country* (Paton 1948), *Portrait with Keys: The City of Johannesburg Unlocked* (Vladislavić 2006) and *Disgrace* (Coetzee 1999). In part, these narratives relate to the notion that crime committed by Black people is the enactment of vengeance for the atrocities of apartheid. Interestingly, in the film *Gangster's Paradise: Jerusalema*, Lucky says as much when he remarks that he and his friend Zakes did not feel bad for carjacking white drivers because they "figured they owed [them]". The fear of crime has largely reshaped the built environment, as white people barricade themselves into their homes (Steinberg in Kynoch 2013: 435), giving rise to the kind of "siege architecture" discussed by Murray (2011) and others. Fear furthermore underpins the phenomenon of white flight, which has shaped the inner city of Johannesburg, and is also evidenced in large numbers of white people emigrating due to uncertainty about their future in the country (Kynoch 2013: 434–439). It is productive here to note, however, that anxiety is not limited to white experiences of Johannesburg, as I mentioned earlier with reference to the book *Anxious Joburg*. The thought of fleeing South Africa seems equally prevalent amongst Black people, according to journalist Sisonke Msimang (2013) in her article on perceptions of crime in the *Daily Maverick*.

Nonetheless, the crisis of white identity and its associated anxieties has become a substantial topic of interest on its own,[2] although not all scholars use the term anxiety. The complexity of feelings such as guilt, melancholia and nostalgia would seem commensurate with how anxiety is embodied in Wikus and his interaction with the camp/township. It is also commensurate with how Charles Gabay (2018:1–45) describes "White anxiety".[3] He discusses "Whiteness" as more than a "phenotypical" condition of being racially white, rather as a system of universalising values, which has, in a Eurocentric manner, constructed the West as superior to the rest of the world. It is the fear of the loss of this "Whiteness" by white people that he describes as "White anxiety". In other words, it is a fear of the loss of the belief that "White people" are superior or possess a mythologised "institutional genius" (Hobson in Gabay 2018: 29).

Wikus as a symbol of white anxiety in the third act of *District 9* invites comparison with Theodore Géricault's *The Raft of the Medusa* (1818–19). Wikus shares several things with the occupants of Gericault's *Raft*. Visually, two aspects of Wikus crawling in the dust remind me of that painting: his languishing and reaching posture, and the section of blue wall which appears to hover above the ruins, giving the composition a triangular quality like Géricault's famous painting. The blue wall is the punctum of the scene; drawing the eye, it symbolises the place beyond the horizon that Wikus is aiming for. The wreckage from which he is crawling is to some degree an extension of the wreck of the mothership hovering above the city – a shipwreck of sorts that Wikus is escaping. And, as with the uncertainty about the future of Gericault's shipwrecked sailors, his crisis and anxiety are unresolved, tied to the transformation that he, as symbol of apartheid-era whiteness, has not fully realised in this sequence (Figures 45a-c).

The township's landscape can likewise be understood as a site of incomplete or unrealised transformation. Township planning under apartheid led to many socio-economic problems, isolating residents from the urban centres where

---

2 White anxiety is investigated by Melissa Steyn (2005: 119–135), Dennis Walder (2014: 143–157) and Anthea Garman (2014: 211–228).
3 Gabay capitalizes the term, and I retain this spelling when clarifying his view of it here.

they worked and symbolising their dispossession from the land. The expectation that this would change with the end of apartheid has been thwarted to a large degree, as noted by Melissa Thandiwe Myambo (2011, 2018: 1–9), among many others.[4] Jack Cilliers (in Akpome 2018: 106) describes South Africa's transition into democracy as incomplete. The township as a symbol of oppression and poverty has not yet transformed into something new; it is in a state of unrealised metamorphosis, just as Wikus is in this scene. The "unformed" or formless landscape (complete with the wreckage of apartheid) in *District 9* symbolises this lack of resolution.

In addition to some shared visual features with *The Raft of the Medusa*, the political implications of Wikus' plight echoes that of Gericault's survivors: they too were victims of a failing dispensation that needed to change. The painting depicts the last few languishing survivors of a failed French mission to re-establish colonial power in Senegal in 1816 (Nicolson 1954: 240–249). When the ship foundered, the soldiers aboard were abandoned by the captain and crew due to a shortage of life rafts, and of the 150 soldiers only ten survived.[5] The message of the painting is not unlike the political allegory of *District 9*, insofar as the last survivor of the old regime has been cast out. The comparison is even more pronounced in a contemporary artwork by the collective named AVANT CAR GUARD.[6]

Active in the late first decade of the 2000s, the collective AVANT CAR GUARD employs irony, and their work is satirical rather than literal. In 2007, they produced a series of photographs called *Africa Biennale*, in which they performed various scenes that reflect cynically on their art careers in South Africa. One of the photographs in the series, *See Ya Later/Triple AVANT CAR GUARD on the Rocks* (Figure 51), depicts the three members of the collective stranded on a raft made of collapsed cardboard boxes. The central figure reaches towards the horizon, mimicking the uppermost figure in Gericault's pyramidal composition, while the other two are prostrate like the dying figures. A pirate flag flies on top of the mast of the raft, perhaps suggestive of their charlatan status as white South Africans of settler descent. One could see the image as symbolic of the fate of the white Afrikaner in South Africa. Like Wikus, the members of the collective struggle with their lack of relevance in contemporary South Africa; they are the political castaways, abandoned by the old regime – a situation

---

4 See scholars such as Mzwanele Mayekiso (1996), Tom Penfold (2012) and Sally Gaule (2005).
5 For more on this history refer to Marie-Helene Huet (2007: 7–31) and Gary Tinterow (1990–1991: 60–61).
6 The collective is made up of three artists who also practise in their solo capacities: Zander Blom, Jan-Henri Booysens and Michael MacGarry.

WHITE ANXIETY

FIGURE 51   *See Ya Later/Triple AVANT CAR GUARD on the Rocks*. Avant Car Guard, 2007. Photofiba print, 54.6cm × 39.8cm. Whatiftheworld Gallery, Cape Town.
IMAGE COURTESY ZANDER BLOM

suggested by the colloquialism of the title "on the rocks". AVANT CAR GUARD's work brings to mind the lyrics of the song *Antibiotika* (2006) by popular Afrikaans rock band Fokofpolisiekar, released around the same time: "Ek's net 'n toeris in my geboorteland, 'n gekweste dier in 'n hok op antibiotika" (I am a mere tourist in my country of birth, a wounded animal in a cage on antibiotics).

The lyrics echo how Steyn (2001: XXI) describes the situation of political transition for white people in South Africa as one of the most momentous mass psychological adjustments to take place in contemporary society across the world.[7] But there are earlier precedents. Coetzee (1988), writing on landscape

---

7   There are parallels with the German concept of *Vergangenheitsbewältigung*, the notion that during the post-war period the German public could 'work through the past', or indeed 'master the past'. Several public intellectuals in Germany critiqued this project after the Second World War, notably Theodor Adorno, who argued that the notion lacked the depth of engagement and confrontation with culpability that would ensure that the Holocaust would never again be repeated (see Sonja Boos' [2015] book on public speeches engaging with *Vergangenheitsbewältigung*). As with white South Africans, facing or even acknowledging the active or passive culpability in the atrocities committed in Nazi Germany seemed to

conventions in South African history between 1800 and the 1950s, speaks of how a crisis of identity among white settlers found expression in a struggle to conceive of new landscape conventions for capturing the South African landscape in literature and the arts. European landscape conventions such as the picturesque seemed a mismatch with the rugged South African terrain and could not effectively represent it. For Coetzee, this was symbolic of their failure to find belonging in the landscape. He suggests that white South Africans in the nineteenth and early twentieth centuries were "no longer European, not yet African" (Coetzee 1988: 11). Applied to contemporary South Africa, it parallels how Wikus in much of *District 9*, and especially the Third Act sequence, is caught between two notions of self, in a state of incomplete transformation from one identity to another. Achille Mbembe (2012) describes the transitional nature of post-apartheid South Africa:

> South Africa entered a historical interval. It is still caught in this interval, between an intractable present and an irrecoverable past; between things that are no longer and things that are not yet.[8]

Intriguing comparisons can be drawn between Coetzee's discussion of landscape and how historic photographic depictions of the country construct the landscape as white. Jeremy Foster (2003) writes about the SAR&H, South African Railways and Harbours, a government corporation established in 1909 that produced an extensive archive of photographs of the South African landscape. The photographs were used in advertising material and as décor in trains, to market the railways to tourists. A prelude to Pierneef's painted landscapes for the Johannesburg Railway Station, the archive was instrumental in constructing and conveying a sense of the South African landscape to local and international travellers. This landscape was of course intended chiefly for white travellers, since the cost of such travel, combined with legislation such as the Land Act, as well as the later pass laws, limited Black South Africans' movements and access to the railways. Foster (2003) considers the photographic archive of the SAR&H as indicative of the relationship between white settlers and the landscape, reading it as a construction related to their sense of belonging, despite their lack of deep historical links, particularly to the landscape of

---

  be met with reluctance or outright denial (Boos 2015: 195–209). Wikus represents a figure that one might compare with the German public in post-war Germany, reluctantly facing his culpability in the country's past.
8 A longer version of this quote also appears in Akpome's (2018) article on Jacob Dlamini's book *Native Nostalgia*.

the South African hinterland that was only settled from the mid-nineteenth century. He describes this process as an "imaginative identification with the country's physical territory" (Foster 2003: 659).

One of the most central aspects of the landscape's historical portrayals rests on the notion of the empty veld. The word, connoting the unspoilt landscape of grassy plains, seemingly empty of human endeavour, came to be associated with the colonial notion of the empty landscape, which Van Robbroeck (2019) and others discuss. Foster describes this empty veld as part of a then emerging white cosmology. He refers to how the nation was naturalised through an association with the landscape, which was marked as a space upon which the white national imagination could be projected, as has happened with rural landscapes elsewhere too (Foster 2012: 48; Van Robbroeck 2019: 676). In this relationship, the landscape shapes the culture of the people who live in it, albeit through imagined relationships rather than working ones. The artist Pierneef, for example, described the Afrikaner nation as "natuurmense" (people of nature) (Van Robbroeck 2019: 54).

The notion of belonging with reference to the landscape had been in some respects a hard-won project for Afrikaners and white settlers in the country, and the anxiety of losing this claim to belonging plays out in nostalgic dystopian portrayals of landscape as well. One might, for example, read the landscapes depicted in *District 9* and by AVANT CAR GUARD as parodies of landscape tropes in South Africa, such as the sublime and the notion of the empty land. The veld is notably always on the periphery of these landscapes, such as the mining landscape, where plant life is returning to the poisoned soil gradually, in the townships, which straddle the categories of rural and urban, and even in the shipwreck scene that AVANT CAR GUARD act out, with its evocations of colonial exploration and maritime travel.

In another artwork entitled *AVANT CAR GUARD Dive into The South African Art Market* (Figure 52), the collective is shown on a site of ruin or demolition, attempting to dive into a small stagnant pool of water.[9] Posturing in parodic versions of themselves performing obscure activities in inhospitable landscapes around Johannesburg like this one, places them in an incongruous relationship with the sites. The setting is not unlike scenes in *District 9*; it appears to be a formerly developed area that is now an incomprehensible landscape of tumbled rocks and dirt. Remains of houses and piles of rubble lurk in the background, while in the foreground the bodies of the young white men perform

---

9 This performance took place at the Rosebank Mall in Johannesburg, where construction was underway at the time. The collective poured Indian ink into the water to make it look dirtier (Zander Blom, email to author, 15 September 2023).

FIGURE 52 *AVANT CAR GUARD Dive into The South African Art Market*. Avant Car Guard, 2007. Photofiba print, 54.6cm × 39.8cm. Whatiftheworld Gallery, Cape Town.
IMAGE COURTESY ZANDER BLOM

a scene that reminds one of an apartheid-era public swimming pool. The nostalgia evoked in AVANT CAR GUARD's work is clearly ironic. The artists cannot feasibly or realistically yearn for apartheid's political oppression, but at the same time its demise has uprooted them, left them stranded, damaged and tainted.

Steyn suggests that one of the coping strategies of whiteness after the fall of apartheid is to identify with other centres of whiteness, such as the United States, Canada, Europe and Australasia. This form of white identity sees itself as part of a white diaspora, keeping ties with global centres of white power (Steyn 2005:127–128). From such a perspective white people in South Africa might identify with a sense of abandonment by their own kind but might also seem like tourists in their country of birth. Perhaps AVANT CAR GUARD are enacting their own sense of being abandoned in the 'backwater' of the South African art market as well, a place where they plainly do not seem to belong, and which they portray as a wrecked wilderness – a parody of a sublime landscape.

Not surprisingly, the collective included Johannesburg's mining landscape in their series of dystopian settings. In an artwork entitled *Stupid Fuckin' White*

FIGURE 53 Stupid Fuckin' White Man. Avant Car Guard. 2007. Photofiba print, 54.6cm × 39.8cm. Whatiftheworld Gallery, Cape Town.
IMAGE COURTESY ZANDER BLOM

Man (2007), the collective is shown dressed in black outfits with white ruffs that resemble seventeenth-century costumes (Figure 53). They have each also donned a ship made of cardboard and other materials, and the men and their crafts seem to be 'stranded' on a mine dump that doubles as a beach in the context of the sailing ships As in *AVANT CAR GUARD Dive into The South African Art Market* (Figure 52), they are ill-matched with the landscape. The absurdity of their performance is amplified by the confrontational title of the artwork. The figure in the centre, probably Jan-Henri Booysens, sports a moustache that like that in the image of Jan van Riebeeck, one of the first Dutch governors of the Cape, whose face was printed on South African currency during apartheid.[10] The absurd performance is a parody of South African history from the Dutch colonial (Afrikaner) point of view, which construed the country's history as

---

10 There has been some historical dispute about whether the face known as Jan van Riebeeck's was actually the portrait of Bartholomew Vermuyden, a Dutch official who never even came to South Africa. The Rand currency erroneously represented Vermuyden's portrait, according to Hermann Giliomee and Bernard Mbenga (2007: 42–43).

beginning with the arrival of the white settlers with Van Riebeeck in 1652. The European trappings seem nonsensical and farcical, exacerbated by the jarring mismatch with the setting. As well as referencing colonial settlement, the performance on this site evokes the mining industry, its wealth and South African currency, the Rand, named after the mining reef. The once lucrative industry is represented here by the residual mine dump, a reminder of the closure of the mines that left behind only the despoiled landscape. Wikus in his crawling sequence is likewise the epitome of such a tragic-comic legacy enacted in a site of similar exploitation – a township landscape – when he is pitifully reduced to dragging himself through the camp for which he had such disdain at the outset of the film. In this setting he is disowned by his own people and belongs nowhere.

Returning to Coetzee, one can draw another parallel with his interpretation of the landscape tradition in South Africa. Coetzee suggests that, in terms of established landscape genres, the country's landscape could have best lent itself to the sublime tradition, although this was never realised in any substantial manner. Considering how the mining landscape may be conceived of as sublime, and the argument around post-industrial and destructive sublime landscapes in the ruinous character of Johannesburg, the images discussed above also speak to what the sublime landscape means for the white men in them. In Wikus's case, the landscape seems inhospitable, but at the same time it is the place where his transformation occurs and where he can redeem himself by choosing to help the aliens, turning on the humans who have rejected him. In that sense, the landscape is a dormant resource for post-apartheid Johannesburg to transform; this seemingly undesirable landscape has unexpected potential for positive transformation. In addition, the sublime tendencies of the Johannesburg landscape in the nostalgic dystopian idiom could transform how urban ruins themselves are seen. To think of these landscapes in ways other than as failed urban settings requires a radical revision of what urban landscapes mean and how people relate to them. Perhaps the contradictory attraction of sublimity can facilitate such a radical revision.

That said, one could also argue that the sublime tradition allows whiteness to reinvent a sense of belonging in the Johannesburg landscape, transforming itself in relation to the landscape rather than transforming the landscape. German Romanticism has been linked historically to Afrikaner nationalist artistic endeavours, as in Pierneef's work (Van Robbroeck 2019: 50–54). The sublime in landscape painting is marked in German Romanticism, especially in the work of Caspar David Friedrich. Van Robbroeck (2019: 50–54) suggests that German idealism featured in nationalist discourse and art, and in ideas brought to South Africa by Afrikaans-speaking intellectuals and artists who had spent time in Europe. In this view, Afrikaners who saw their identity and their nationhood as bound up with the land understood this bond as a spiritual, and indeed Protestant (or Calvinist), claim to belonging (Van Robbroeck 2019: 52). Instead of subverting apartheid agendas, therefore, the notion of Johannesburg as sublime landscape may turn out to reinforce Afrikaner notions of affinity with the land. In terms of how the nostalgic dystopian idiom interacts with notions of whiteness, I would argue that the anxiety experienced in connection with dystopian places in Johannesburg still seems dominant. But it is important to recognise the complexity of distinct layers in the interaction between landscape and identity.

•••

The last three chapters have engaged with 'the what' of Johannesburg in *District 9* and other representations – how the materiality of the landscape itself contributes to nostalgic dystopia. Urban ruination in *District 9* points toward the sublime qualities that Johannesburg takes on when it appears in the guise of nostalgic dystopia. These sublime qualities in turn point to the contradictions in nostalgic dystopia as reflecting a dynamic of attraction and repulsion. When interrogated through analyses of post-industrial sublime landscapes, the possibility of transformation emerges prominently as part of nostalgic dystopia's vocabulary. In the case of post-industrial landscapes in Johannesburg, this could translate into critical potential.

When seeking to understand how the landscape informs these nostalgic dystopian depictions of Johannesburg, the mining landscape emerges as an iconic dystopian setting. The history of mining in the area is characterised by the sullied socio-economic and physically toxic legacy of this industry, its radioactive waste, acid mine drainage and airborne pollution. For people living near these sites, this presents a very real health risk. In depictions, however, these sites often appear incongruously sublime, although this does not mean they offer a Kantian transcendence. In depictions such as those by Larkin and Jansson, the landscape transforms in a manner that rearticulates the human connection to nature. In relation to post-industrial sublime landscapes, humankind is not triumphant in the face of nature's power, in the way it was thought to be in relation to earlier sublime landscapes. Instead, humankind needs to articulate its relationship with landscape and nature anew, as humans are once more at the mercy of nature's power. This is a re-framed sublimity, which does not place humanity in a position of superiority with regard to the landscape.

Toxic landscapes such as those around Johannesburg are unsafe to inhabit, no longer viable for industry or agricultural output: they are useless landscapes from an economic perspective. Yet I have argued that such landscapes can have a different kind of value. In endeavouring to understand this, the materiality of these landscapes emerges as crucial. Although they resemble hills or outcrops, mine waste areas are fundamentally topsy-turvy, revealing what was previously below ground. There is nothing 'natural' about them. As products of the ecotechnological, they are dystopian, uncanny, and materially disturbing. However, considering them as formless, defying form rather than reflecting the absence of form, may allow one to think of them as sublime in a new sense. They do not offer the triumph the Kantian sublime would, but they may offer something beyond the "solace of good forms": they are landscapes with aesthetic *potential* in their very formlessness. The affinity of the formless with entropy, one of the fundamental forces of physics, demands a new way of thinking about landscape, one that points to new sorts of contact humankind could have with nature in the Anthropocene.

Mine waste areas may be iconic in Johannesburg, but they are not the only ruins or the only ones to be represented in new ways. The formal characteristics of urban ruin in the inner city and the township are equally prevalent in representations, and they likewise carry social meaning. In *District 9*, rubble and structural decay pervade the camp, which speaks of the decay of apartheid and colonial planning regimes. Devolution into organic disorder is evident in photographs of buildings in the inner city, such as Ponte City. The abhorrent state of these buildings and their material decay into base matter, renders them part of a seemingly dystopian sublime landscape, formless rather than romantic. This type of landscape depiction denies the viewer resolution and may be profoundly disconcerting in its "abject allure". The effect is concomitant with the anxiety that these landscapes embody, which appears as racialised, for these are the spaces affected by the white flight of the 1980s, 1990s and even 2000s. While often thought of as abhorrent, these images may, however, also contain the germ of critical potential; their occupation and regeneration can be read as a signal of resilience and resistance against the apartheid regime's oppressive planning agendas and the ongoing geopolitical inequality of its aftermath.

The mining industry and the ideologies of the apartheid regime are represented as part of a collapsing past in *District 9*, where the landscape itself is the setting for, and indeed the gambit in, white anxiety, but also the setting for Wikus' redemption for his transgressions against the aliens and his ultimate transformation. White anxiety is understood here as the white fear of the collapse of its hegemony, a fear which has allegorically come to pass for Wikus. His anxiety is also linked to a fear of transforming into the other he abhors. In act three of the film, Wikus is caught in a discomfiting state of incomplete transformation. The Johannesburg landscape in the nostalgic dystopian idiom echoes this limbo state, characterised by incomplete transformation that fosters experiences of non-belonging for its citizens. This unrealised state of being is mirrored in the landscape of the camp, in effect the township in contemporary Johannesburg, which shows little geopolitical transformation since apartheid ended. Instead, like the township in *District 9*, it is a space of decay, still perpetuating the social and spatial inequalities of colonial township planning and the apartheid era.

Conclusion: The *District 9* Cache

The project I undertook at the outset of this book, to excavate *District 9*'s Johannesburg from the sediment of recent history, has revealed some compelling things about this city as nostalgic dystopia. Although I have shown the nostalgic dystopian idiom *District 9* engages to have a much wider orbit, I asked what it is that is so special about *District 9*'s Johannesburg. Why does this hardcore depiction of Johannesburg linger in the popular imagination? One thing has become abundantly clear: the film has made more of a mark than many have given it credit for. At the outset, I suggested that it might be considered a Rosetta stone, a key to understanding depictions of the city that are contemporaneous with it. *District 9*'s idiosyncratic portrayal of the city of gold has rippled outward, impacting many other portrayals and crystallising in a visual shorthand that, in retrospect, seems a new *Johannesburg idiom*. This is Johannesburg during the 'Zuma years' – when Jacob Zuma was elected leader of the ANC in 2007, and became president of South Africa two years later – a snapshot of a time where the city congeals as a nostalgic dystopia.

Apart from *District 9*, depictions that paint the city as dystopian, yet nostalgic, include the films discussed in this book: *Gangster's Paradise: Jerusalema*, *The Battle for Johannesburg* and *Berea*, along with the work of photographers, such as Goldblatt, Tshabangu, Mofokeng, and Subotzky and Waterhouse, as well as fashion bloggers and popular depictions in music videos, such as those of Die Antwoord and Skrillex. The idiom, a shared visual vocabulary identifiable and distinct in its formal features, appears spontaneously, perhaps unconsciously, in the work of all these practitioners.

The obvious qualities of the shared idiom relate to some important points of contention that I identified when I embarked on this expedition. To begin with, it depicts the city as dystopian, as a city haunted by poverty, violence and urban decay, and trapped in the past. Although it captures some of the realities of contemporary Johannesburg, such a view can be reductive and could contribute to a place-image of the city shaped by depictions of gratuitous poverty porn or ruin porn. In addition, the vocabulary is nostalgic. A recurring preoccupation with the past romanticises the city's history. And this is deeply problematic, given the history of the city and of the country, drenched in atrocities of the apartheid era. The questionable nature of these modes of representation raised the question of why *District 9*'s depiction is so influential, and why so many practitioners elect to depict the city so incongruously. And a further question arose: how can depictions of the city be dystopian and nostalgic at the same time?

To probe these questions, I considered whether the very contradiction at work in the idiom – its simultaneously nostalgic and dystopian elements – could be at the core of its prominence in the history of depictions of the city. I was particularly aware of the representation of the city as far more than a passive background to the narrative; it was a proactive *landscape*, an aspect that has been neglected in discussions of the film, and which pointed me in the direction of landscape traditions. The idea shaped my thinking in the different parts of this book, where I sought to plumb *District 9*'s compelling view of Johannesburg.

In the first part of the book, I drilled down into the bedrock of Johannesburg's appearance in *District 9* and recent popular media. Three concepts emerged from this – dystopia, nostalgia and the sublime. Both dystopia and nostalgia have a critical orientation, evident in scholarship on critical dystopias and reflective nostalgia, though less often considered in discussion of *District 9*.[1] However, the third concept is glaring in its omission from academic discourse on the city: the sublime. Johannesburg has rarely been described as a landscape, and almost never as having features of the sublime. In South African landscape representation historically, the sublime does not feature prominently either, a phenomenon Coetzee (1988) explores in his seminal book on landscape in the country.

Two specific inflections of these concepts emerged as worthy of deeper consideration: analogue nostalgia and the post-industrial sublime. Both are important in *District 9* in characterising 'the how'– the media technologies and techniques that shaped *District 9*'s vision of Johannesburg – and 'the what' – the post-industrial landscape of urban ruins that lends itself to becoming a nostalgic dystopia. Analogue nostalgia speaks to the context for nostalgia in *District 9* as part of a larger phenomenon in contemporary (digital) popular media and film, and shapes *District 9*'s analogue aesthetics. Drawing on scholarship on the post-industrial sublime and its ruin aesthetics in turn enabled me to re-frame the notion of the sublime in terms of the particular post-colonial and post-apartheid context of contemporary Johannesburg. In this re-framed sense, the sublime fundamentally resists colonial and modernist notions of what landscapes should look like and unravels the sublime's transcendental function into one that reflects humanity's ultimate demise in the face of its own environmental destruction.

---

1 Scholars that engage with the city, such as Murray (2011), Robinson (2010, 2004), Myambo (2018, 2011) and Mayekiso (1996) have interrogated these qualities in recent years.

Delving into current interpretations of both *District 9* and other Johannesburg representations, it becomes clear that there is a need to focus on the techniques of representing the city in popular depictions, and to think of the city as more than a backdrop in such representations. In general scholars have neglected the formal features of depictions of the city in film, photography and popular media, and *District 9* has also suffered from this treatment. *District 9* provides such a significant portrait of Johannesburg that it can be recognised as a landmark portrayal of the city. In the film the elements of dystopia, nostalgia and the sublime interact in complex ways, contributing to an understanding of *District 9* itself, and enabling one to interpret several contemporary portrayals as not only reflecting similar techniques, but as forming part of a body of representations that retrospectively cohere in a visual-stylistic sense.

In the book's second part, I used a media archaeological approach to reflect on the dominant techniques in *District 9*'s rendering of Johannesburg as nostalgic dystopia. These techniques evoke analogue nostalgia by emulating analogue effects despite using digital media. They are also informed by generic conventions underpinning the film: mockumentary and science fiction. Comparable techniques appear in several other films and amateur fashion photographers' work, although they construct analogue nostalgia to very different effect. The consistent use of an analogue vocabulary in these portrayals of Johannesburg affords an important insight: that the nostalgic dystopian idiom exemplified by *District 9* is evident across the work of practitioners from diverse socio-cultural backgrounds who were active during the period under discussion. This does not mean that factors such as race have no impact on how the city is depicted: different practitioners use the vocabulary to different ends. Rather, it suggests that the nostalgic dystopian idiom encompasses these diverse strands within its overall fabric, and that it cannot be reduced to a singular view of the city. *District 9* is but one permutation of nostalgic dystopia; not all depictions share its focus on white anxiety, for example. Furthermore, the techniques practitioners use to depict Johannesburg within the idiom may be put to subversive uses, as with the fashion photographers who visually rewrite the past through "subversive resistance" to suit their own narrative (Farber 2015).

There are several further implications for deepening our understanding of *District 9*'s techniques and aesthetics. *District 9*'s complex use of mockumentary elements affects how nostalgic dystopia is depicted in the film. Several aspects of the film reflect the generic features of mockumentary: using digital footage to create a "low-resolution realism" (Lucas 2014:143–146); evoking 1980s newsreel footage through analogue nostalgia; using mock interviews that include apparently incidental landscapes; employing existing settings

CONCLUSION

that often introduce landmark buildings; and referencing the militarised character of the city's architecture. These strategies add to our sense of how the landscape is constructed, which is all the more poignant as the landscape is so integral to the transformation of the protagonist Wikus. Part of the transformative potential in how *District 9* portrays the city is that Johannesburg appears 'as if in documentary'. This is true for the film's idiom as a larger phenomenon as well, in that its critical potential is inextricably tied up with its apparent documentary qualities. In fact, the idiom of nostalgic dystopia depends on these documentary qualities to function in the way it does. The irony inherent in the mockumentary genre softens the documentary grit of the harsh depiction of the city in *District 9*, allowing the viewer to indulge in a more nostalgic view of its embattled past. It is furthermore especially by means of remediation, inasmuch as analogue media evokes a media nostalgia, that viewers are at liberty to indulge in a nostalgia that is not overtly directed towards the apartheid era itself.

In conjunction with the mockumentary genre, the film's formal features draw heavily on science fiction. While mockumentary plays a large role in the film's portrayal of the city because it parodies documentary renditions so closely, science fiction is equally significant in how it affects the film's nostalgic tone. To begin with, it is a genre known for its temporal acrobatics, especially in retrofuturist depictions of the future. This is evident in *District 9*'s two temporal settings, which are in the past and in the future, 1982 and 2010. The film is retrofuturist in that it represents how the 1980s would have imagined futuristic technology like spaceships; in addition, it nostalgically draws on retrofuturist films from the 1980s. These films, especially those in the new bad future subgenre, share several motifs with *District 9*, not least of which is a recurring dystopian setting. The film is thus nostalgic on multiple levels, on a generic level, evoking 1980s science fiction cinema, as well as on the level of representing Johannesburg as it would have looked in newsreels and documentary media in the 1980s. Director Blomkamp dovetails these forms of nostalgia in a manner that foregrounds its role in this depiction of the city: he maps the nostalgic depiction of Johannesburg in *District 9* onto the science fiction genre's nostalgic conventions with the effect of accentuating the nostalgic qualities of the idiom itself. Ultimately, this merging of nostalgia rooted in 1980s science fiction films reinforces the analogue nostalgia of the film, creating yet a further layering of nostalgia.

In Part 3 of the book, the focus shifted from the impact of media technologies and techniques to the Johannesburg landscape itself. Theories of the sublime provided a lens for examining the landscape more closely as one significantly marked by post-industrial ruins.

The mining landscape, which features prominently in the opening sequence of *District 9*, is also iconic in other representations of Johannesburg. Even in terms of traditional theories of the sublime, these mining vistas can be viewed as sublime landscapes. However, questioning the implication of mining landscapes as sublime is important because it helps articulate how we may understand the sublime's work in *District 9*, and within the idiom of nostalgic dystopia. Here, the sublime is not premised on transcending the forces of nature in the way the Kantian mathematical sublime was theorised. Instead, humankind is dwarfed by the havoc they themselves have wreaked on nature; we are forced to rearticulate our relationship to this new, formless and abject eco-technological nature. In other words, the mining landscapes of Johannesburg as they appear in representations are not merely sublime; they represent a rearticulation, indeed a re-framing of the sublime's implications for humanity's relationship to landscape, in this case Johannesburg. Here humans are not triumphant over nature but recede into a secondary role in relation to the landscape.

Another aspect of the sublime that emerges as important is that, when applied to post-industrial spaces and urban ruins, it could be understood as representing the disruption of modernist urban planning agendas, in particular apartheid planning agendas. Thus, although the landscapes appear abhorrent in the township of Chiawelo in *District 9*, urban slums like San Jose in *Gangster's Paradise: Jerusalema*, or Ponte City captured by Mikhael Subotzky and Patrick Waterhouse, the extreme deterioration in such depictions also indicates a latent generative potential insofar as they radically disrupt apartheid structures in the city.

The critical potential of the depiction of the city in *District 9* is inevitably also entangled in the notion of white anxiety. Wikus is the epitome of this affective condition associated with post-apartheid South Africa. The fear of losing white hegemony is realised in Wikus as he flees from the white suburbs, where he resides at the beginning of the film, to find involuntary shelter in the township, the camp where the aliens live. *District 9*'s plot pivots around Wikus's process of transformation into the other, and his incomplete transformation is mirrored in the landscape throughout the film. The township, and indeed the city of Johannesburg, is depicted as a place of unfulfilled transformation – a quality embedded in the idiom of nostalgia dystopia itself. The geopolitics of colonial and apartheid urban planning are neither resolved nor transformed in the contemporary city itself. Johannesburg is fundamentally in need of transformation. The idiom of nostalgic dystopia captures the uneasy moment in which the city is trapped – a moment when the much-yearned-for transformation has yet to come to fruition. *District 9* is an important index of

CONCLUSION

this state of limbo in post-apartheid history, which is bound up with white anxiety in the film.

Consolidating the insights gained here, I can draw several concluding points. First, *District 9* is a landmark film. This film provides such a clear portrait of Johannesburg that it should be given its due place in prevailing discussions of the city. The film portrays Johannesburg in a manner both iconic and very particular to a period in the city's post-apartheid history. And digging a little below the surface reveals that *District 9* is not an isolated portrayal of Johannesburg as a dystopian, backwards-looking, and painfully contradictory landscape. An entire stratum of visual history has *District 9*'s Johannesburg at its core, including cinema, documentary photography and popular media. Films that are *District 9*'s contemporaries, *Gangster's Paradise: Jerusalema*, *The Battle for Johannesburg*, and *Berea*, likewise reflect Johannesburg in what may now be understood to be a shared idiom for the city: nostalgic dystopia.

My second concluding point is that the formal features of *District 9* and its nostalgic dystopian idiom draw heavily on the appearance of analogue media, particularly analogue photography and film. In digital media, the appearance of analogue media is evoked by using older-generation digital cameras, filters and visual effects to emulate flaws, noise, scratches and particular distortions and colour palettes associated with analogue film stock. Developing processes of analogue filmmaking and photography are similarly emulated, such as the bleach bypass process. These techniques give *District 9* a distinct visual texture: a washed-out colour palette dominated by browns, oranges and dusty blues; an emphasis on noise and other imperfections such as colour distortions; and a look of decay further emphasised by focusing on languishing landmark buildings that represent the era when such analogue media (and apartheid) was at its peak in the 1980s. In short, the film is steeped in analogue nostalgia. In counterpoint to this, the film *Gangster's Paradise: Jerusalema* uses actual analogue cameras to evoke this nostalgia. And there are photographers representative of the idiom, such as Goldblatt and Subotzky and Waterhouse, who also work with analogue cameras, even though they may convert their photographs to digital prints. Significantly, the nostalgic dystopian idiom emerges in the decade of transition from analogue to digital cameras and related technologies, where there is much interaction between these two media paradigms.[2] *District 9* is therefore a remarkable index of changes in the media ecology of the time.

---

2 See Kristen Whissel (2007: 2–4).

Third, *District 9* and the nostalgic dystopian idiom have a strong affinity for, and in fact a reliance upon, documentary practices. The film is concerned largely with conveying a sense of the realities of the city, its geographic character, and how people inhabit it. Its affinity with documentary also lends it a particular appearance, thanks partly to its dependence on recording devices such as cameras that capture the city as it appears, and the (questionable) authenticity still associated with these media (Mitchell 1992: 23–57). Aspects of documentary fidelity include the light conditions peculiar to the city, which Blomkamp exploited so successfully by shooting *District 9* in winter. He captured the distinct light and colour of the season, affected by the smog from open fires used for cooking and heating in the townships that pervades the city's atmosphere. *District 9* often portrays the more challenging parts of the city, exposing the underbelly of the city of gold, where poverty, decay, violence and environmental pollution are prevalent.

A key insight, however, is that the documentary quality of *District 9* and the broader idiom can counteract a devolution into gratuitous poverty porn rather than reinforce it. The film acquires a critical potential that is strongly informed by the mockumentary conventions at work in *District 9*, which draws heavily on the documentary genre and analogue nostalgia, endowing the film with its constructed authenticity. This critical promise, which remains potential rather than fulfilled, warrants further investigation to interrogate problematic aspects in the subversive practices that have come to light here.

Fourth, in line with the focus on documentary qualities, *District 9* is also characterised by capturing the ruins of the past as they linger in the city. The decay evident in portrayals like *District 9* is so prominent that ruins are essentially a motif in the nostalgic dystopian vocabulary. The motif relates specifically to remnants of the recent past, ruins of the mining industry, and ruins of urban planning as they appear in inner-city and township slums. In fact, decaying townships feature to the point of almost being its own distinct motif. John Matshikiza (2004: 491), the famous playwright who returned from exile in 1991, describes the townships as hovels built by the government, trapping people "shoulder to shoulder", and Mzwanele Mayekiso's (1996) and Johannes Rantete's (1984) accounts of the periods of unrest in the 1980s affirm the hardship, violence and danger associated with township life from insider perspectives. There is a remarkable focus on Johannesburg *as a township* in the broader idiom, as if over the years the township has become a *pars pro toto* for

CONCLUSION

the city as such. The "township metropolis"[3] quality is deeply characteristic of the idiom's portrayal of Johannesburg.

The prevalence of ruins and ruination also indicates a preoccupation with unresolved spaces in *District 9* and the idiom. Typical of post-industrial ruins is that they are in a state of ongoing decay, which is evident in many of the depictions covered in the book. The unresolved quality is also evident in the nature of the spaces themselves, often peri-urban, between stages of development, between urban zones and, most importantly, in a state of untransformed limbo after the end of the apartheid era. This unrealised transformation, a seemingly pending transformation, tinges the idiom of nostalgic dystopia itself and makes it all the more compelling.

Ultimately the city's unresolved, untransformed, contradictory character allows the idiom to disclose new possibilities, for it to have the potential to subvert the geopolitical structures that still govern the city *through representation*, even if on a small and quotidian scale, and to create the "freedom to" engage with its challenges (Lees 2004: 23). However, I need to be emphatic: such potential is *not* a "get out of jail free card" for *District 9* and its broader idiom. The critical potential, which has already been broached in some appraisals of nostalgic depictions of Johannesburg's past,[4] beckons further development. This capacity nonetheless goes some way towards explaining why *District 9*'s nostalgic dystopian idiom has been taken up by such diverse practitioners – professionals and amateurs; Black practitioners and white practitioners; those who lived in the city during the apartheid era and those living in it in the aftermath. Nostalgic dystopia marks a moment of pending transformation in Johannesburg as "ever-changing" city (Matshikiza 2004: 482), a moment of potential, if not a guarantee. And, irrespective of how it unfolds, it is a moment that will long captivate both practitioners working in Johannesburg, and viewers of *District 9*.

3 This description belongs to Fanuel Motsepe (in Nuttall & Mbembe 2004: 197).
4 See Megan Jones' (2014) article on Jacob Dlamini's use of nostalgia in his book *Native Nostalgia*.

Afterword

Looking Back on *District 9* – An Interview with Neill Blomkamp

In April 2020, I interviewed director Neill Blomkamp via email to discuss *District 9*. Our conversation centred on techniques, technologies and pertinent motifs in the film, as well as Johannesburg's importance to the film and its making. In what follows, I present a transcription of the conversation, with some light editing, and look back on some of the interview's pertinent points in the light of my subsequent research. My reflections on some of our exchanges follow them in italics.[1]

LR: What is the relationship between Alive in Joburg and District 9? Did you work with a concept artist for either of the films, or did the short film serve as the concept for District 9? How did you conceive of the technologies in the film, such as the mechanical armour that Wikus dons or the spaceship itself?

NB: I worked with many concept artists on *District 9*, but none on *Alive in Joburg*. At the time I had no idea I was making something that would serve as a template for a larger film. I just wanted to make what I considered a piece of artwork. It had no label 'short film' in my head. I actually often do this – if you look at something like RAKKA from Oats Studios, it is very similar. There is no traditional beginning, middle and end: it's rather a presentation of a place and a world. The real story came out in *District 9*, and I hope it would be the same if I make a film version of RAKKA.

So much of writing and directing is subconscious, it's hard to answer sometimes. The relationship between humans and technology, and the idea of transformation or augmentation of the human hold huge fascination for me, so the mechanical suit represents a desire to play with that idea. The same goes for Wikus changing into an alien.

LR: I am interested in how you conceptualised *District 9* to have a nostalgic analogue look. It is often described as 'washed-out'. From reading interviews with you and cinematographer Trent Opaloch, it seems your initial idea was based on newsreel footage from the 1980s. Why did you decide to conceptualise an essentially futuristic film in this way?

---

[1] Although I have edited the interview for ease of reading this does not alter the substance of Blomkamp's answers or views.

AFTERWORD

NB: I guess nostalgia is there, but it's a smaller part of the equation. For me, as a viewer, my favourite thing is to be transported to a place or a world that doesn't exist, and the more 'real' the presentation of that place, the more heightened my interest is in it. So the goal for me was absolute realism, and a trick is being played on the audience, which is that usually VFX and CGI are so expensive you would never waste them – but if you use them in a way that seems banal, it seems more real. Because you are not putting the special FX on a pedestal and [you are] entrusting the audience to *look*, it makes it all feel more real. This could mean that science fiction motifs are embedded in places they would not normally be found (such as 1980s SABC footage).

> *The way Blomkamp describes his use of visual effects echoes what scholars such as Lucas (2014) suggest when they write about how they are used in cinema, especially around the end of the first decade of the 2000s when cinema moved into the digital realm. At the time, and increasingly since then, visual effects were used to create a greater sense of 'realism' in cinema, rather than to create something fantastical or overtly otherworldly. The tension between the fictional qualities of such a 'world', as Blomkamp calls it, and its aspects of realism seems to play out in the documentary qualities of* District 9's *Johannesburg, which always seems very realistic. The city looks so much the way it does in documentary photography that even the aliens do not seem glaringly (science-)fictional. Intriguingly, Blomkamp seems less taken with the idea of nostalgia, which in my view is a very prominent quality of the film. He seems to consider the nostalgia in* District 9 *as an indication of the portrayal being 'real', and I have argued that nostalgia does in fact lend some authenticity to depictions, or at least seeks to simulate an authenticity or historicity, which becomes an important constituent of the nostalgic dystopian idiom. Although the visual effects are not flaunted in* District 9, *media effects are, often resulting in a strongly nostalgic quality as 1980s media forms are evoked.*

LR: The 1980s, a period marked by several States of Emergency in the country, is known (apart from newsreels) for a lot of documentary photography which often captured unrest in the townships. Are there any photographers whose work is important to you, or are there images from the time that stand out in your mind?

NB: For me it was the experience of living it as a child. I was born in '79, so in the real flashpoint years of 1987–1994 I was 7 to 14 years old. I remember the feeling of that time, and the level of militarisation of everything really affected me. Seeing tan Casspirs on the highway going into Soweto or having bomb defusal blankets in malls are just some examples. Every suburban household was awash with guns. Terrorist drills in school were commonplace. Watching the separation and also mixing of white and Black under these circumstances left an impression on me. [The families of] every white kid in the northern suburbs had Black domestic workers, and in my case I soaked up a ton of information from them, along with their point of view. I would say [that my view of that time in South Africa] was 99.99% influenced by real life. In fact, it wasn't until I moved to Canada, by the time I was 18 or 19, that I realised that I was in fact obsessed with South Africa and Johannesburg and its history. This interest accelerated, and I would travel back often and begin venturing into townships like Alexandra and Soweto and Khayelitsha.

LR: Media scholars are speculating on a "nostalgia boom" in popular culture, and part of this is what scholars have termed "analogue nostalgia". Do you think that *District 9* may have influenced filmmakers and photographers in South Africa to look at Johannesburg through analogue nostalgia?

NB: I agree with them about a nostalgia boom – it's also a boom specifically for my generation of filmmakers. You will begin to see more films set in the 90s rather than the 80s, that kind of thing. But like above, I do think *District 9* is less nostalgia and more hyper-realism. When I think of *District 9*'s influence, I don't think of it so much stylistically as conceptually – meaning, when I wanted to be a film director, having just moved to Canada, it felt like no South African would ever consider a commercial Hollywood film [set] in South Africa. Instead, it was a process of emulating or aspiring to American film and filmmakers; the biggest stamp of approval would be to shoot in Los Angeles or New York, and set a film there. To me, the one thing *District 9* did was open up the ability to say, "I want to shoot a blockbuster – where I grew up". I would be tagged on Twitter a lot with up-and-coming filmmakers all over the world, making their version of *Alive in Joburg* – in Jakarta, or Lagos, or Ho Chi Minh city. It validated places that didn't "make the cut" before.

> *Blomkamp's reference to his own childhood reinforced my conviction that nostalgia about the past was an important underpinning in* District 9*'s construction of Johannesburg, even if he thinks of it in a slightly different way. However, his impulse to set a Hollywood-scale film in Johannesburg is also revealing, because it shows his motivation as something beyond the urge to revisit South Africa's past. Speaking as a director, he points to the often*

> *pragmatic or hidden factors and circumstances that contribute to making films. Setting the film in South Africa was, at least in part, more a matter of challenging generic conventions and customs and less about telling a story of the country's past than one might expect. In some ways this speaks of his desire to claim his South African identity and to find ways in which cinema from the global South can engage the canon of Hollywood films. To him, it was important to represent Johannesburg from his own point of view, not least because of his childhood in the country, which gave him first-hand 'real' experience of apartheid's segregation and urban politics.*

LR: The late 2000s are known as a period of transition from analogue to digital filmmaking processes. Peter Jackson, who produced *District 9*, is often described as an early adopter of digital technologies. What are your own views on this transition?

NB: Yes, digital is a million times better, pretty much on all levels. It does make life way easier, and it gives you far, far more options. Peter Jackson is a prolific adopter of all things digital and, when I began making *District 9*, he had a really good relationship with RED cinema. He actually bought many RED cameras; I think he was the first person to own them at all.

LR: There seems to be a particular relationship between analogue and digital technologies in the filmmaking process of *District 9*. Even though the film was shot on digital cameras, the Red One and the EX1, it often has an analogue look. Do you often work with evoking older media forms?

NB: I am not sure I totally agree. To me, analogue means 16mm film, or super 8mm. I am really interested in these formats, but *District 9* is more of what I described above. It is the banal, burnt-out, washed-out look that makes it look 'unpolished', rather than analogue. The closest to analogue would be the SABC [South African Broadcasting Corporation] video footage at the start, but the rest is decidedly digital, and we didn't really add much synthetic grain or anything to achieve a film look. We kept it digital and shitty.

> *As a scholar of film rather than a filmmaker myself, I had half expected that Blomkamp would romanticise shooting on film. His response to the contrary was a genuine surprise considering the analogue nostalgia that pervades* District 9. *Thinking of the complex exchanges between digital and analogue media at the time* District 9 *was made, I am reminded of how Minniti (2020) sees this when he writes about the amateur practice of Lomography.*

He argues that digital media brings about analogue nostalgia, and that digital media continue to complicate how analogue media are used and regarded by users. While Blomkamp as an expert sees the two paradigms as quite separate, I cannot but notice their inextricable entanglement. Digital media at the time of nostalgic dystopia, during the first decade of the 2000s, offer new ways to understand the meanings and possibilities of analogue media. Instead of supplanting analogue technologies, they prompt users and viewers to reinvent the uses and associated visual language of analogue media forms.

While a "film look" is not exactly what District 9 *seems to be after, the "shitty" character that Blomkamp regards as essentially digital does seem to complement the fixation on ruins, decay and deterioration that the nostalgic qualities of older media and aged cities evoke in the cases I have unearthed in this book. The hypermediacy in how digital cameras are deployed in* District 9 *to create such a sense of decay is interesting in light of much literature that asserts that digital cameras lack defects. In the digital context, scholars and users often describe images as crisp, clear and of superior quality. They can be easily reproduced without losing quality, and digital cameras are much easier to use than their analogue counterparts: lighter, with a broader range of lighting conditions that they can render, and with seemingly unlimited storage space, along with the immediacy of footage captured. They do seem in every way to improve the process of filmmaking and perhaps even photography. The way Blomkamp uses them to evoke the antithesis of technological advancement is therefore strikingly ironic, much like* District 9 *itself. One might even say he uses them against the grain to evoke a sense of flawed technology.*

LR: Many academics writing on the film describe it as a science fiction film, but the mockumentary genre is also very important to its structure and its cinematography. I would argue that it allows an ironic humour which softens the difficult subject matter, was this the intention?

NB: Yes, 'fake documentary' has always intrigued me. I love the realism of performances, it's like a different kind of acting, and it also heightens the realism of the whole thing to me. You get more of a window into the characters, or at least a slightly different kind, and it feels like they are closer to you, there is no separation. I would not say it softens the subject matter, however. Personally, I always try to get to the worst of the subject matter. I do not shy away from it, so it certainly is not used to dull anything.

> *Mockumentary, like documentary, relates to the difficult and often debated notion of reality. What is the film's relationship to Johannesburg; did you intend to imbue the film with a feeling of the 'actual' city?*

LR: Yes for sure; Johannesburg was almost a character in the movie to me. The feeling of that city is so specific, and for me riddled with so much personal history, that it all had to be in there. I know it's a heightened version of the city; it's not like I was making a real documentary about the city. But that's the amazing thing about cinema and science fiction: you can create for the audience how it feels to you specifically. I can let them view the world through my eyes. I have spent many an hour trying to figure out why I want to be a filmmaker, and the best answer I have is that I want to show people the way I see the world – this is Neill's view.

> *In writing this book, it has been tempting to 'digress' into an excavation of Johannesburg's images, with* District 9 *emerging as one artefact of importance among many in the historical moment of the nostalgic dystopian idiom. However, I realised in the process that the film and the city are almost interchangeable.* District 9, *as quintessential nostalgic dystopia, is Johannesburg, as I suggested at the very outset of the book. The film is so representative of the city in its visual language that it offers all the material needed to better understand Johannesburg in representation in general during this period. As Blomkamp points out, Johannesburg takes its place as one of the characters in* District 9.

LR: *District 9* depicts Johannesburg as a city that seems to me to appear dated, as if it is trapped in the past. Foregrounding the mine dumps early on in the film seems to me to highlight the city's fraught history. Do you think that the city is recognisable by these structures?

NB: Yes, absolutely. The [mine dumps] were etched into my mind from a young age. All parts of Johannesburg link back to this powerful history of conflict, and gold is often at the core of it.
I think those mine dumps also served as a bottleneck into Soweto, creating only one way in and out.

LR: In terms of science fiction, the film seems to reference motifs from 1980s science fiction films, such as *Robocop* and *The Terminator*. Are there 1980s films that are important to you, or perhaps that you grew up watching, and that might relate to *District 9*?

NB: Those films are really important to me, but it feels like *Robocop* is closer to *District 9* than *The Terminator*. The dark satire and dark humour of the film resonates; it's a critique of modern culture. Paul Verhoeven and I share a somewhat similar outlook, I think.

LR: I posit in my research that *District 9* is nostalgic, but also that it is dystopian. Do you think it could be described as visually attractive and challenging at the same time – and what could this invite from viewers?

NB: To me, subjectively, it's hugely visually attractive. It's my favourite kind of imagery (which I guess is why I directed it). It presents the impossible *as everyday*. There is something infinitely more interesting to me about the burnt-out sun-bleached way the alien mothership is presented in *District 9*, than the more typical Hollywood, well-lit, well-balanced, 'perfect' presentation in most other films. I love the style of it, and to me it's absolutely attractive.

> *Irony is clearly very important to Blomkamp's thinking. His personal approach to filmmaking dovetails (much like his use of nostalgia) with the post-apartheid period in South Africa, and the widespread irony, satire and parody that permeate the country's popular media. This is of course particularly prevalent in how the past is revisited, remembered and engaged with in the work of practitioners such as the fashion bloggers discussed in this book, but also in contemporary art of the period such as that by* AVANT CAR GUARD. *The ironic attraction that gritty and decaying spaces and representations offer, and the glamour of ruins or even poverty, seems to fascinate Blomkamp as much as it does audiences. South Africa's ruined past is no exception, and the uncomfortable pleasure received from looking at such ruin is evident in the widespread use of the nostalgic dystopian vocabulary to imagine and capture Johannesburg. The practitioners I have covered were chosen specifically for how they engage with the contradictions implicit in this visual vocabulary. Yet there are countless portrayals of gratuitous poverty and ruin. High-profile photographers who come to mind include Guy Tillim, Roger Ballen and Pieter Hugo: although their work has often been critiqued as exploitative, it deserves to be carefully interrogated before being dismissed out of hand as offering nothing more.*

LR: Some scholars have described the film as a journey that leads to Wikus's redemption. I argue that the landscape of Johannesburg in the film represents elements of transformation that mirror Wikus's own transformation.

Do you think that dystopian landscapes hold a conceptual potential for transformation?

NB: I have never consciously thought of the landscape as also part of the transformation. But there is so much that comes out, from a psychological perspective, when you work on a project day in and day out for three years, and you put everything of yourself into it – there could be so many layers I am not aware of. I would say the entire film is built around the transformation of Wikus. Both ideologically and also physically. This is the reason the film exists.

> *Finally, Blomkamp's comments on the transforming landscape reveal that, while the manner in which* District 9 *portrays the city is echoed by so many other depictions, this vocabulary evolved spontaneously, without a contrived agenda. To my mind this is further testament to the significance of these portrayals.* District 9's *Johannesburg, the city* as District 9 *resonates with the (often unacknowledged) sentiments shared by citizens and practitioners towards the city – that it is a nostalgic dystopia. The city offers views of the past and the future, most of them not pleasant, and yet seductive in ways that may make us forget why they are so objectionable.*

Bibliography

1974 Johannesburg Street Scenes, Skyline, Architecture, 1970s South Africa. 2017. [Online]. Available: https://www.youtube.com/watch?v=OzteAu-8NbU&list=PL_YmYGJCfb0VAynY3u5jvX5_41PIfkAyE&index=17&t=0s&ab_channel=thekinolibrary. Accessed 15 February 2021.

Adorno, T.W. & Horkheimer, M. 1993 [1944]. The Culture Industry: Enlightenment as Mass Deception, in *The Cultural Studies Reader*, edited by S. During. London: Routledge: 31–41.

Agamben, G. 1998. *Homo Sacer: Sovereign Power and Bare Life.* Stanford: Stanford University Press.

AgentNo. [n.d.]. [Online]. Available: https://agentno.wordpress.com/2012/03/14/asphalt-rundown/smithson-asphalt-rundown-rome-italy-1969-2/. Accessed 14 September 2018.

Akpome, A. 2017. "Zones of Indistinction" and Visions of Post-reconciliation South Africa in *District 9. Safundi: The Journal of American and South African Studies* 18(1): 85–97.

Akpome, A. 2018. Memory, Ethics and the Re-temporalisation of South African National History in the Works of Jacob Dlamini. *Current Writing: Text and Reception in Southern Africa* 30(2): 105–115.

Altman, R. 1984. Toward a Theory of the History of Representational Technologies. *Iris* 2(2): 115.

Anno, H. (creator). 1995. *Neon Genesis Evangelion* [Television series]. Tokyo: Gainax.

Anti-Apartheid Protest. [n.d.]. Wikimedia Commons. Available: https://commons.wikimedia.org/w/index.php?curid=26754890. Accessed 6 October 2023.

Antrop, M. 2013. A Brief History of Landscape Research, in *The Routledge Companion to Landscape Studies*, 1st ed, edited by P. Howard, I. Thompson, E. Waterton & M. Atha. London: Routledge: 12–22.

Appiah, K. A. 2020. The Case for Capitalizing the B in Black. *The Atlantic*, 18 June. [Online] Available: https://www.theatlantic.com/ideas/archive/2020/06/time-to-capitalize-blackand-white/613159/. Accessed 20 February 2024.

Arendt, H. (ed). 1973. *Illuminations/Walter Benjamin*, translated by H Zohn. London: Fontana/Collins.

Artnet. [n.d.]. Artists. [Online]. Available: http://www.artnet.com/artists/david-goldblatt/johannesburg-from-the-southwest-ZSdBASgucqhcANAHCF9f2w2. Accessed 12 Oct 2022.

Arya, R. 2014. *Abjection and Representation. An Exploration of Abjection in the Visual Arts, Film and Literature.* Basingstoke: Palgrave Macmillan.

Bagnall, R.G. 1999. *Discovering Radical Contingency: Building a Postmodern Agenda in Adult Education.* (Series: Counterpoints vol. 81). Berlin: Peter Lang.

Barasch, M. 1997. *The Language of Art: Studies in Interpretation.* New York: New York University Press.

Bartholeyns, G. 2014. The Instant Past: Nostalgia and Digital Retro Photography, in *Media and Nostalgia: Yearning for the Past, Present and Future*, edited by K. Niemeyer. Basingstoke: Palgrave Macmillan: 51–67.

BBC News, 2009. Nigeria 'Offended' by Sci-fi Film, 19 August [Online]. Available: http://news.bbc.co.uk/2/hi/8264180.stm. Accessed 31 March 2010.

Beavon, K. 2004. *Johannesburg: The Making and Shaping of a City.* Leiden: Koninklijke Brill.

Belton, J. 2008. Painting by the Numbers: The Digital Intermediate. *Film Quarterly* 61(3): 58–65.

Beningfield, J. 2006. *The Frightened Land: Land, Landscape and Politics in South Africa in the Twentieth Century.* London: Routledge.

Benjamin, W. 1972 [1931]. A Short History of Photography. [Online]. Available: https://monoskop.org/images/7/79/Benjamin_Walter_1931_1972_A_Short_History_of_Photography.pdf. Accessed 30 September 2020.

Benjamin, W. 2002 [1982]. *The Arcades Project*, translated by H. Eiland & L McLaughlin. London: Bellknap Press.

Benjamin, W. 2004 [1936]. The Work of Art in the Age of Mechanical Reproduction, translated by H. Zohn, in *Film Theory and Criticism*, edited by L. Braudy & M. Cohen. Oxford: Oxford University Press: 791–811.

Benjamin, W. 2006. *The Writer of Modern Life: Essays on Charles Baudelaire*, translated by H. Eiland, E. Jephcott, R. Livingstone & H. Zohn, edited by M. W. Jennings. London: Bellknap Press.

Bethlehem, L. 2022. Hydrocolonial Johannesburg, *Interventions* (Special Issue: Reading for Water) 24(3): 340–354.

Beukes, L. 2010. *Zoo City*. Johannesburg: Jacana.

Bila, A. 2014. #AlexandraTownship #Kasi #Joburg. [Online] Available: https://khumbula.files.wordpress.com/2014/07/bila.jpg. Accessed 22 July 2020.

Blomkamp, N. (dir). 2006. *Alive in Joburg*. [Film]. Wellington: Spy Films. Available: https://vimeo.com/1431107. Accessed 24 July 2020.

Blomkamp, N. (dir). 2009. *District 9*. [Film]. Culver City: Tristar Pictures.

Blomkamp, N. (dir). 2013. *Elysium*. [Film]. Culver City: Tristar Pictures.

Blomkamp, N. (film director, Oats Studios). 2020. Electronic interview by author [transcript]. 17 April.

Boetzkes, A. 2010. Waste and the Sublime Landscape. *Canadian Art Review* (Special Issue: Landscape, Cultural Spaces, Ecology) 35(1): 22–31.

Bois, Y.A. & Krauss, R.E. 1997. *Formless: A User's Guide.* New York: Zone Books.

Bolter, J.D. & Grusin, R. 2000. *Remediation: Understanding New Media*. Cambridge, MA: MIT Press.

Boos, S. 2015. *Speaking the Unspeakable in Postwar Germany: Toward a Public Discourse on the Holocaust*. New York: Cornell University Press.

Booyens, I. & Rogerson, C.M. 2019. Re-creating Slum Tourism: Perspectives from South Africa. *Urbani Izziv* (Special Issue: Urban and Spatial Challenges in South Africa: Continuing the Conversation) 30: 52–63.

Bordwell, D. 2008. *Poetics of Cinema*. London: Routledge.

Bouman, A. C. 1955. *Painters of South Africa*. Cape Town: HAUM h/a JH De Bussy.

Boym, S. 2001. *The Future Nostalgia*. New York: Basic Books.

Brady, E. 2012. *The Sublime in Modern Philosophy: Aesthetics, Ethics and Nature*. Cambridge: Cambridge University Press.

Bremner, L. 2010. *Writing the City into Being. Essays on Johannesburg 1998–2008*. Johannesburg: Fourthwall Books.

Brodie, N. (ed). 2008. *The Joburg Book: A Guide to the City's History, People & Places*. Johannesburg: Pan Macmillan.

Bronner, S.E. 2011. *Critical Theory: A Very Short Introduction*. Oxford: Oxford University Press.

Brott, S. 2013. Dead or Alive in Joburg, in *Architecture Post Mortem: The Diastolic Architecture of Decline, Dystopia and Death*, edited by D.D. Bertolini, S.D. Brott & D.P. Kunze. Ashgate: Farnham: 31–43.

Brook, I. 2012. Aesthetic Appreciation of Landscape, in *The Routledge Companion to Landscape Studies*, 1st ed, edited by P. Howard, I. Thompson, E. Waterton & M. Atha. London: Routledge: 108–118.

Bruzzi, S. 2015. Observational ("Fly-on-the-Wall") Documentary, in *The Television Genre Book*, 3rd ed, edited by G. Creeber. Basingstoke: Palgrave Macmillan: 150–151.

Bryson, N. 1993. House of Wax, in *Cindy Sherman 1975–1993*, edited by R. Krauss. New York: Rizzoli: 216–223.

Bunn, D. 2008. Art Johannesburg and its Objects, in *Johannesburg: The Elusive Metropolis*, edited by A. Mbembe & S. Nuttall. Durham, NC: Duke University Press: 137–169.

Burgin, V. 1991. Geometry and Abjection, in *Psychoanalysis & Cultural Theory: Thresholds*, edited by J. Donald. New York: St Martins: 11–26.

Burke, E. 1996 [1757]. *A Philosophical Enquiry into the Origin of our Ideas of the Sublime and Beautiful*, edited by A. Ashfield & B. De Bolla. Cambridge: Cambridge University Press: 131–143.

Caccia, A. 2016. Moses Tladi (1906–1959): South Africa's First Black Landscape Painter? *de arte*, 28(48): 3–22. DOI: 10.1080/00043389.1993.11761164.

Cameron, J. (dir). 1984. *The Terminator*. [Film]. Los Angeles: Orion Pictures.

Cameron, J. (dir). 1986. *Aliens.* [Film]. Los Angeles: Twentieth Century Fox Film Corporation.

Caoduro, E. 2014. Photo Filter Apps: Understanding Analogue Nostalgia in the New Media Ecology. *Networking Knowledge* 7(2): 67–82.

Carroll, J. 2008. The Limits of the Sublime, the Sublime of Limits: Hermeneutics as a Critique of the Postmodern Sublime. *The Journal of Aesthetics and Art Criticism* 66(2): 171–181.

Chipkin, C. 1993. *Johannesburg Style: Architecture & Society 1880s-1960s.* Johannesburg: Thorold's Africana books.

Chong, W.L. 1995. Alienation in the Modern Metropolis: The Visual Idiom of Taiwanese Director Tsai Ming-liang. *China Information* 9(4): 81–95. DOI: 10.1177/0920203X9500900408.

Claeys, G. 2013. Three Variants on the Concept of Dystopia, in *Dystopia(n) Matters: On the Page, on Screen, on Stage,* edited by F. Vieira. Newcastle upon Tyne: Cambridge Scholars Publisher: 14–18.

Clarke, J. 2017. Elegies to Cinematography: The Digital Workflow, Digital Naturalism and Recent Best Cinematography Oscars, in *Collaborative Production in the Creative Industries,* edited by J. Graham & A. Gandini. London: University of Westminster Press: 105–123.

Clay, P. & Griffiths G. 1982. *Hillbrow.* Cape Town: National Book Printers.

Clute, J., Langford, D., Nicholls, P. & Sleight, G. (eds). [n.d.]. Religion. *Encyclopedia of Science Fiction.* [Online]. Available: http://www.sf-encyclopedia.com/entry/religion. Accessed 14 September 2018.

Clute, J., Langford, D., Nicholls, P. & Sleight, G. (eds). [n.d.]. Spaceships. *Encyclopedia of Science Fiction.* [Online]. Available: http://www.sf-encyclopedia.com/entry/spaceships. Accessed 14 September 2018.

Coen, E. & Coen, J. 2000. *O Brother, Where Art Thou?* [Film]. Burbank: Touchstone Pictures.

Coetsee, Y. 2013. Transvaal Romantic: An Exploration of Romantic Elements in the Landscape Paintings of Moses Tladi. *South African Journal of Art History* 28(3): 1–11.

Coetzee, H., Horstmann, U., Ntsume, G. & Croukamp, L. 2003. The Potential Environmental Impact of the Decant of Water from Witwatersrand. *8th International Congress on Mine Water & the Environment, Johannesburg, South Africa.* [Online]. Available: https://www.imwa.info/docs/imwa_2003/imwa_2003_201-217.pdf. Accessed 14 September 2018.

Coetzee, J.M. 1988. *White Writing: On the Culture of Letters in South Africa.* New Haven: Yale University Press.

Coetzee, N.J. 1992. *Pierneef, Land and Landscape: The Johannesburg Station Panels in Context.* Johannesburg: CBM Publishing.

Coetzee, J.M. 1999. *Disgrace.* London: Secker & Warburg.

Connolly, J. & Evans, K. 2014. Cracking Ray Tubes: Reanimating Analog Video in a Digital Context. *Leonardo Music Journal* 24: 53–56.
Coogler, R. (dir). 2018. *Black Panther*. [Film]. Burbank: Marvel Studios.
Cook, P. 2005. *Screening the Past: Memory and Nostalgia in Cinema*. London: Routledge.
Coppola, F.F. (dir). 1979. *Apocalypse Now*. [Film]. San Francisco: American Zoetrope.
Corner, J. 2015. Form and Content in Documentary Study, in *The Television Genre Book*, 3rd ed, edited by G. Creeber. Basingstoke: Palgrave Macmillan: 147–148.
Cramer, F. 2014. What is 'Post-Digital'? *APRJA* 3(1): 10–24.
Cramer, F. & Jandrić, P. 2021. Postdigital: A Term That Sucks but Is Useful. *Postdigital Science and Education* 3: 966–989.
Crowther, P. 1996. *Critical Aesthetics and Postmodernism*. Oxford: Oxford University Press.
Crowther, P. 2009. *Phenomenology of the Visual Arts (Even the Frame)*. Palo Alto, CA: Stanford University Press.
Cukrowska, E.M., Yalala, B.M., Tutu, H. & Chimuka, L. 2017. Spatial Distribution and Source Identification of Mercury in Dust Affected by Fold Mining in Johannesburg, South Africa. *Proceedings of the International Conference of Recent Trends in Environmental Science and Engineering* (RTESE'17), Toronto, Canada, 23–25 August 2017: 104.1–104.8.
Cullinan. [n.d.]. South African History Online [Online]. Available: https://www.sahistory.org.za/place/cullinan. Accessed 27 September 2024.
Davis, M. 2006. *Planet of Slums*. London: Verso.
De Bolla, P. 1989. *The Discourse of the Sublime: Readings in History, Aesthetics, and the Subject*. New York: Oxford University Press.
De Satgé, R. & Watson, V. 2018. *Urban Planning in the Global South: Conflicting Rationalities in Contested Urban Space*. Cham: Palgrave Macmillan.
De Satgé, R., Cartwright, K., Kingwill, R. & Royston, L. 2017. The Role of Land Tenure and Governance in Reproducing and Transforming Spatial Inequality. [Online]. Available: https://www.parliament.gov.za/storage/app/media/Pages/2017/october/High_Level_Panel/Commissioned_Report_land/Commissioned_Report_on_Spatial_Inequality.pdf. Accessed 29 January 2019.
Decommissioning Projects – South Africa. 2021. [Online]. Available: https://www.wise-uranium.org/udza.html. Accessed 5 October 2022.
Deleuze, G. 1983. *Cinema 1: The Movement Image*, translated by H. Tomlinson & B. Habberjam. Paris: Les Éditions de Minuit.
Deleuze, G. 1985. *Cinema 2: The Time Image*, translated by H. Tomlinson & R. Galeta. Paris: Les Éditions de Minuit.
DeLong, M., Heinemann, B. & Reiley, K. 2005. 'Hooked on Vintage!'. *Fashion Theory* 9(1): 23–42.

Desai, R. (dir). 2010. *The Battle for Johannesburg*. [Film]. Johannesburg: Uhuru Productions.

DeSilvey, C. & Edensor, T. 2012. Reckoning with Ruins. *Progress in Human Geography* 37(4): 465–485.

Dhlomo, H.I.E. 1985. *H.I.E. Dhlomo: Collected Works*, edited by T. Couzens and N. Visser. Johannesburg: Ravan Press.

"*District 9*" goes huge. 2009. *Mail & Guardian*, 2 August. [Online]. Available: https://mg.co.za/article/2009-08-22-district-9-goes-huge/. Accessed 12 February 2021.

Dlamini, J. 2009. *Native Nostalgia*. Johannesburg: Jacana.

Dlamini, J. 2014. *Askari: A Story of Collaboration and Betrayal in the Anti-apartheid Struggle*. Johannesburg: Jacana.

Dlamini, P.V. 2019. Nostalgia in Reimagining the Past: The Subjectivity of Memory in the Representation of History. A Textual Analysis of Rehad Desai's Documentary Films. PhD thesis, University of Johannesburg, Johannesburg.

Domestic top 250. 2010. *Variety*, 11–17 January, 417(8): 12–13.

Dondolo, L.M. 2018. Apartheid Spatial Plan. Heritagisation and Museumification of the Past at Vilakazi Street in Soweto, in *Reversing Urban Inequalities in Johannesburg*, edited by M. T. Myambo. London: Routledge: 95–108.

Doss, E. 2010. *Memorial Mania. Public Feeling in America*. Chicago, IL: University of Chicago Press.

Douglas, M. 2002. *Purity and Danger: An Analysis of Concepts of Pollution and Taboo*. London: Routledge.

Douglas, T. 2018. The Final Frame: An Interview with David Goldblatt. [Online]. Available: https://www.mca.com.au/stories-and-ideas/final-frame-interview-david-goldblatt/. Accessed 13 February 2021.

Dovey, K. & King, R. 2011. Forms of Informality: Morphology and Visibility of Informal Settlements. *Built Environment* 37(1): 11–29.

Duffer, M. & Duffer, R. 2016. *Stranger Things*. [Television series]. Netflix.

Dumas, M. J. 2016. Against the Dark: Antiblackness in Education Policy and Discourse. *Theory Into Practice* 55(1): 11–19. DOI: 10.1080/00405841.2016.1116852.

Edensor, T. 2005. *Industrial Ruins: Space, Aesthetics, Materiality*. Oxford: Berg.

Eliashberg, J., Elberse, A. & Leenders, M.A.A.M. 2006. The Motion Picture Industry: Critical Issues in Practice, Current Research, and New Research Directions. *Marketing Science* 25(6): 638–661.

Elkins, J. 2005. *Art History Versus Aesthetics*. London: Routledge.

Elkins, J. 2011. Against the Sublime. [Online]. Available: https://www.scribd.com/document/54086153/Against-the-Sublime. Accessed 23 June 2020.

Elkins, J. 2012. An Introduction to the Visual as Argument, in *Theorizing Visual Studies: Writing Through the Discipline*, edited by J. Elkins, K. McGuire M. Burns, A. Chester & J. Kuennen. London: Routledge.

Elkins, J. 2013. *Beyond the Aesthetic and the Anti-aesthetic*. Pennsylvania: Penn State University Press.

Elkins, J. 2015. First Introduction: Starting Points, in *Farewell to Visual Studies*, edited by G. Frank, S. Manghani & J. Elkins. Pennsylvania: Penn State University Press.

Ellapen, J.A. 2009. The Cinematic Township: Cinematic Representations of the "Township Space" and Who Can Claim the Right to Representation in Post-apartheid South Africa. *Journal of African Cultural Studies* 19(1): 113–137.

Elsaesser, T. 2016. *Film History as Media Archaeology: Tracking Digital Cinema*. Amsterdam: Amsterdam University Press.

Enwezor, O. 2013. Rise and Fall of Apartheid, in *Rise and Fall of Apartheid*, edited by O. Enwezor and R. Bester. Munich: Prestel: 20–45.

Everything You Need to Know About Government Housing. 2017. GROUNDUP. [Online]. Available: https://www.groundup.org.za/article/everything-you-need-know-about-government-housing/. Accessed 14 September 2018.

Falkof, N. & Van Staden, C. (eds). 2020. *Anxious Joburg: The Inner Lives of a Global South City*. Johannesburg: Wits University Press.

Farber, L. 2010. *Representation & Spatial Practices in Urban South Africa*. Johannesburg: Research Centre, Visual Identities in Art and Design, Faculty of Art Design and Architecture, University of Johannesburg.

Farber, L. 2015. Hypersampling Black Masculinities, Jozi Style. *Image & Text* 26: 111–136.

Foster, J. 2003. "Land of Contrasts" or "Home We Have Always Known"? The SAR&H and the Imaginary Geography of White South African Nationhood, 1910–1930. *Journal of Southern African Studies* 29(3): 657–680.

Foster, J. 2012. The Wilds and the Township: Articulating Modernity, Capital, and Socio-nature in the Cityscape of Pre-apartheid Johannesburg. *Journal of the Society of Architectural Historians* 71(1): 42–59.

Foucault, M. & Gordon, C. (ed). 1980. *Power/Knowledge: Selected Interviews and Other Writings 1972–1977*. New York: Pantheon Books.

Francaviglia, R.V. 1997. *Hard Places: Reading the Landscape of America's Historic Mining Districts*. Iowa City: University of Iowa Press.

Frassinelli, P.P. 2015. Heading South: Theory, '*Viva Riva!*' and '*District 9*'. *Critical Arts* 29(3): 293–309.

Frassinelli, P.P. 2022. Documentary Film as Political Communication in Post-apartheid South Africa, in *Decolonising Political Communication in Africa: Reframing Ontologies*, edited by B. Karam & B. Mutsvairo. London: Routledge: 64–78.

Freschi, F. 2019. From Volksargitektuur to Boere Brazil: Afrikaner Nationalism and the Architectural Imaginary of Modernity, 1936–1966, in *Troubling Images: Visual Culture and the Politics of Afrikaner Nationalism*, edited by F. Freschi, B. Schmahmann & L. van Robbroeck. Johannesburg: Wits University Press: 66–91.

Friedman, S. 2021. *Prisoners of the Past*. Johannesburg: Wits University Press.

Gabay, C. 2018. *Imagining Africa. Whiteness and the Western Gaze*. Cambridge: Cambridge University Press.

Gabriel, I. 2013. *Four Corners*. [Film]. Johannesburg: Indigenous films.

Garman, A. 2014. Troubling White Englishness in South Africa: A Self-interrogation of Privilege, Complicity, Citizenship and Belonging. In *Unveiling Whiteness in the Twenty-first Century: Global Manifestations, Transdisciplinary Interventions*, edited by V. Watson, D. Howard-Wagner & L. Spanierman. New York: Lexington Books: 211–228.

Gaudreault, A. & Marion, P. 2015. *The End of Cinema? A Medium in Crisis in the Digital Age*. New York: Columbia University Press.

Gaule, S. 2005. Alternating Currents of Power: From Colonial to Post-apartheid Spatial Patterns in Newtown, Johannesburg. *Urban Studies* 42(13): 2335–2361.

Gaylard, G. (ed.) 2011. *Marginal Spaces: Reading Ivan Vladislavić*. Johannesburg: Wits University Press.

Gerber, J. 2021. Elections 2021: "Stop the Decay" – FF Plus at Manifesto Launch, 9 October. *News 24*. [Online]. Available: https://www.news24.com/news24/southafrica/news/elections-2021-stop-the-decay-ff-plus-at-manifesto-launch-20211009. Accessed 7 September 2022.

Gevisser, M. 2014. *Lost and Found in Johannesburg*. Johannesburg: Jonathan Ball Publishers.

Gikandi, S. 2001. Race and the Idea of the Aesthetic. *Michigan Quarterly Review* 11(2). [Online]. Available: https://quod.lib.umich.edu/cgi/t/text/text-idx?cc=mqr;c=mqr;c=mqrarchive;idno=act2080.0040.208;g=mqrg;rgn=main;view=text;xc=1. Accessed 20 November 2017.

Giles, J.M. 2012. Of Gods and Dogs: The Post-colonial Sublime in Coetzee's Disgrace, or, David Lurie's Aesthetic Education, in *The Sublime Today: Contemporary Readings in the Aesthetic*, edited by G.B. Pierce. Newcastle upon Tyne: Cambridge Scholars Publishing: 13–48.

Giliomee, H. & Mbenga, B. 2007. *New History of South Africa*. Cape Town: Tafelberg.

Ginsberg, R. 2004. *The Aesthetics of Ruins*. Amsterdam: Rodopi.

Glass, F. 1989. The "New Bad Future": *Robocop* and 1980s' Sci-fi Films. *Science as Culture* 1(5): 7–49.

Gobodo-Madikizela, P. 2012. Remembering the Past: Nostalgia, Traumatic Memory, and the Legacy of Apartheid. *Peace and Conflict: Journal of Peace Psychology* 18(3): 252–267.

Godby, M. 2014. Thinking South African Photography. *Safundi: The Journal of American and South African Studies* 15(2–3): 149–154. DOI: 10.1080/17533171.2014.925646.

Godfrey, I. [n.d.]. Legacy of the Mine. [Online]. Available: https://www.lensculture.com/ilangodfrey?modal=project-431480. Accessed 8 September 2020.

Goldblatt, D. 2006. *David Goldblatt Photographs*. Rome: Contrasto.

Gordimer, N. 1958. *A World of Strangers*. Harmondsworth: Penguin.

Gorman, S. 2009. Alien Action Film "*District 9*" Tops Box Office. *Reuters.* 17 August 2009. [Online]. Available: https://www.reuters.com/article/us-boxoffice/alien-action-film-district-9-tops-box-office-idUSTRE57D06Y20090817. Accessed 19 October 2018.

Gumede, V. 2015. *Political Economy of Post-apartheid South Africa*. [Ebook]. Oxford: African Books Collective. Project MUSE.

Hallet, G. & Mckenzie, P. (eds). 2007. *District Six Revisited*. Johannesburg: Wits University Press.

Hansen, M. 1987. Benjamin, Cinema and Experience: "The Blue Flower in the Land of Technology". *New German Critique* 40: 179–224.

Hansen, M. 2008. Benjamin's Aura. *Critical Inquiry* 34(2): 336–375.

Hansen, M. 2015. *Feed-forward: On the Future of Twenty-first-century Media*. Chicago: University of Chicago Press.

Harries, P. 1997. Under Alpine Eyes: Constructing Landscape and Society in Late Pre-colonial South-East Africa. *Paiduema: Mitteilungen zur Kulturkunde* 43: 171–191.

Harrison, P. & Harrison, K. 2014. Soweto: A Study in Socio-spatial Differentiation, in *Changing Space, Changing City: Johannesburg After Apartheid,* edited by P. Harrison, G. Gotz, A. Todes & C. Wray. Johannesburg: Wits University Press.

Harrison, P. & Zack, T. 2012. The Power of Mining: The Fall of Gold and the Rise of Johannesburg. *Journal of Contemporary African Studies* 30(4): 551–570.

Helgesson, S. 2010. The Global South as Science Fiction ("*District 9*": A Roundtable). *Safundi: The Journal of South African and American Studies* 11(1–2): 155–175.

Hight, C. 2008. Mockumentary. A Call to Play, in *Rethinking Documentary: New Perspectives and Practices,* edited by A. Thomas & W. de Jong. New York: McGraw-Hill Education: 204–216.

Hoad, P. 2009. *District 9*: Where Aliens Come to Earth and Handheld Comes of Age. *The Guardian.* 26 August 2009. [Online]. Available: https://www.theguardian.com/film/filmblog/2009/aug/26/district-9-handheld. Accessed 19 October 2018.

Hogan, P.C. 2016. *Beauty and Sublimity: A Cognitive Aesthetics of Literature and the Arts*. Cambridge: Cambridge University Press.

Holben, J. 2009. Aliens in South Africa. *American Cinematographer* 90(9): 26–31.

Hood, G. (dir). 2005. *Tsotsi*. [Film]. Johannesburg: Industrial Development Corporation of SA.

Hook, D. 2012. Screened History: Nostalgia as Defensive Formation. *Peace and Conflict: Journal of Peace Psychology* 18(3): 225–239.

Hook, D. 2014. *(Post)apartheid Conditions: Psychoanalysis and Social Formation*. Cape Town: HSRC Press.

Huchzermeyer, M. 2011. *Cities with Slums: From Informal Settlement Eradication to a Right to the City in Africa*. Claremont: Juta Academic.

Huchzermeyer, M. 2014. Troubling Continuities: Use and Utility of the Term "Slum", in *The Routledge Handbook on Cities of the Global South*, edited by S. Parnell & S. Oldfield. London: Routledge: 86–97.

Huchzermeyer, M., Karam, A. & Maina, M. 2014. Informal Settlements, in *Changing Space, Changing City: Johannesburg After Apartheid*, edited by P. Harrison, G. Gotz, A. Todes, & C. Wray. Johannesburg: Wits University Press: 154–175.

Huet, M. 2007. The Face of Disaster. *Yale French Studies* (Special Issue: Myth and Modernity) 111: 7–31.

Huhtamo, E. & Parikka, J. 2011. *Media Archaeology. Approaches Applications and Implications*. Oakland: University of California Press.

Human rights watch. World Report 2009. Events of 2008. [Online]. Available: https://www.hrw.org/sites/default/files/reports/wr2009_web.pdf. Accessed 11 February 2021.

Huyssen, A. 2006. Nostalgia for Ruins. *Grey Room* 23: 6–21.

I See A Different You. 2016. Johannesburg//Home. Instagram. [Online]. Available: https://www.instagram.com/p/BFipWD5QeXx/?taken-by=iseeadifferentyou. Accessed 14 September 2018.

I See A Different You. 2016. Power Park//Soweto. Instagram. [Online]. Available: https://www.instagram.com/p/BFgT39DweQH/?taken-by=iseeadifferentyou. Accessed 14 September 2018.

Isenberg, N. & Benjamin, W. 2001. The Work of Walter Benjamin in the Age of Information. *New German Critique* (Special Issue: Walter Benjamin) 83: 119–150.

J.M. Coetzee – Biographical. NobelPrize.org. Nobel media AB 2003. Thu. 5 Nov 2020. [Online]. Available: https://www.nobelprize.org/prizes/literature/2003/coetzee/biographical/. Accessed 6 November 2020.

Jameson, F. 1984. Postmodernism, or the Cultural Logic of Late Capitalism. *New Left Review* 146: 53–94.

Jansen van Veuren, M. 2012. Tooth and Nail: Anxious Bodies in Neill Blomkamp's *District 9*. *Critical Arts* 26(4): 570–586.

Jansson, E. 2015. *An Acid River Runs Through It*. San Francisco: Blurb Incorporated.

Jay, M. & Leavell, V. 2017. Material Conditions of Detroit's Great Rebellion. *Social Justice* 44(4): 27–54.

Jethro, D. 2009. "Waar Val Jy Uit?" District Six, Sacred Space, and Identity in Cape Town. *Journal for the Study of Religion* 22(1): 17–41.

Joburg Heritage Walking Tour - Art Deco Johannesburg. [n.d.]. Johannesburg In Your Pocket. [Online]. Available: https://www.inyourpocket.com/johannesburg/joburg-heritage-tour-art-deco-johannesburg_5161e. Accessed 27 September 2024.

Joburg's Rissik Street Post Office Revamp. 2016. Brand South Africa. 22 April. [Online]. Available: https://www.brandsouthafrica.com/people-culture/history-heritage/rissik-street-post-office-220416. Accessed 13 February 2021.

Jones, M. 2014. Fracture and Selfhood in Jacob Dlamini's "Native nostalgia". *African Studies* 73(1): 107–123.
Josephy, S. 2017. Acropolis Now: "Ponte City" as "Portrait of a City". *Thesis Eleven* 141(1): 67–85.
Judin, H. 2021. *Falling Monuments, Reluctant Ruins: The Persistence of the Past in the Architecture of Apartheid.* Johannesburg: Wits University Press.
Kant, I. 2001 [1790]. The Critique of Judgement, in *Continental Aesthetics, Romanticism to Postmodernism: An Anthology,* edited by R. Kearney & D. Rasmussen. Malden, MA: Blackwell: 5–42.
Kant, I. 2007 [1790]. *The Critique of Judgement*, translated by J. C. Meredith, edited by N. Walker. Oxford: Oxford University Press.
Kapinos, T. 2007–2014. *Californication.* [Television series] Beverly Hills: Aggressive Mediocrity.
Kapstein, H. 2014. The Hysterics of *"District 9". English Studies in Canada* 40(1): 155–175.
Kind, J. 1964. Sphinx of the Plains: A Chicago Visual Idiom. *New Chicago Writing and Art* 2(3): 38–55.
King, G. & Krzywinska, T. 2006. *Science Fiction Cinema: From Outerspace to Cyberspace.* London: Wallflower.
Kinnear, K. 2010. The Aesthetics of Science Fiction Spaceship Design. Masters dissertation, University of Ontario, Ontario.
Kirkwood, M.L.E. 2019. Land as Natural Resource: Representations of Mining in Contemporary South African Landscape Photography. *Photography and Culture* 12(4): 429–452.
Klein, K. 2021. Post-digital, Post-internet: Propositions for Art Education in the Context of Digital Cultures, in *Post-Digital, Post-Internet Art and Education: The Future is All-Over*, edited by K. Tavin, G. Kolb & J. Tervo. Cham: Palgrave Macmillan: 27–44.
Krauss, R.E. 1999. Reinventing the Medium. *Critical Inquiry* 25(2): 289–305.
Kruger, L. 2006. Filming the Edgy City: Cinematic Narrative and Urban Form in Postapartheid Johannesburg. *Research in African Literatures* 37(2): 141–163.
Kruger, L. 2013. Imagining the Edgy City: Writing, Performing and Building Johannesburg. [Ebook]. Oxford Scholarship Online. DOI: 10.1093/acprof:oso/9780199321902.001.0001.
Koolhaas. R. 2002. Junkspace. *October* 100: 175–190.
Kovel, J. (cinematographer). 2022. Electronic Interview by Author [transcript]. 18 July.
Kynoch, G. 2013. Fear and Alienation: Narratives of Crime and Race in Post-apartheid South Africa. *Canadian Journal of African Studies* 47(3): 427–441.
Larkin, J. 2013. After the Mines/Tales from the City of Gold. [Online]. Available: http://jasonlarkin.co.uk/work/tales-from-the-city-of-gold-3/#PHOTO_29. Accessed 14 September 2018.

Läuferts, M. & Mavunganidze, J. 2009. Ruins of the Past: Industrial Heritage in Johannesburg. *WIT Transactions on the Built Environment* 109: 533–542.

Lavery, C. & Gough, R. 2015. Introduction. *Performance Research. A Journal of the Performing Arts* 20(3): 1–8.

Law-Viljoen, B. 2010. "Bang-Bang Has Been Good to Us": Photography and Violence in South Africa. *Theory, Culture & Society* 27(7–8): 214–238. DOI: 10.1177/0263276410383711.

Le Roux, H. 2019. Designing KwaThema: Cultural Inscriptions in the Model Township. *Journal of Southern African Studies* 45(2): 273–301.

Leeb Du-Toit, J. 2010. Land and Landlessness: Revisiting the South African Landscape, in *Visual Century. South African Art in Context*, volume 1, edited by J. Carman. Johannesburg: Wits University Press.

Lees, L. 2004. "The Emancipatory City": Urban (Re) visions, in *The Emancipatory City? Paradoxes and Possibilities*, edited by L. Lees. London: SAGE: 13–26.

Lefebvre, H. 1974. La Production de L'espace. *L'Homme et la Société* 31–32: 15–32.

Lefebvre, H. 1991. *The Production of Space*, translated by D. Nicholson-Smith. Oxford: Basil Blackwell.

Lehman, D. 2011. "When We Remembered Zion": The Oscar, the Tsotsi, and the Contender. *English in Africa* 38(3): 113–129.

Lewis, M. & Zack, T. 2015. *Good Riddance*. Johannesburg: Fourthwall Books.

Li, A. 2013. Tudor Shaft: As Dangerous as Chernobyl? *Mail & Guardian*, 18 July 2013. [Online]. Available: https://mg.co.za/multimedia/2013-06-18-tudor-shaft-as-dangerous-as-chernobyl. Accessed 14 September 2018.

Liefferink, M. [n.d.]. Rehabilitation of Mine Contaminated Eco-systems: A Contribution to a Just Transition to a Low Carbon Economy to Combat Unemployment and Climate Change. Just Transition for All. [Online]. Available: https://justtransitionforall.com/reports/southafrica/page/5/. Accessed 27 September 2024.

Lockheed F-117 Nighthawk Low-observable / Stealth Strike Aircraft. 2019. [Online]. Available: https://www.militaryfactory.com/aircraft/detail.asp?aircraft_id=38. Accessed 1 April 2020.

Louw, L. 2021. Documentary Film Politics and the Politics of Documentary Film: Miners Shot Down (2014). *Communicare* 40(1): 49–66.

Lowenthal, D. 2015. *The Past is a Foreign Country – Revisited*. Cambridge: Cambridge University Press.

Lucas, C. 2014. The Modern Entertainment Marketplace, 2000–Present, in *Cinematography (Behind the Silver Screen)*, edited by P. Keating. New Brunswick: Rutgers University Press: 132–157.

Lütge Coullie. J. 2014. The Ethics of Nostalgia in Post-apartheid South Africa. *Rethinking History* 18(2): 195–210.

Lyons, S. (ed). 2018. *Ruin Porn and the Obsession with Decay*. London: Palgrave Macmillan.

Lyotard, J. 1990. After the Sublime: The State of Aesthetics, in *The States of "Theory": History, Art, and Critical Discourse*, edited by D. Carrol. New York: Columbia University Press: 297–304.

Lyotard, J. 1984 a. The Sublime and the Avant-garde. *Art Forum* 22(8): 36–43.

Lyotard, J. 1984 b. *The Postmodern Condition: A Report on Knowledge*, translated by Geoff Bennington & Brian Massumi. Manchester: Manchester University Press.

Maceck, C. (prod). 1985. *Robotech*. [Television series]. Los Angeles: Harmony Gold USA.

Magome, M. 2022. New Attacks Against Illegal Miners after South Africa Rapes. *AP News*, 5 August. [Online]. Available: https://apnews.com/article/africa-johannesb urg-south-government-and-politics-37dab356aedc7e1697af65afe2926d7b. Accessed 27 September 2024.

Makama, R., Helman, R., Titi, N. & Day, S. 2019. The Danger of a Single Feminist Narrative: African-centred Decolonial Feminism for Black men. *Agenda* 33(3): 61–69. DOI: 10.1080/10130950.2019.1667736.

Malpas, S. 2002. Sublime Ascesis: Lyotard, Art and the Event. *Journal of the Theoretical Humanities* 7(1): 199–212.

Manathunga, C. 2018. Decolonising the Curriculum: Southern Interrogations of Time, Place and Knowledge. *SOTL in the South* 2(1): 95–111.

Mandaza, I. 1997. *Race, Colour and Class in Southern Africa*. Harare: Sapes Books.

Mann, M. (dir). 1995. *Heat*. [Film]. Burbank: Warner Brothers Pictures.

Manovich, L. 1995. What is Digital Cinema? [Online]. Available: http://manovich.net /index.php/projects/tag:1995. Accessed 24 February 2021.

Manovich, L. 2005. *The Language of New Media*. Cambridge, MA: MIT Press.

Manovich, L. 2017. Aesthetics, "Formalism", and Media Studies, in *Keywords in Media Studies*, edited by L. Ouellette & J. Gray. New York: NYU Press: sp.

Maré, E.A. & Coetzee, N.J. (2016). Altered Landscapes: A Comparison Between Works by J. H. Pierneef and John Clarke. *Filozofski Vestnik* 22(2). Available: https://ojs.zrc -sazu.si/filozofski-vestnik/article/view/3608. Accessed 9 April 2024.

Martin, D. 2014. Introduction: Towards a Political Understanding of New Ruins. *International Journal of Urban and Regional Research* 38(3): 1037–1046. DOI: 10.1111/ 1468-2427.12116.

Marx, G. & Marx, M. 2007. Rewind (Extract). [YouTube]. Available: https://www.yout ube.com/watch?v=GaUorqyY2Ys&list=PL_YmYGJCfboUOxjqBLtNrIrzGmt5cB kdE&index=7&ab_channel=PhilipMiller. Accessed 6 September 2022.

Marx, L. 2010. "Technology": The Emergence of a Hazardous Concept. *Technology and Culture* 51(3): 561–577.

Maseko, Z. (dir). 1997. *The Foreigner*. [Film]. MNET/Mac-D-TV/National Film and Video Foundation.

Maseko, Z. (dir). 2002. *A Drink in the Passage*. [Film]. La Sept Arte/Channel Four/Primedia.

Maskit, J. 2007. "Line of Wreckage": Towards a Postindustrial Environmental Aesthetics. *Ethics, Place and Environment* 10(3): 323–337. DOI: 10.1080/13668790701586309.

Masweneng, K. 2022. Seven Suspects in the Krugersdorp Mine Dump Attack Charged with Rape. *Sunday Times Live*, 10 August. [Online]. Available: https://www.timeslive.co.za/news/south-africa/2022-08-10-seven-suspects-in-the-krugersdorp-mine-dump-attack-charged-with-rape/. Accessed 2 September 2022.

Mateer, J. 2014. Digital Cinematography: Evolution of Craft or Revolution in Production? *Journal of Film and Video* 66(2): 3–14.

Matshikiza, J. 2004. Instant City. *Public Culture* 16(3): 481–497.

May, A. 2018. *Rockets and Ray Guns: The Sci-fi Science of the Cold War*. Cham: Springer International Publishing AG.

Mayekiso, M. 1996. *Township Politics: Civic Struggles for a New South Africa*. New York: Monthly Review Press.

Mbembe, A. 2012. Rule of Property Versus the Rule of the Poor? *Mail & Guardian*, 15 June. Available at http://mg.co.za/article/2012-06-15-rule-of-property-versus-rule-of-the-poor. Accessed 3 September 2022.

Merrett, C. 1990. In a State of Emergency: Libraries and Government Control in South Africa. *The Library Quarterly* 60(1): 1–22.

Metz, C. 1977. *Psychoanalysis and Cinema. The Imaginary Signifier*, translated by C. Britton, A. Williams, B. Brewster & A. Guzzetti. London: The Macmillan Press.

Mhlongo, E.S. & Amponsah-Dacosta, F. 2016. A Review of Problems and Solutions of Abandoned Mines in South Africa. *International Journal of Mining, Reclamation and Environment* 30: 279–294.

Mhlongo, N. 2007. *After Tears*. Athens, OH\: Ohio University Press.

Mhlongo, N. 2010. Zwakal'eMsawawa, in *Soweto*, edited by J. Beiber. Johannesburg: Jacana: 11–15.

Mhlongo, N. 2018. *Soweto, Under the Apricot Tree*. Cape Town: Kwela books.

Mijs, J.J.B. 2014. In Pictures: Detroit's Wealth of Ruins. *Contexts* 13(2): 62–69.

Mikhael Subotzky Archive. [n.d.]. [Online]. Available: http://www.subotzkystudio.com/ponte-city/ponte-city-160-207/. Accessed 14 September 2018.

Milaras, M., Ahmed, F. & McKay, T.J.M. 2014. Mine Closure in South Africa: A Survey of Current Professional Thinking and Practice, in *The Book of Proceedings of the 9th International Conference on Mine Closure: Mine Closure 2014*, edited by I.M. Weiersbye, A.B. Fourie, M. Tibbett & K. Mercer. University of the Witwatersrand: Johannesburg: 1–13.

Mills, G. 1989. Space and Power in South Africa: The Township as a Mechanism of Control. *Ekistics* (Special Issue: Space Syntax: Social Implications of Urban Layouts) 56(334/335): 65–74.

Milner, A. 2004. Darker Cities. Urban Dystopia and Science Fiction Cinema. *International Journal of Cultural Studies* 7(3): 259–279.

Minniti, S. 2020. "Buy Film not Megapixels": The Role of Analogue Cameras in the Rematerialization of Photography and the Configuration of Resistant Amateurism, in *The Camera as Actor: Photography and the Embodiment of Technology*, edited by A. Cox Hall. London: Routledge: 78–102. DOI: 10.4324/9781003086932.

Mitchell, W.J. 1992. *The Reconfigured Eye. Visual Truth in the Post-photographic Era*. Cambridge, MA: MIT Press.

Mob Attacks Illegal Miners After Rapes Shock South Africa. 2022. Aljazeera, 4 August. [Online]. Available: https://www.aljazeera.com/news/2022/8/4/mob-attacks-illegal-miners-after-rapes-shock-south-africa. Accessed 2 September 2022.

Moloi, V. (dir). 2013. *Berea*. [Film]. Johannesburg: Gauteng Film Commission.

Moloi, V. (dir). 2017. *Tjovitjo*. [Television series]. Johannesburg: Puo Pha.

Mooifontein 225-Iq. 2018. Google Maps. [Online]. Available: https://www.google.com/maps/place/Mooifontein+225-Iq,+Johannesburg,+2093,+South+Africa/@-26.2189794,27.9549351,3763m/data=!3m2!1e3!4b1!4m5!3m4!1s0x1e950a283828cb53:0x17f5e66c7da578af!8m2!3d-26.2183506!4d27.9629752. Accessed 14 September 2018.

Morris, A. 1999. *Bleakness & Light: Inner-city Transition in Hillbrow, Johannesburg*. Johannesburg: Wits University Press.

Moser, W. 2002. The Acculturation of Waste, in *Waste-site Stories: The Recycling of Memory*, edited by B. Neville & J. Villeneuve. Albany: State University of New York Press: 85–105.

Moses, M.V. 2010. The Strange Ride of Wikus van de Merwe. *Safundi: The Journal of American and South African Studies* 11(1–2): 156–161.

Moyer-Duncan, C. 2015. Review: Miners Shot Down by Rehad Desai. *African Studies Review* 58(1): 281–283.

Moylan, T. 2000. *Scraps of the Untainted Sky: Science Fiction, Utopia, Dystopia*. London: Routledge.

Mpe, P. 2001. *Welcome to Our Hillbrow*. Athens, AL: Ohio University Press.

Msimang, S. 2013. When Will Crime Stop Being a White Thing? *Daily Maverick*, 6 March. [Online]. Available: https://www.dailymaverick.co.za/opinionista/2013-03-06-when-will-crime-stop-being-a-white-thing/. Accessed: 1 September 2022.

Mukherjee, R. 2017. Anticipating Ruinations: Ecologies of 'Make Do' and 'Left With'. *Journal of Visual Culture* 16(3): 287–309.

Mulvey, L. 1975. Visual Pleasure and Narrative Cinema. *Screen* 16(3): 6–18. DOI: 10.1093/screen/16.3.6.

Munakamwe, J. 2017. Zamazama – Livelihood Strategies, Mobilisation and Resistance in Johannesburg, South Africa, in *Mining Africa: Law, Environment, Society and Politics in Historical and Multidisciplinary Perspectives*, edited by A. Nhemachena & V. Warikandwa. Oxford: African Books Collective: 155–186.

Murray, M.J. 2008. *Taming the Disorderly City: The Spatial Landscape of Johannesburg after Apartheid*. Cape Town: Juta and Company.

Murray, M.J. 2011. *Politics, History, and Culture: City of Extremes: The Spatial Politics of Johannesburg*. Durham, NC: Duke University Press.

Murray, P. 1971. *Piranesi and the Grandeur of Rome*. London: Thames and Hudson.

Mututa, A.S. 2020. Customising Post-apartheid Johannesburg: The Dialectic of Errancy in Ralph Ziman's 'Jerusalema'. *Safundi: The Journal of American and South African Studies* 21(2): 206–223.

Myambo, M.T. (ed). 2018. *Reversing Urban Inequality in Johannesburg*. London: Routledge.

Myambo, M.T. 2011. Capitalism Disguised as Democracy: A Theory of "Belonging", Not Belongings, in the New South Africa. *Comparative Literature* 63(1): 64–85.

Myrick, D. & Sánchez, E. 1999. *The Blair Witch Project*. [Film]. Orlando: Haxan Films.

Naidoo, L. 2016. Contemporary Student Politics in South Africa: The Rise of Black-led Movements of #RhodesMustFall and #FeesMustFall in 2015, in *Students Must Rise: Youth Struggle in South Africa Before and Beyond Soweto '76*, edited by A. Heffernan & N. Nieftagodien. Johannesburg: Wits University Press: 180–190.

Natives Land Act. 2013. South African History Online. [Online]. Available: https://www.sahistory.org.za/topic/natives-land-act-1913. Accessed 19 March 2019.

Ndebele, N.S. 1983. *Fools and Other Stories*. Johannesburg: Ravan Press.

Ndebele, N.S. 2010. Foreword. Sol T. Plaatjie and "The Power of All", in *Sol Plaatjie's Native Life in South Africa*, edited by J. Remmington, B.W. Peterson, B.M. Sabatampho, S. Maake, & P. Limb. Johannesburg: Wits University Press: IX–XIV.

Neale, S. 2003. Hollywood Blockbusters. Historical Dimensions, in *Movie Blockbusters*, edited by J. Stringer. London: Routledge: 47–60.

Neale, T. (dir). 2014. *Ragga Bomb*. [Music video]. Johannesburg: Egg Films.

Nearpass Ogden, K. 1990. Sublime Vistas and Scenic Backdrops: Nineteenth-century Painters and Photographers at Yosemite. *California History* 69(2): 134–153.

Neille, D. 2020. Gauteng Demolitions: Red Ants in All-out War on the Poor. *Daily Maverick* 22 April. [Online]. Available: https://www.dailymaverick.co.za/article/2020-04-22-gauteng-demolitions-red-ants-in-all-out-war-on-the-poor/. Accessed: 1 September 2022.

Nel, A. 2012. The Repugnant Appeal of the Abject: Cityscape and Cinematic Corporality in *District 9*. *Critical Arts* 26(4): 547–569.

Nichols, B. 2017. *Introduction to Documentary*, 3rd ed. Bloomington: Indiana University Press.

Nicolson, B. 1954 The "Raft" from the Point of View of Subject-matter. *The Burlington Magazine* 96(617): 241–246.

Nieftagodien, N. & Gaule, S. (eds). 2012. *Orlando West, Soweto: An Illustrated History*. Johannesburg: Wits University Press.

Niemeyer, K. (ed). 2014. *Media and Nostalgia. Yearning for the Past, Present and Future*. Basingstoke: Palgrave Macmillan.

Niemeyer, K. 2016. Digital Nostalgia. *Media Development* 4: 27–30.

Nigeria Bans *District 9*. 2009. News24. 19 September. [Online]. Available: https://www.news24.com/news24/xarchive/entertainment/international/nigeria-bans-district-9-20090919. Accessed 15 March 2021.

Nkosi, V., Wichmann, J. & Voyi, K. 2017. Indoor and Outdoor PM10 Levels at Schools Located Near Mine Dumps in Gauteng and North West Provinces, South Africa. *BMC Public Health* 17(42): 1–7.

Nsele, Z. 2019. Post-apartheid Nostalgia and its Images of Common Sense, in *Diverse Unfreedoms: The Afterlives and Transformations of Post-Transatlantic Bondages*, edited by S. Balagopalan, C. Coe & K.M. Green. London: Routledge: 77–95. DOI: 10.4324/9780429321665.

Nuttall, S. & Mbembe, A. (eds). 2008. *Johannesburg: The Elusive Metropolis*. Durham, NC: Duke University Press.

Nuttall, S. & Mbembe, A. 2007. Afropolis: From Johannesburg. *PMLA* 122(1): 281–288.

Nuttall, S. & Mbembe, A. 2004. A Blasé Attitude: A Response to Michael Watts. *Public Culture* 17(1): 193–201.

Nye, E.D. 1994. *American Technological Sublime*. Cambridge, MA: MIT Press.

Nyoni, P. 2017. Unsung Heroes? An Anthropological Approach into the Experiences of "Zamazamas" in Johannesburg, South Africa, in *Mining Africa: Law, Environment, Society and Politics in Historical and Multidisciplinary Perspectives*, edited by A. Nhemachena, & V. Warikandwa. Oxford: African Books Collective: 133–154.

Olivier, B. 1998. The Sublime, Unpresentability and Postmodern Cultural Complexity, in *Critique, Architecture, Culture, Art*, edited by B. Olivier. Port Elizabeth: University of Port Elizabeth: 197–214.

Olsin-Lent, T. 1987. The Dark Side of the Dream: The Image of Los Angeles in Film Noir. *Southern California Quarterly* 69(4): 329–348.

Opalach, B. 1997. Political Space: The Architecture of Squatter Settlements in São Paulo, Brazil. *Traditional Dwellings and Settlements Review* 9(1): 35–50.

Opper, A. 2014. Foreword. Catalogue for the Exhibition *Dark city*: 17–28.

Orvell, M. 2013. Photographing Disaster: Urban Ruins and the Destructive Sublime. *Amerikastudien/American Studies* 58(4): 647–671.

Palmary, I. Rauch, J. & Simpson, G. 2003. Violent Crime in Johannesburg, in *Emerging Johannesburg*, edited by R. Tomlinson, R. Beauregard, L. Bremmer & X. Mangcu. London: Routledge: 101–122.

Parikka, J. 2012. *What is Media Archaeology?* Hoboken: Wiley.

Parker, A.M. 2012. Gangsters' Paradise: The Representation of Johannesburg in Film and Television. *International Journal of the Image* 2(3): 167–178.

Parker, A.M. 2014. Images and Influence: The Role of Film in Representing Johannesburg and Shaping Everyday Practice in the City. PhD thesis, University of the Witwatersrand, Johannesburg.

Parker, A.M. 2016. *Urban Film and Everyday Practice: Bridging Divisions in Johannesburg.* New York: Palgrave Macmillan.

Parker, A.M. 2018. The Ghetto in the Cities and Films of Johannesburg and Cape Town. *Journal of African Cinemas* 10(1,2): 65–80.

Paton, A. 1948. *Cry, the Beloved Country.* London: Jonathan Cape.

Peeples, J. 2011. Toxic Sublime: Imaging Contaminated Landscapes. *Environmental Communication* 5(4): 373–392.

Peffer, J. 2009. *Art and the End of Apartheid.* Minneapolis: University of Minnesota Press.

Penfold, T. 2012. Public and Private Space in Contemporary South Africa: Perspectives from Post-apartheid Literature. *Journal of South African Studies* 38(4): 993–1006.

Penprase, B.E. 2018. The Fourth Industrial Revolution and Higher Education, in *Higher Education in the Era of the Fourth Industrial Revolution*, edited by N.W. Gleason. [Ebook], 207–228. Available: https://library.oapen.org/bitstream/handle/20.500.12657/23279/1006877.pdf?sequence=1#page=216. Accessed 24 July 2020.

Peters, M.A. 2017. Technological Unemployment: Educating for the Fourth Industrial Revolution. *Educational Philosophy and Theory* 49(1): 1–6.

Phooko, K. 2022. Cele Claims Krugersdorp Gang Rape Suspects Have Been Identified. *The Citizen*, 10 August. [Online]. Available: https://www.citizen.co.za/news/south-africa/3169800/cele-krugersdorp-gang-rape-suspects-identified-10-august-2022/. Accessed 2 September 2022.

Pierce, G.B. (ed). 2012. *The Sublime Today: Contemporary Readings in the Aesthetic.* Newcastle upon Tyne: Cambridge Scholars Publishing.

Pinnavaia, L. 2018. *Food and Drink Idioms in English: "A Little Bit More Sugar and Lots of Spice".* Newcastle upon Tyne: Cambridge Scholars Publishing.

Plaatjie, S.T. 1998 [1915]. Native Life in South Africa, Before and Since the European War and the Boer Rebellion. [Ebook]. Project Gutenberg. Available: http://www.gutenberg.org/ebooks/1452. Accessed 12 February 2021.

Ponte City. 2022. *Wikipedia.* [Online]. Available: https://en.wikipedia.org/wiki/Ponte_City. Accessed 14 September 2018.

Posel, D. 1990. Symbolizing Violence: State and Media Discourse in TV Coverage of Township Protest, 1985–7, in *Political Violence and the Struggle in South Africa*, edited by N.C. Mangyani & A. du Toit. London: Palgrave Macmillan: 154–171.

Poyner, J. 2011. Dismantling the Architecture of Apartheid: Vladislavić's Private Poetics in *Portrait with Keys*, in *Marginal Spaces: Reading Ivan Vladislavić*, edited by G. Gaylard. Johannesburg: Wits University Press: 309–326.

Prakash, G. (ed). 2010. *Noir Urbanisms: Dystopic Images of the Modern city.* Princeton: Princeton University Press.

Prince, S. 2004. The Emergence of Filmic Artefacts: Cinema and Cinematography in the Digital Era. *Film Quarterly* 57(3): 24–33.

Prince, S. 2011. *Digital Visual Effects in Cinema: The Seduction of Reality*. London: Rutgers University Press.

Qviström, M. 2012. Peri-urban Landscapes: From Disorder to Hybridity, in *The Routledge Companion to Landscape Studies*, edited by P. Howard, I. Thompson, E. Waterton & M. Atha. London: Routledge: 427–437.

Rancière, J. 2004. *Aesthetics and its Discontents*, translated by S. Corcoran. Cambridge: Polity Press.

Rancière, J. 2009. *The Emancipated Spectator*, translated by G. Elliott. London: Verso.

Rancière, J. 2013. *Aisthesis*. London: Verso.

Rankin, E. 2010. Lonely Road: Formative Episodes in the Development of Black Artists in Early Twentieth-century South Africa, in *Visual Century: South African Art in Context*, volume 1, edited by J. Carman. Johannesburg: Wits University Press: 92–113.

Rantete, J. 1984. *The Third Day of September: An Eye-witness Account of the Sebokeng Rebellion of 1984*. Johannesburg: Ravan Press.

Raubenheimer, L. 2020. Nostalgic Dystopia: Johannesburg as Landscape after *White Writing*. *Journal of Literary Studies* 36(4): 123–142.

Reddy, T. 2004. *Higher Education and Social Transformation, South Africa Case Study*. Pretoria: Council on Higher Education.

Reichardt, M. 2013. The Wasted Years: A History of Mine Waste Rehabilitation Methodology in the South African Mining Industry from its Origins to 1991. PhD thesis, University of the Witwatersrand, Johannesburg.

Riegl, A. 1996 [1903]. The Modern Cult of Monuments: Its Essence and its Development, translated by K. Bruckner & K. Williams, in *Historical and Philosophical Issues in the Conservation of Cultural Heritage*, edited by N. Stanley-Price, N. Price, M. Kirby Tally & A. Melucco Vaccaro. Los Angeles: Getty Publications: 69–83.

Rijsdijk, I. & Lawrence, A. 2019. Editorial, *Journal of African Cinemas* 11(1): 1–9.

Robinson, J. 2004. The Urban Basis of Emancipation: Spatial Theory and the City in South African Politics, in *The Emancipatory City? Paradoxes and Possibilities*, edited by L. Lees. London: SAGE: 142–155.

Robinson, J. 2010. Living in Dystopia: Past, Present and Future in Contemporary African cities, in *Noir Urbanisms: Dystopic Images of the Modern City*, edited by G. Prakash. Princeton: Princeton University Press: 218–240.

Robinson, T. 2009. *District 9* Director Neill Blomkamp. *AV Club*. 8 December. [Online]. Available: https://www.avclub.com/district-9-director-neill-blomkamp-1798217462. Accessed 15 September 2020.

ROBOTECH – INTRO HD 720P. 2011. [Online]. Available: https://www.youtube.com/watch?v=qEeokzyFOyU&ab_channel=FelipeSoto. Accessed 24 July 2020.

Rodney, L. & Lauder, A. 2018. The Tremendous Image: Viceland TV's Abandoned Series and the Persistence of Ruin Porn, in *Feelings of Structure. Explorations in Affect*, edited by K. Engle & Y. Wong. Montreal: McGill-Queen's University Press: 76–85.

Rogerson, C.M. 2004. Towards the World-class African City: Planning Local Economic Development in Johannesburg. *Africa Insight* 34(4):12–21.

Rosello, M. 2016. A Grammar of Peripheralisation: Neill Blomkamp's *"District 9"*, in *Peripheral Visions in the Globalizing Present. Space, Mobility, Aesthetics*, edited by E. Peeren, H. Stuit & A. Weyenberg. Leiden: Koninklijke Brill: 31–47.

Ryan, C. 2016. Reviewed Work(s): African Metropolis: Six Stories from African Cities. *African Studies Review* 59(3): 322–324.

Ryan, L. 2007. Art + Ecology: Land Reclamation Works of Artists Robert Smithson, Robert Morris, Helen Mayer Harrison and Newton Harrison. *Environmental Philosophy* 4(1&2): 95–116.

Saks, L. 2010. Cities, Citizenship, and Other 'Joburg Stories', in *Ruins of Modernity*, edited by J. Hell & A. Schönle. Durham, NC: Duke University Press: 151–165.

Sapio, G. 2014. Homesick for Aged Home Movies: Why Do We Shoot Contemporary Family Videos in Old-fashioned Ways?, in *Media and Nostalgia: Yearning for the Past, Present and Future*, edited by K. Niemeyer. Basingstoke: Palgrave Macmillan: 39–50.

Sapire, H. 2013. Township Histories, Insurrection and Liberation in Late Apartheid South Africa. *South African Historical Journal* 65(2): 167–198.

Sargent, L.T. 2013. Do Dystopias Matter?, in *Dystopia(n) Matters: On the Page, on Screen, on Stage*, edited by F. Vieira. Newcastle upon Tyne: Cambridge Scholars Publisher: 10–13.

Scanlan, T. 2005. *On Garbage*. London: Reaktion Books.

Scott, C. 2018. The Truths/Fictions/Traumas of Marikana: Exploring Violence and Trauma in Three Films, "The Marikana Massacre: Through the Lens" (2013), "Miners Shot Down" (2014), and "Night is Coming: A Threnody for the Victims of Marikana" (2014). *Communicatio* 44(4): 18–31.

Scott, R. (dir). 1982. *Blade Runner*. [Film]. Los Angeles: Warner Brothers.

Schatz, T. 2003. New Hollywood, in *Movie Blockbusters*, edited by J. Stringer. London: Routledge: 15–44.

Schmitz, O. & Tilley, B. 1997. *Joburg Stories*. [Television film]. Paris: La Sept/arte, London: Channel Four.

Schneider, A. & Strauven, W. 2013. Waste: An Introduction. *NECSUS European Journal of Media Studies* 2(2): 409–418.

Schön, H. 1973. *The Johannesburg Station Panels by J.H. Pierneef*. Catalogue, Pretoria Art Museum.

Schrey, D. 2014. Analogue Nostalgia and the Aesthetics of Digital Remediation, in *Media and Nostalgia: Yearning for the Past, Present and Future*, edited by K. Niemeyer. Basingstoke: Palgrave Macmillan: 27–38.

Schwab, K. 2016. *The Fourth Industrial Revolution*. New York: Crown Business.
Seabi, J., Seedat, J., Khoza-Shangase, K. & Sullivan, L. 2014. Experiences of University Students Regarding Transformation in South Africa. *International Journal of Educational Management* 28(1): 66–81.
Seale, K. & Hamilton, C. 2010. Waste. *M/C Journal* 13(4): [n.p.].
Shapiro, M. J. 2018. *The Political Sublime*. Durham, NC: Duke University Press.
Shapshay, S. 2017. Feeling Not at Home in the Twenty-first Century World. The Sublime in Contemporary Environmental Aesthetics, in *Contemporary Visual Culture and the Sublime*, edited by T. Trifonova. London: Routledge: 164–174.
Shaw, P. 2017. *The Sublime*. London: Routledge.
Shields, R. 1991. *Places on the Margin: Alternative Geographies of Modernity*. London: Routledge.
Siegenthaler, F. 2013. Visualizing the Mental City: The Exploration of Cultural and Subjective Topographies by Contemporary Performance Artists in Johannesburg. *Research in African Literatures* (guest editors Z. Norridge, C. Baker & E. Boehmer) 44(2): 163–176.
Simone, A. 2004. People as Infrastructure. *Public Culture* 16(3): 407–429.
Simone, A. 2010. *City Life from Jakarta to Dakar: Movement on the Crossroads*. London: Routledge.
SmartMonkeyTV. 2014. Vincent Moloi on His Film in African Metropolis Berea and His Next Film Project. [YouTube video]. Available: https://www.youtube.com/watch?v=esx5l9olssU&ab_channel=SmartMonkeyTV. Accessed 7 September 2022.
Smith-Rowsey, D. 2018. *Blockbuster Performances: How Actors Contribute to Cinema's Biggest Hits* (Series: Palgrave Studies in Screen Industries and Performance). London: Palgrave Macmillan.
Sobchack, V. 1998. *Screening Space: The American Science Fiction Film*. New Brunswick: Rutgers University Press.
Sobchack, V. 2008. American Science Fiction Film: An Overview, in *A Companion to Science Fiction*, edited by D. Seed. Hoboken: John Wiley & Sons: 261–274.
Solomons, I. 2017. Govt, NGOs, Industry Combining to Fend off Acid Mine Water Threat. *Mining Weekly*, 11 November 2017. [Online]. Available: http://www.miningweekly.com/article/govt-ngos-and-industry-joining-forces-to-fend-off-acid-mine-water-threat-2017-11-10. Accessed 14 September 2018.
Sontag, S. 1977. *On Photography*. London: Penguin Books.
Sontag, S. 1980. *Under the Sign of Saturn*. London: Penguin Books.
South Africa. 2014. The Presidency. 2014. Act No. 46 of 2013: Broad-Based Black Economic Empowerment Amendment Act, 2013. *Government Gazette* 583(37271), 27 January.
South Africa State of Emergency 1980's. 2008. [Online]. Available: https://www.youtube.com/watch?v=Ej-KqF5CJes&ab_channel=Rui. Accessed 14 September 2018.

South Africa's Tower of Trouble. 2014. [Online]. Available: https://www.youtube.com/watch?v=3EIKmmSifqw&ab_channel=Vocativ. Accessed 14 September 2018.

Spaulding, J. 1996. Yosemite and Ansel Adams: Art, Commerce, and Western Tourism. *Pacific Historical Review* 65(4): 615–639.

Special Feature: Focus on *District 9*. Gauteng Film Commission. 2009. [Online]. Available: https://gautengfilm.org.za/2009/09/special-feature-focus-on-district-9/. Accessed 19 October 2018.

Staiger, J. 1988. Future Noir: Contemporary Representations of Visionary Cities. *Film Journal* 3(1): 20–40.

Stassen, W. 2015. Gauteng's Mine Dumps Brimming with Radioactive Uranium. *Health E-News*, 15 October. [Online]. Available: https://www.health-e.org.za/2015/10/15/gautengs-mine-dumps-brimming-with-radioactive-uranium/. Accessed 14 September 2018.

States of Emergency in South Africa: the 1960s and 1980s. 2019. 27 August [Online]. Available:https://www.sahistory.org.za/article/states-emergency-south-africa-1960s-and-1980s. Accessed 10 March 2020.

Steinmetz, G. 2008. Harrowed Landscapes: White Ruingazers in Namibia and Detroit and the Cultivation of Memory. *Visual Studies* 23(3): 211–237.

Steyn, L. 2022. Krugersdorp Rapes: Govt Failed to Enforce Mine Cleanup. Now it's a Crime Scene. *News 24*, 6 August. [Online]. Available: https://www.news24.com/fin24/economy/krugersdorp-rapes-govt-failed-to-enforce-mine-cleanup-now-its-a-crime-scene-20220806. Accessed 2 September 2022.

Steyn, M. 2001. *Whiteness Just Isn't What it Used to Be: White Identity in a Changing South Africa*. Albany: State University of New York Press.

Steyn, M. 2005. "White Talk": White South Africans and the Management of Diasporic Whiteness, in *Post-colonial Whiteness: A Critical Reader on Race and Empire*, edited by A.J. Lopez. Albany: State University of New York Press: 119–135.

Straker, G. 2013. Unsettling Whiteness, in *Race, Memory and the Apartheid Archive: Towards a Transformative Social Praxis*, edited by G. Stevens, N. Duncan & D. Hook. Basingstoke: Palgrave Macmillan: 91–108.

Strauss, H. 2016. Managing Public Feeling: Temporality, Mourning and the Marikana Massacre in Rehad Desai's "Miners Shot Down". *Critical Arts* 30(4): 522–537.

Su, J.J. 2011. Amitav Ghosh and the Aesthetic Turn in Post-colonial Studies. *Journal of Modern Literature* 34(3): 65–86.

Sundaram, R. 2010. Imaging Urban Breakdown: Delhi in the 1990s, in *Noir Urbanisms: Dystopic Images of the Modern City*, edited by G. Prakash. Princeton: Princeton University Press: 241–260.

Tatsumi, T. 2015. Transnational Interactions: *District 9*, or Apaches in Johannesburg, in *Science Fiction Double Feature: The Science Fiction Film as Cult Text*, edited by G. Duchovnay & J.P. Telotte. Liverpool: Liverpool University Press.

Teays, W. (ed). 2012. *Seeing the Light: Exploring Ethics through Movies*. Chichester: Wiley Blackwell.

The Dark City. 2017. [Online]. Available: https://www.inyourpocket.com/johannesburg/dark-city_4541e. Accessed 15 February 2021.

The Raft of the Medusa. 2018. Wikipedia. [Online]. Available: https://en.wikipedia.org/wiki/The_Raft_of_the_Medusa#/media/File:JEAN_LOUIS_TH%C3%89ODORE_G%C3%89RICAULT_-_La_Balsa_de_la_Medusa_(Museo_del_Louvre,_1818-19).jpg. Accessed 14 September 2018.

The Third Day of September. 1985. *Index on Censorship* 14(3): 37–42.

Thompson, C. & Wood, M.A. 2018. A Media Archaeology of the Creepshot. *Feminist Media Studies* 18(4): 560–574. DOI: 10.1080/14680777.2018.1447429.

Time. 1985. South Africa, 5 August. [Online]. Available: http://content.time.com/time/covers/0,16641,19850805,00.html. Accessed 31 July 2020.

Tinterow, G. 1990–1991. Gericault's Heroic Landscapes: The Times of Day. *The Metropolitan Museum of Art Bulletin*, New Series 48(3): 1,4,7,18–76.

Toffa, T.N. 2013. Reinstating Water, Resurrecting the Witwatersrand. *Journal of Landscape Architecture* 8(2): 24–31.

Tomino, Y. & Yatate, H. (creators). 1979. *Gundam*. [Television series]. Tokyo: Sunrise Inc.

Trangos, G. & Bobbins, K. 2015. Gold Mining Exploits and the Legacies of Johannesburg's Mining Landscape. *Scenario Journal 05: Extraction*. [Online]. Available: https://scenariojournal.com/article/gold-mining-exploits/. Accessed 12 September 2018.

Travis, P. 2012. *Judge Dredd*. [Film]. London: DNA Films.

Trigg, D. 2006. *The Aesthetics of Decay. Nothingness, Nostalgia and the Absence of Reason*. New York: Peter Lang.

Turquety, B. 2014. Toward an Archaeology of the Cinema/Technology Relation: From Mechanization to "Digital Cinema", in *Technē/Technology. Researching Cinema and Media Technologies – Their Development, Use, and Impact*, edited by A.M.A. van den Oever. Amsterdam: Amsterdam University Press: 50–64.

Turquety, B. 2017. On Viewfinders, Video Assist systems, and Tape Splicers: Questioning the History of Techniques and Technology in Cinema, in *Technology and Film Scholarship: Experience, Study, Theory*, edited by S. Hidalgo. Amsterdam: Amsterdam University Press: 239–259.

UN-Habitat. 2018. Goal 11: Make Cities and Human Settlements Inclusive, Safe, Resilient and Sustainable. [Online]. Available: https://unstats.un.org/sdgs/metadata/files/Metadata-11-01-01.pdf. Accessed 16 September 2020.

Vahed, G. 2021. 'Where's Our Monument?' Commemorating Indian Indentured Labour in South Africa, in *Falling Monuments, Reluctant Ruins: The Persistence of the Past in the Architecture of Apartheid*, edited by H. Judin. Johannesburg: Wits University Press: 256–277.

Van den Oever, A.M.A. (ed). 2014. *Technē/Technology. Researching Cinema and Media Technologies – Their Development, Use, and Impact*. Amsterdam: Amsterdam University Press.

Van den Oever, A.M.A. 2011. The Prominence of Grotesque Figures in Visual Culture Today: Rethinking the Ontological Status of the (Moving) Image from the Perspective of the Grotesque. *Image & Text* 18: 101–102.

Van den Oever, A.M.A. 2013. The Medium-sensitive Experience and the Paradigmatic Experience of the Grotesque, "Unnatural", or "Monstrous". *Leonardo* 46(1): 88–89.

Van Robbroeck, L. 2019. Afrikaner Nationalism and Other Settler Imaginaries at the 1936 Empire Exhibition, in *Troubling Images: Visual Culture and the Politics of Afrikaner Nationalism*, edited by F. Freschi, B. Schmahmann & L. van Robbroeck. Johannesburg: Wits University Press: 43–65.

Venables, E. 2011. "We are Proud of this Tower": Health and High-rises in Inner-city Johannesburg. *Etnofoor* 23(1): 124–143.

Veracini, L. 2011. "District 9" and "Avatar": Science Fiction and Settler Colonialism. *Journal of Intercultural Studies* 32(4): 355–367.

Verhoeven, P. (dir). 1987. *Robocop*. [Film]. Los Angeles: Orion Pictures.

Verhoeven, P. (dir). 1990. *Total Recall*. [Film]. Boca Raton: Carolco Pictures.

Vidler, A. 1994. *The Architectural Uncanny: Essays in the Modern Unhomely*. Cambridge, MA: MIT Press.

Vladislavić, I. 2006. *Portrait with Keys: The City of Johannesburg Unlocked*. London: W.W. Norton & Co.

Vladislavić, I. 2014. Ponte City Book Introduction. [Online]. Available: http://www.subotzkystudio.com/works/ponte-city-text/. Accessed 12 February 2021.

Vundla, M. 2017. [Online]. Vincent Moloi: These Streets Made Me. *Actor Spaces*. 27 March. Available: https://www.actorspaces.co.za/vincent-moloi/. Accessed 16 September 2024.

Waetjen, T. & Maré, G. 2009. The Politics of Culture in the Rape Trial of Jacob Zuma. *Theoria: A Journal of Social and Political Theory* 56(118): 63–81.

Wagner, K.B. 2015. *"District 9"*, Race and Neoliberalism in Post-apartheid Johannesburg. *Race & Class* 57(2): 43–59.

Walder, D. 2014. Hysterical Nostalgia in the Postcolony: From "Coming Home" to "District 9". *Consumption Markets & Culture* 17(2): 143–157.

Wamba, P. 2003. Here Comes the Neighborhood. *Transition* 94: 8–15.

Wells, K. 2018. Detroit Was Always Made of Wheels: Confronting Ruin Porn in its Hometown, in *Ruin Porn and the Obsession with Decay*, edited by S. Lyons. London: Palgrave Macmillan: 13–30.

Westerholt, R., Mocnik, F., & Zipf, A. 2018. *Introduction to the PLATIAL'18 Workshop on Platial Analysis*. Heidelberg, Germany, 20–21 September.

Whissel, K. 2007. Digital Visual Effects and Popular Cinema: An Introduction. *Film Criticism* (Special Issue: Digital Visual Effects and Popular Cinema) 32(1): 2–4.

Whitehouse, T. 2018. *How Ruins Acquire Aesthetic Value: Modern Ruins, Ruin Porn, and the Ruin Tradition*. London: Palgrave Pivot.

Wilhelm-Solomon, M. 2022. *The Blinded City: Ten Years in Inner-city Johannesburg*. Johannesburg: Picador Africa.

Williams, R. 1978. Utopia and Science Fiction. *Science Fiction Studies* 5(3): 203–214.

Willis, D. 2003. The Sociologist's Eye: W.E.B. DuBois and the Paris Exposition, in *A Small Nation of People: W.E.B. DuBois and African American Portraits of Progress*, edited by D. Levering Lewis & D. Willis. Washington DC: Amistad Books and The Library of Congress.

Winkler, T. 2009. Prolonging the Global Age of Gentrification: Johannesburg's Regeneration Policies. *Planning Theory* 8(4): 362–381.

Wittenberg, H. 2004. The Sublime, Imperialism and the African Landscape. PhD thesis, The University of the Western Cape, Cape Town.

Woerner, M. 2009. *District 9*'s Director Tells Us All about His Alien Back Story. *Gizmodo*, 8 July. [Online]. Available: https://gizmodo.com/district-9s-director-tells-us-all-about-his-alien-back-5331799. Accessed 14 September 2018.

Wolff, J. 1993. Memoires and Micrologies: Walter Benjamin, Feminism and Cultural Analysis. *New Formations* 20 (Summer): 113–122.

Womack, Y.L. 2013. *Afrofuturism: The World of Black Sci-fi and Fantasy Culture*. Chicago: Lawrence Hill Books.

Woods, A. 1984. Death and the Instamatic. *The Cambridge Quarterly* 13(2): 147–163.

Worby, E. & Ally, S. 2013. The Disappointment of Nostalgia: Conceptualising Cultures of Memory in Contemporary South Africa. *Social Dynamics: A Journal of African Studies* 39(3): 457–480.

Yuen, E. 1997. Social Movements, Identity Politics and the Fenealogy of the Term "People of Color". *New Political Science* 19(1–2): 97–107.

Zemeckis, R. (dir). 1985. *Back to the Future*. [Film]. Universal City: Universal Pictures.

Ziman, R. 2021. [Online]. Casspir the Vehicle. Available: https://ralphziman.com/project/the-casspir-vehicle/. Accessed 6 September 2024.

Ziman, R. (dir). 2008. *Gangster's Paradise: Jerusalema*. [Film]. London: United International Pictures.

Ziman Steals the Screen. 2008. [Online]. *Mail & Guardian*. 30 August. Available: https://mg.co.za/article/2008-08-30-ziman-steals-the-screen/. Accessed 29 September 2022.

Zylinska, J. 2017. *Nonhuman Photography*. Cambridge, MA: MIT Press.

Index

Page numbers in italics refer to figures.

abandoned mines   143–145
abjection   65, 121, 174–175, 177, 178*n*
acid mine drainage   144, 145*n*, 149–150
Acid River Runs through It, An   149–150
Adorno, Theodor   165, 185*n*
aesthetics   6, 11–12, 43–44, 46, 49, 61–67, 118, 147–149, 154–157
Afrapix   15, 27
Africa Biennale (series of photographs)   184–185
African National Congress (ANC)   13*n*, 44–45
Afrikaner identity   1, 23, 94–95, 149, 181, 187, 190–191
Afrikaner nationalism   99, 149, 181, 190–191
Afrofuturism   120*n*4
After the Mines   139, 140, 145, 146, 149–150, 150
Agamben, Giorgio   23, 33–34
age value   173
aggressive customization   176
air pollution. *See* pollution; smog
Akpome, Aghogho   23, 33, 76
aliens, in *District 9*   1–2, 24, 33–34, 96, 175, 178, 181
Alive in Joburg (film)   21, 80, 80, 100, 130, 131, 202
Ally, Shireen   35–37
amateur filmmaking and photography   85, 94
America. *See* United States
analogue aesthetics   4, 53–61, 66, 77–90, 98, 133
analogue cameras   85, 109, 134
analogue media   4–6, 53–56, 80–81, 84–89, 97–98, 133, 199, 205–206
analogue nostalgia   4, 11, 36, 59–60, 66, 103, 106–117, 135, 195–199
analogue photography   14*n*22, 97–98, 110, 114–115
analogue renaissance   53, 89
ANC. *See* African National Congress
anime films and television series   126
Antibiotika (song)   185
Antichita Romane (series of etchings)   165

anxiety   30, 63, 120, 167, 177. *See also* white anxiety
Anxious Joburg   30*n*20, 183
apartheid
    Afrikaner identity and   1
    Black artists under   45
    braziers   130
    end of   2, 4
    floodlights   124, 125
    legislation   75, 178*n*
    in mockumentary genre   93, 100, 107
    nostalgia   6–7, 10–11, 37, 112–113, 134
    police force   74–75, 79, 87, 103, 123–124, 170
    protests against   27, 35, 74–75, 74
    ruins   163, 167, 171
    townships   77
    urban planning and   29, 32, 73
    white anxiety and   179, 181–182, 192
Apartheid Archives Project research project   182
Appiah, Kwame Anthony   29*n*19
Arcades Project   57
archaeology   17, 130–131
archival footage   80–81, 82, 92
armour suit. *See* mechanical suit, in *District 9*
Arnold, Kenneth   123
Arya, Rina   65, 175
Askari   113
attraction and repulsion   7, 66, 154, 174*n*16, 176–177
aura of authenticity   57–59
authenticity
    in mockumentary genre   77, 81, 84–86, 90, 94, 106–107
    nostalgia and   55–59, 64, 66
    ruins and   173
    in science fiction genre   134
    township nostalgia and   115–116
Avant Car Guard   16, 184–190, 185, 188, 189
avant-garde art   40–41, 50, 165
Avatar (film)   21*n*

Back to the Future (film)   119
bad buildings   26, 90
Barasch, Moshe   8
Bartholeyns, Gil   83
Bataille, George   64
Battle for Johannesburg, The (film)   2–3, 24–26, 88, *89*, 90–91, *91*, 93–95, 100–101, 103, 106, 176
belonging   180, 187, 190–191
Beningfield, Jennifer   36, 48
Benjamin, Walter   55–59, 66, 115, 173
Berea   100
Berea (film)   24–26, 179–180, *180*
Bethlehem, Lael   *91*
Bhengu, Gerard   45
Bila, Anthony   115
Black artists   45–47
Black Consciousness   29*n*19
Black History Tribute series   115
Black people   44–45, 170*n*, 179, 181
Blade Runner (film)   33, 118–120
Blair Witch Project (film)   93
Blinded City, The   90*n*
blockbusters   21*n*
bloggers. *See* fashion bloggers
Blomkamp, Neill
   on aliens   122
   background of   3, 15, 21, 119, 139
   on braziers   130
   on digital media   4, 120
   interview with   202–209
   on location shooting   78, 104
Boetzkes, Amanda   40, 42, 49, 152–154
Bois, Yves Alain   64–65, 154
Bolter, David Jay   56, 88
Bordwell, David   16–17
Botha, P.W.   34
boundaries   29, 166
Boym, Svetlana   37, 165
Brazier – Joubert Park I (photograph)   129–130, *130*
braziers   129–130, *130*, *131*
Brodie, Nechama   167
Brook, Isis   156–157, 166
Bryson, Norman   174*n*15
buildings in Johannesburg   31, 98–102, 118*n*, 192. *See also* Hillbrow Tower; Ponte City
Burgin, Victor   174–175

Burke, Edmund   12, 39–40, 43
Burtynsky, Edward   150–154, *152*

Californication (television series)   55
call to play   107
cameras   4, 14, 85–87, 93–94, 109, 120*n*3, 134, 205
camps. *See* refugee camps
Caoduro, Elena   4*n*4, 58–59, 84, 114
Carceri d'Invenzione   165–166
Carlton Centre   102, *102*, 118*n*
Casspirs   25*n*12, 103, *104*, *170*
censorship   22*n*5, 76
Chiawelo   22, 33, 71–73, 104, 114
Chicago   7, 99, 102
children   151–152, 156–157
Chong, Woei Lien   7
Cilliers, Jack   184
cinematography   60–61, 77–78, 81–83, 85–86, 88–89, 109–110, 117, 133, 206
cinéma vérité   77, 92–93, *94*
Clarke, Jamie   88–89
classical ruins   42*n*39, 61, 63, 164, 166, 173, 175
Cleaning the Core (360 Degree Panorama) (photograph)   *100*, 172–173
closure, lack of   164, 166
Coetzee, J. M.   46–48, 185–186, 190, 195
Coetzee, N. J.   148
cold character of digital media   55, 60, 85
collectives   16, 110, 134–135, 184–190
colonialism   29, 43–44, 46, 49, 73, 149, 179, 187
colour palettes   3, 61, 82–83, 85–86, 98, 109–110, 161
command module, of spaceship   131, *132*
contamination   122, 178
contradictory dynamic   11, 135, 172, 195
Cook, Pam   115
corrugated iron   126
Cramer, Florian   54
crime   14, 22*n*5, 28*n*17, 30, 102, 156, 169, *170*, 182
critical dystopia   35, 195
critical potential   13, 34–35, 38, 49–51, 61, 63, 151, 176, 191–192, 197–198, 200–201
Crowther, Paul   7
cyberpunk subgenre   118–119
cyborgs   120–121, 127

INDEX   239

cynicism   119–120

Davis, Mike   35
Deakins, Roger   61
debris. *See* waste
decay
    Johannesburg   6–7, 200–201, 206
    mining landscapes   145, 147, 155
    post-industrial landscapes   42–43, 62
    science fiction genre   120–121
    urban ruins   158–159, 171–174, 176–177
    white anxiety   180, *180*, 192–193
delight. *See* terror and delight
depthlessness   119
Desai, Barney   25
Desai, Rehad   2–3, 15, 25–26, 88, 90, 172–173
destruction   *105*, 106
*Destruction of District Six under the Group
    Areas Act, The* (photograph)   *162*
destructive sublime   172
desublimation   65
detention without trial   75
Detroit   34, 172
Dhlomo, Herbert   45
Die Antwoord (pop musicians)   6
Diepkloof   124, *125*
digitalisation   60
digital media   4–5, 53–55, 60–61, 86–89,
    120*n*3, 133, 205–206
digital turn   60, 81, 85
dispositive   9*n*12
dispossession   44–45
disruption   40–42, 63
District 9 (film)
    background to   1–2, 21
    introductory sequence   80, *81*
    reasons for research on   2–5, 51
District Six   23, 161–163, *162*
Dlamini, Jacob   11*n*17, 36, 112–114
documentary genre   3, 27, 33, 77–78,
    86–88, 106, 168, 200, 203. *See also*
    mockumentary genre
documentary photography   27, 33, 76*n*13, 86,
    90, 103, 106, 168, 171, 199, 203
Doornkop Gold Mine   *152*
Drink in the Passage, A (film)   173*n*13
Drum magazine   27
dystopia   6, 10–11, 32–35, 45, 51, 106, 117–118,
    191, 195–196. *See also* nostalgic dystopia

ecotechnological   152–153
Edensor, Tim   63
edgy cities   29–30
electricity pylons   95, *96*, 97, 145
Elkins, James   38*n*32
Elysium (film)   124
emancipation   49–50
'empty' landscape   149, 187
engaged photography   27
English Garden Suburb   71
Enlightenment   35, 46, 49, 164–165
entropy   155, 174–178
Enwezor, Okwui   27
escape   131
European landscape traditions   44–48, 186
evictions   103
experts, interviews with   90, *91*, *92*, 131

family photographs   84, 110
Farber, Leora   110–111, 134
fashion bloggers   16, 84, 109, 114–116, 134–135
fear   177–178, 182–183
film noir genre   95
filters, use of   83–84
fire. *See* braziers
floodlights   124, *125*
fly-on-the-wall style   90, 93
focus, cameras   79–80, 88
Fokofpolisiekar (rock band)   185
Football World Cup   15
forced removals   2, 23, 72, 162
forgetting   36–37
formless   43, 64–65, 67, 146–157, 173–175, 192
Formless, A User's Guide (exhibition)   64–65
Foster, Jeremy   186–187
Foucault, Michel   9*n*12, 17
found footage   78–79
Four Corners (film)   31
Fourth Industrial Revolution   120
Francaviglia, Richard V.   146–147
Frassinelli, Pier Paolo   23
freedom   50, 52, 63, 111, 134–135, 156
Freedom Front Plus   62
Freschi, Federico   99
Frightened Land, The   36
future noir genre   118*n*
Future of Nostalgia, The   37

Gabay, Charles   181, 183

gangster genre   25, 168
Gangster's Paradise: Jerusalema (film)
    background to   24–25
    documentary genre and   84–86, *84*, 93, 95, *96*, 100–101, 103, 106
    mining landscapes in   151–152, 156–157
    nostalgic dystopia in   31, 199
    urban ruins in   167–171, 168, 169, 170, 176
    white anxiety and   182
garbage. *See* waste
garden, landscape as   46
Gaudreault, André   60*n*9
gentrification   6*n*7, 167
Géricault, Theodore   183–184
German Romanticism   190–191
Gevisser, Mark   144*n*9
Gikandi, Simon   49
Ginsberg, Robert   63, 158
Glass, Fred   119–121
global North   34*n*29, 72
global South   34*n*29
Gobodo-Madikizela, Pumla   36
Godby, Michael   27
Godfrey, Ilan   151, *153*, 156–157
Goldblatt, David   15, 36, 97–98, *97*, 109, 134, 145, 161–163, *162*, 165–166
gold mines   139, 142–145, *152*
grading   60–61, 82–83, *83*
Griffioen, James D.   10
grittiness   85, 88, 205–206
grotesque   174–175
Grusin, Richard   56, 88

Hamese, Harness   110–111, *112*
hand-held camera techniques   78, 93–94, 161
Hansen, Mark   153–154
Hansen, Miriam   58, 66
hard places   146–147
Hayden, Robert   49
Hight, Craig   90, 94, 107
Hillbrow   24–26, 90, 100–102, 109, 167–171, 169, 173
Hillbrow Tower   *99*, 101–102, 168, 169
historical poetics   17
historicity   109, 114–116, 134
Hogan, Patrick Colm   16*n*28
Hollywood films   21, 25, 88–89, 118–119, 135, 204–205

Hook, Derek   36
House of Wax   174*n*15
housing   30, 71–72, 147, 152, 161, 167
Hudson River School   7, 47
human figures, absence of   149–153
humanity   33–34
human rights   76
humour   78, 94, 106–107, 134
Huyssen, Andreas   63–64, 164–166
hypermediacy   56, 79, 84–86, 107

idiom   7–9, 194–195
illegal miners (*zama zamas*)   156
immigrants. *See* migrant labour
imperfections   85–86, 173
incidental details   89–98, *94*
industrialisation   41–42, 44, 145, 147–149, 156
informality   31, 72, 126, 170
informal settlements   29, 72–73, 95, 144
inner city of Johannesburg   167, 171, 179, 183
Instagram photography   109, 114–115, 134–135
interviews, in *District 9*   90–94, *91*, *92*, *94*, 121, 131
irony   11, 37–38, 78, 106, 109, 157, 171, 188, 208
I See A Different You   109–110, *110*, 134–135
Isenberg, Noah   57

Jackson, Peter   21, 205
Jameson, Fredric   118–119
Jansen van Veuren, Mocke   23
Jansson, Eva-Lotta   149–150
Jerusalem   5, 24–25, 101, 167–171
Johannesburg
    adjectives and phrases for   29–31
    Blomkamp on   204–207
    history of   139–142
    inner city of   167, 171, 179, 183
    nicknames of   9–10
    representations of   2–8, 21–27
    research on   22–24
Johannesburg from the Southwest (photograph)   *97*, 145, 165
Johannesburg//Home (photograph)   109–110, *111*
Johannesburg Railway Station panel series   147–149
Josephy, Svea   10*n*14, 31, 100–102

INDEX

Kant, Immanuel   12, 39, 43, 49, 64*n*, 154, 166
Kapstein, Helen   23, 77, 95, 178*n*
Katlehong   113–114
Kentridge, William   36
Khumbula   109, 115, 134–135
Kind, Joshua   7
King, Geoff   117–118
Kinnear, Kate   123–124
Kirkwood, Meghan   151
Klein, Kristin   54*n*
Kovel, Jonathan   88
Krauss, Rosalind   64–65, 154
Kristeva, Julia   174
Kruger, Loren   29–30, 99
Krzywinska, Tanya   117–118
KwaThemba   72
Kynoch, Gary   182

Land Act   44–45, 73–74
landlords   167
landmarks   98–102, *99*, *102*
land ownership   29, 44–45, 73–74, 95, 149, 179
landscape conventions   18, 46, 66–67, 186
landscapes   12–13, 36–39, 44–48, 77–108, 146–157, 163, 186–187, 190–191, 195–198
landscape tradition   5, 12–13, 44–48, 190–191, 195–197
Larkin, Jason   139, *140*, 145, *146*, 149–150, *150*, 154
Läuferts, Monika   146
Law-Viljoen, Bronwyn   27
Leeb-du Toit, Juliette   7*n*, 44–45
Lees, Loretta   13, 50, 52, 111
Lefebvre, Henri   9*n*12, 50
Legacy of the Mine   151, *153*
location shooting   78, 95
Lockheed F-117A aircraft   123, *124*
Lomography movement   56, 85–86, 205
Lost and Found in Johannesburg   144*n*9
low-resolution realism   33, 77–89
Lucas, Christopher   60, 81, 87
Lyons, Siobhan   10*n*14, 64
Lyotard, Jean-Francois   40, 177

Mabote, Goodman   76*n*, 103
Malpas, Simon   40
Manovich, Lev   4*n*4, 16, 53

Maré, Gehard   14*n*24
Marion, Philippe   60*n*9
Maseko, Zola   173*n*13
Maskit, Jonathan   155, 157
Matshikiza, John   5, 200
Mavunganidze, Judith   146
Mbembe, Achille   31, 186
mechanical suit, in *District 9*   126–127, *128*, 159–161, *160*, 202
media archaeology   4, 17, 196
melancholia   182–183
memento mori   159
Merrett, Christopher   75–76
metamorphosis   157, 162, 177–178. See also transformation
Mhlongo, Niq   71, 114
migrant labour   24, 122, 142
militarisation   87, 103–104, 106, 122–123, 203–204
mine dumps   97, 102, *102*, 139–146, *140*, *143*, 149–152, *150*, 156–157, 166, 207. See also mining waste
Mine scene (painting)   147–148
mine waste areas (MWAs)   61, 63, 95–97, 141–142, *141*, 145, 147, 153–155, 174, 191–192
mining, history of   61, 139–142
mining industry
    abandoned mines   143–145
    boundaries   29
    colonialism and   149
    history of   61, 139–142
    migrant labour   122
    science fiction genre and   122, 129, *129*
    white anxiety and   179, 188–192
mining landscapes
    aesthetics of   147–149, 154–157
    formlessness   146–157
    mining apparatus in   *96*, 147
    mining waste in   139, *140*, 141–147, *141*, *143*, 149–157, *152*
    sublime   148–151, 153–156, 198
    white anxiety and   179, 188–191
mining waste   61, 95–97, *97*, 139, *140*, 141–157, *141*, *143*, *152*, 191–192. See also mine dumps; waste
Minniti, Sergio   56, 85–86, 205
Mngxitama, Andile   112
MNU. *See* Multi National United

mockumentary genre
  Blomkamp on   206
  call to play   107
  incidental details   89–98
  irony   78, 106, 208
  landmarks   98–102, *99, 102*
  low-resolution realism   77–89
  militarisation   *87*, 103–104, 106
  newsreel footage   22, 75, 78–80, *79, 81*, 86, *87*, 94, 104
  1980s   74–75, 92, 98–104, 133–134
  nostalgic dystopia   196–197
  See also documentary genre
modernity   37, 127, 166
Mofokeng, Santu   15, 124, *125*
Mohl, John Koenakeefe   45
Mokonyane, Nomvula   145*n*
Moloi, Vincent   15, 26, 179
Mooifontein mine dumps   142–143, *143*, 157
mothership. *See* spaceship, in *District 9*
Motsepe, Fanuel   31
Moylan, Tom   34–35
Mpanza, James   72
Mpe, Phaswane   28*n*17
Msimang, Sisonke   183
Multi National United (MNU)   102–103, *102*, 104
Murray, Martin   6*n*7, 30, 34
Mututa, Addamms Songe   10*n*13, 167–169, 176
MWAS. *See* mine waste areas
Myeni, Eric   112

Nancy, Jean Luc   152–153
Nationalism. *See* Afrikaner nationalism
Native Life in South Africa   44
Native Nostalgia   11*n*17, 36, 112–114
Neale, Steve   21*n*
Nel, Adele   23, 33, 77–78, 106
new bad future   117–121, 127, 135
new media. *See* digital media
New South Africa   5–6
newsreel footage   22, 33, 75, 78–80, *79, 81*, 86, *87*, 92–94, 104, 121, 133
Niemeyer, Katharina   55, 84
Nigeria   22*n*5
1980s
  Blomkamp on   203–204, 207–208
  in mockumentary genre   74–75, 92, 98–104
  photography from   110
  science fiction genre of   33, 118–120, 123, 126, 133, 135, 197
Noir Urbanisms   34
nostalgia
  for analogue media   53–56
  Blomkamp on   202–204
  boom   55, 66, 204
  for Johannesburg   6–7, 10–11, 25–26, 35–38, 51–52, 194–196
  mining landscapes and   157
  mockumentary genre and   84, 89–90, 98, 107
  science fiction genre and   117, 119, 126, 134–135
  townships and   109–116
  urban ruins and   164–165, 173
  white anxiety and   188
nostalgic dystopia   3, 7–11, 117, 133, 191, 194–199, 201, 209
Nsele, Zamansele   5*n*5, 36
Nuttall, Sarah   31
Nye, David   41, 42*n*38, 47, 147

O Brother, Where Art Thou? (film)   61
office, in *District 9*   92–93, *94*
Okorafor, Nnedi   120*n*4
Olivier, Bert   40
on-location shooting   78, 95
Opaloch, Trent   78, 80, 87, 104, 120
open plan office, in *District 9*   92–93, *94*
Orlando   71–72
Orvell, Miles   42, 172–173
otherness   177–178, 181

Parker, Alexandra   31, 167, 176
parody   78–79, 84, 90–91, 93–95, 117
participatory aesthetics   156*n*23
Peeples, Jennifer   11–12
pentimenti   59
pessimism   119–120, 166
photography   27–28, 47*n*42, 58–59, 71, 83–84, 134–135, 159
picturesque   47
Pierce, Gillian B.   39, 43
Pierneef, J. H.   36, 48*n*, 147–149, 187, 190

INDEX

Pinnavaia, Laura   9
Piranesi, Giovanni Battista   164–166
Plaatjie, Sol   44, 73–74
place-image   9–10, 31n23, 164
plant life   97, *97*, 147, 161, 166, 187
poetics   104–108, 117–121, 135
poisoned landscapes   143–145, 149–151, *152*, 156
polaroidism   56, 83–84, 110
police force, apartheid   74–77, *79*, *87*, 103–104, 123–124, *170*
pollution   78, 95, 97, 129–130, *130*, 143–145, 149–151, *152*, 156. See also waste
Ponte City   15, 26, 31–32, 86, *89*, 99–101, *99*, *100*, 118n, 134, 171–175
Ponte City book project   32, 86, 134, 171–172
popular culture   6, 14–15
Posel, Deborah   75–76
post-apartheid   3–4, 8, 10–11, 24–26, 35–36, 43–44, 108, 163, 177–178, 180–182, 186, 198–199
post-colonial   41, 43–44, 49, 52, 195
post-industrial landscapes   61–64, 67, 143–157, 163–166, 173, 201
post-industrial sublime   12n20, 18, 38–43, 66–67, 173, 191, 195–196
postmodernism   40, 65, 118–119
potential, spaces of   48–51, 63
poverty   7, 10–11, 73, 176
poverty porn   10–11
Power Park//Soweto (photograph)   109–110, *110*
Poyner, Jane   31
Prakash, Gyan   34–35
prawns, in *District 9*   1–2, 24, 33–34, *96*, 175, 178, 181
Prince, Stephen   60, 82–83
protests   14, 74–75, *74*
public spaces   30–31
pylons. See electricity pylons

quarantine   122, 178

race and racism   1–2, 43–44, 49, 75, 95, 129, 181–182
radiotoxicity   144
Raft of the Medusa, The (painting)   183–184
railways   145, 186–187
Rakka (film)   202

Rancière, Jacques   16n28
Rand Gold Mine (painting)   148
Randlords   29, 129, 139, 141
Rankin, Elizabeth   45
Rantete, Johannes   76, 103, 122–123, 200
Ravan Press   76
realism   77–89, 106, 203–204, 206
Red Ants   103
redemption   107–108, 121, 134
reflective nostalgia   37–38, 52, 106
refugee camps   33, 178, 183
religion   131, 133
remediation   56, 88
Remediation: Understanding New Media   56
Repulsion. See attraction and repulsion
restorative nostalgia   5n5, 37
retrofuturism   117–121, 135, 197
Rewind (interactive video)   104, *105*
Riegl, Alois   63, 173–174
Robinson, Jennifer   35, 50
Robocop (film)   33, 118–121, 126–127, 207–208
Robotech (television series)   126, *127*
robots   126, *127*
romanticism   110, 164–165, 190–191
Rosello, Mireille   23–24, 117, 122
Rosetta stone   7–10, 194
rubble. See waste
ruin porn   10–11, 62–64, 172
ruins. See urban ruins
rural spaces   45–46

sameness   176n
San Jose   26, 90, 95, 176
Sapio, Giuseppina   81, 115
SAR&H. See South African Railways and Harbours
Sartists   109, 134–135
Scholem, Gershom   58
Schrey, Dominic   4n4, 36, 56, 59
science fiction genre
    Blomkamp on   203, 207–208
    cyborgs   120–121, 127
    dystopia   33–35
    mechanical suit   126–127, *128*, 159–161, *160*, 202
    new bad future   117–121, 127, 135
    1980s   118–120, 123, 126, 133, 135
    retrofuturism   117–121, 135, 197
    spaceship   121–133, *122*, *126*, 129, *132*, 135

Screening Space   118
See Ya Later/Triple Avant Car Guard on the Rocks (photograph)   184–185, *185*
segregation   2, 30, 72–73, 95, 141–142. *See also* apartheid
self-reflexivity   4, 37–38, 52, 106
Shapiro, Michael J.   41, 44, 49
Shapshay, Sandra   41*n*, 49
Shields, Rob   9
Short History of Photography, A   57
Simmel, Georg   50
Simone, Abdoumaliq   158, 170
Singh, Naunihal   120*n*4
Skrillex   6
slavery   49
slums   22*n*4, 31*n*24, 35, 61–62, 72, 167. *See also* townships
smartphones   83–84
Smithson, Robert   155
smog   95, 129–130, *130*
Sobchack, Vivian   117–119, 133
social media   83–84. *See also* Instagram photography
South African Railways and Harbours (SAR&H)   186–187
Soweto   15*n*26, 22, 35, 71–72, 109
spaceship, in *District 9*   99, 121–133, *122*, *126*, *129*, *132*, 135, *140*
special effects   60
Staiger, Janet   118*n*
States of Emergency   34, 74–77, *79*, 104, 122
stereotypes   7, 9–10, 35, 46, 75, 94–95, 106
Steyn, Melissa   185, 188
Straker, Gillian   182
Stupid Fuckin' White Man (photograph)   188–190, *189*
sublime   10–13, 38–52, 66–67, 148–149, 155–156, 165–166, 174–175, 190–192, 195–198
sublime landscapes
  mining   148–151, 153–156, 198
  post-industrial   191
  urban ruins   5, 158–159, 163–166, 172–175
Subotzky, Mikhael   15, 32, 86, 100–101, *100*, 134, 171–172
subversive resistance   50–51, 109–111, 134
Su, John   43–44
surveillance   122–123

tactility   114–115

Taste for Life, A (photograph)   125
Tatsumi, Takayuki   118–119, 126
technological sublime   12*n*20
television   79–80, 121
temporality   42, 86, 103, 117, 119
Terminator, The (film)   33, 118–120, 126, 207–208
terror and delight   40, 42, 64–65
Theweleit, Klaus   174
Third Day of September, The   76*n*
Three Stages of Preparing Tea, The (photograph)   111, *112*
Tladi, Moses   48*n*, 147–148
topography   10–13, 147–148
tourism   35
townships
  history of   15*n*26
  around Johannesburg   29, 31–34, 200–201
  in mockumentary genre   71–75, 77, 104, 107–108
  nostalgia   109–116
  in science fiction genre   121–125, 128–129, 133–135
  white anxiety and   181, 183–184, 190, 193
toxicity   12, 26, 143–145, 152, 154, 191–192. *See also* pollution
trains. *See* railways
transcendence   39–40, 42, 49
transformation
  Blomkamp on   202, 208–209
  of cities   13, 50–51, 201
  of landscapes   190–193
  socio-political transformation   13*n*21
  spaceship, in *District 9*   135
  of townships   183–184
  of Wikus van de Merwe   18, 23, 107–108, 127–128, 159–162, *160*, 174–178, 186, 198–199, 202, 208–209
trauma   10
Trigg, Dylan   39, 41–43, 50, 63, 67, 148*n*16, 163–166, 173, 177
Tsai Ming-liang   7
Tshabangu, Andrew   15, 129–130, *130*
Tudor Shaft   144

UFOS   123
United States (US)   7, 34, 47, 99, 102, 118–119, 147, 172

INDEX

unpresentable   165, 177
Urban Film and Everyday Practice   31
urbanism   33, 118, 170*n*
urban landscapes   5, 45
urban planning   72–73, 163*n*4, 179
urban renewal   26
urban ruins
   abjection   174–175, 177, 178*n*
   analogue media   59
   decay   147, 158–159, 171–174, 176–177, 200–201
   District Six   161–163, *162*
   entropy   174–178
   formlessness   173–175
   Hillbrow   167–171, *169*, 173
   nostalgia   164–165, 173
   Ponte City   171–175
   post-industrial   61–67, 163–166, 173
   ruin porn   10–11, 62–64, 172
   sublime landscapes   158–159, 163–166, 172–175
   waste   161, 168–173, *170*
   white anxiety   179, 187–188, 191–192
US. *See* United States
used future   124, 127
utopia   32–35, 37, 45, 117

Van de Merwe, Wikus. *See* Wikus van de Merwe (character in *District 9*)
Van Riebeeck, Jan   189–190
Van Robbroeck, Lize   148–149, 187, 190
vedute etchings   164–165
vegetation. *See* plant life
Venables, Emilie   101, 171
Vergangenheitsbewältigung   185*n*
Verhoeven, Paul   208
Vidler, Anthony   34
violence   7, 27, 74–76, 93–94, 107–108, 121, 156, 169
Virilio, Paul   166
visual effects   59–61, 203
visual idiom   3, 7–8
Vladislavić, Ivan   28*n*17
voyeuristic view   77, 93

Waetjen, Thembisa   14*n*24
Wagner, Keith   24, 102
Walder, Dennis   10, 37
Wamba, Phillipe   30*n*20

waste   161, 168–173, *170*, 180, *180*, 191–192. *See also* mining waste
watchtowers   123, *125*
Waterhouse, Patrick   15, 32, 86, 100–101, 134, 171–172
Weinberg, Paul, photograph by   *74*
Wells, Kate   63
white anxiety
   Afrikaner identity and   181, 187, 190–191
   apartheid and   179, 181–182, 192
   Avant Car Guard art   184–190, *185*, *188*, *189*
   belonging and   180, 187, 190–191
   Berea (film)   179–180, *180*
   concept of   181–184, 192
   decay and   180, *180*, 192–193
   landscape conventions and   186–187, 190–191
   melancholia and   182–183
   mining industry and   179, 188–192
   nostalgia and   26
   Ponte City   101
   townships and   181, 183–184, 190, 193, 198–199
   transformation and   183–184, 186, 190–193
   waste and   180, *180*, 191–192
white flight   28*n*17, 98, 101, 167, 182–183
Whitehouse, Tanya   62–63
whiteness   23, 29*n*19, 44, 128, 163*n*4, 181–183, 188, 190–191
white supremacy   182
White Writing   46
Wikus van de Merwe (character in *District 9*)
   Afrikaner identity of   1–2
   Blomkamp on   202, 208–209
   mockumentary genre and   78, 92, 94–95, *94*, *96*, *105*
   science fiction genre and   120–121, 127–128, *128*, 134
   transformation of   18, 23, 107–108, 127–128, 159–162, *160*, 174–178, 186, 198–199, 202, 208–209
   white anxiety and   181, 183–184, 186, 190, 192–193
Wilhelm-Solomon, Matthew   90*n*
Wittenberg, Herman   43
Worby, Eric   35–37
Writer of Modern Life, The   115

xenophobia   14, 22, 24, 156*n*24

YouTube   79–80

Ziman, Ralph   15, 24–25, 167

zone of indistinction   23, 33, 76
Zuma, Jacob   14, 194
Zylinska, Joanna   164

Printed in the United States
by Baker & Taylor Publisher Services